ZENO'S
PARADOXES

ZENO'S PARADOXES

Edited by **WESLEY C. SALMON**

Hackett Publishing Company, Inc.
Indianapolis/Cambridge

TO MY DAUGHTER TORI

Copyright © 1970 by The Bobbs-Merrill Company, Inc.
Reprinted 2001 by Hackett Publishing Company, Inc.
New material copyright © 2001 by Hackett Publishing Company, Inc.

14 13 12 11 10   2 3 4 5 6 7

For further information, please address
    Hackett Publishing Company, Inc.
    P.O. Box 44937
    Indianapolis, IN 46244-0937

    www.hackettpublishing.com

Cover design by Abigail Coyle

Library of Congress Cataloging-in-Publication Data
Zeno's paradoxes / edited by Wesley C. Salmon.
    p. cm.
  Originally published: Indianapolis: Bobbs-Merrill, [1970].
  Includes bibliographical references and index.
  ISBN 0-87220-561-4 (cloth) — ISBN 0-87220-560-6 (pbk.)
  1. Zeno of Elea. 2. Paradoxes. 3. Space and time. I. Salmon, Wesley C.
QC131.Z46 2001
531—dc21   00-065035

ISBN-13: 978-0-87220-560-4 (pbk.)
ISBN-13: 978-0-87220-561-1 (cloth)

PREFACE

It is natural enough to ask at the outset, "Why an anthology on Zeno's paradoxes?" Perhaps the reader shares the widespread feeling that they are mere anachronisms that can, at best, befuddle undergraduates who have not taken any calculus yet. Their utility, on this view, continually diminishes as calculus comes to be ever more commonly taught at the high school level. As mathematical sophistication becomes more universal, one may feel, Zeno's paradoxes will serve only to show how mathematically naive were the Greeks of the fifth century B.C.

No evaluation could be further from the truth, as I trust the contents of this anthology demonstrate beyond reasonable doubt. All of the selections are taken from mathematically literate twentieth-century authors, and all but the first two, which are modern classics by Russell and Bergson, are from the second half of the twentieth century. Indeed, one of the leading reasons for contemplating such a project in the first place was the high level of philosophical discussion of Zeno's paradoxes in the current literature, and the belief that materials were available for a highly cohesive anthology.

Since 1950, there have been many articles in the British journal *Analysis,* starting with Max Black's "Achilles and the Tortoise," and including J. O. Wisdom's "Achilles on a Physical Racecourse" and James Thomson's "Tasks and Super-Tasks," all three of which are reprinted here. Paul Benacerraf's "Tasks, Super-Tasks, and the Modern Eleatics," though published in a different journal, is a direct response to Thomson. These four articles, plus the second section of Adolf Grünbaum's "Modern Science and Zeno's Paradoxes of Motion," constitute a highly unified discussion of a number of fascinating devices known as "infinity machines."

Zeno's paradoxes of plurality, though less well-known than the paradoxes of motion, present difficulties even more perplexing and profound. In the early fifties Adolf Grünbaum published "A Consistent Conception of the Extended Linear Continuum as an Aggregate of Unextended Elements"—an article which was a precursor to "Zeno's Metrical Paradox of Extension" in this volume—in which he attempted to deal directly with the most significant of the paradoxes of plurality. The paradoxes of plurality are not logically independent of the paradoxes of motion, as is shown by the transition in Thomson's reply to Benacerraf from the paradox of the dichotomy to a paradox of plurality. Indeed, G. E. L. Owen's "Zeno and the Mathematicians" attempts to fit all of the paradoxes of motion and plurality into one coherent pattern. Owen's article also gives interesting indications of the problems in historical scholarship posed by Zeno's paradoxes.

As I attempt to explain in the Introduction, the issue of the infinity machines is a special case of the more general problem of whether and how abstract mathematics can describe the physical world. In its general form, this issue was taken up by Grünbaum in another early article, "Relativity and the Atomicity of Becoming," upon which I draw heavily in the section of the Introduction entitled "Zeno's Paradoxes and Modern Physics." His interest in this problem, as well as in the infinity machines and the paradox of plurality, have culminated in his recent monograph, *Modern Science and Zeno's Paradoxes*, in which he offers extended systematic treatment of all of the paradoxes. The latter two selections by Grünbaum in this anthology are taken from it. The last, "Modern Science and Zeno's Paradoxes of Motion," however, incorporates more recent material, not contained in Grünbaum's book, which makes his treatment of the infinity machines considerably more definitive.

Although the Bibliography makes no pretense of being complete—in fact, it is largely confined to works in English subsequent to Russell's *Our Knowledge of the External*

World (1914)—it is fairly extensive. Even a cursory scan will reveal how actively the current discussion of Zeno's paradoxes continues in the philosophical literature, and a number of the very recent contributions are extremely significant. There are several comprehensive and well-documented sources available. H. D. P. Lee's *Zeno of Elea* contains all of the important ancient source materials. Florian Cajori's "The History of Zeno's Arguments on Motion" traces the discussion from antiquity to Bertrand Russell. Gregory Vlastos' article "Zeno of Elea" in the new *Encyclopedia of Philosophy* provides an excellent brief survey of the current state of research on Zeno. Adolf Grünbaum's *Modern Science and Zeno's Paradoxes* contains a thorough systematic analysis in terms of the resources of modern mathematics and physics. These works collectively provide comprehensive and detailed treatment of all aspects of the subject.

This anthology, I hope, gives clear indication of the tenor of contemporary philosophical discussion of the paradoxes, but has a further motivation as well. These paradoxes have extensive ramifications both within philosophy and outside of it. As I try to show in the Introduction, they have deep significance for metaphysics and epistemology, but also occur on the borderline where philosophy must make positive contact with modern mathematics and physics. They constitute problems in the philosophy of science in the sense that their resolution demands that philosophy be made to bear upon science, and science upon philosophy. While it may go without saying that philosophy of science should increase our understanding of science, perhaps not so evident is the fact that it ought also to shed light on philosophy in general. Zeno's paradoxes, I believe, provide a superlative example of the two-way illumination that can result from philosophy of science done well.

Thanks are due many people for many kinds of help in connection with this anthology. I am grateful, in the first instance, to the authors, editors, and publishers who have

kindly granted permission for the reprinting of the selections herein contained. Specific acknowledgement will be
found on the page beginning each article. I owe special
thanks to Abner Shimony for making available his previously
unpublished philosophical playlet, and to James Thomson
for writing a reply to Paul Benacerraf's paper expressly for
inclusion here. To Nuel Belnap I am grateful for a number
of helpful suggestions concerning the Appendix, and my
thanks go to Joel Feinberg for much sage counsel.

My greatest debt, however, is to Adolf Grünbaum for his
encouragement, advice, and help throughout the entire
enterprise, as well as his generosity in allowing me to include large quantities of his work on Zeno. He has given
unstintingly of his time and the fruit of his labor; moreover,
I cannot overestimate the amount I have learned from
him regarding the basic philosophical issues that are involved in the analysis, clarification, and resolution of Zeno's
marvelous paradoxes.

W. C. S.
September, 1967

PREFACE TO THE 2001 REPRINT

When *Zeno's Paradoxes* was first printed in 1970, I likened these problems to an onion, which has many layers. When one layer is removed, another—often richer—is found beneath it. The metaphor is still apt. Not only are the original paradoxes (as best we know them) endlessly fascinating, but new aspects continue to appear. Among the various topics that had been recently discussed at that time, 'infinity machines' received a great deal of attention. They are no less fascinating at the beginning of the twenty-first century than they were in middle decades of the twentieth. To illustrate the *ongoing saga* of these paradoxes, I should like to mention three developments that have emerged since 1970.

1. A boy, a girl, and a dog take a walk along a path; they depart from a common starting point. The boy walks at four miles per hour and the girl walks at three miles per hour; the dog trots back and forth between them at ten miles per hour. Question: at the end of one hour, what is the position of the dog and in which direction is it facing? Answer: the dog can be at any point between the boy and the girl, and it can be facing in either direction. Pick any arbitrary point and either direction. If you time-reverse the whole process, you will find that it invariably leads back to the stated starting conditions.

In January of 1971, the year after the first printing of *Zeno's Paradoxes,* this problem was published in *Mathematics Magazine* as a straightforward mathematical puzzle. Several readers protested that the initial conditions were either insufficiently specified or logically inconsistent. Martin Gardner, then the author of the "Mathematical Games" column in *Scientific American,* seems to have been the first person to suspect the Zenonian character of this problem. He wrote to me, and I confirmed his hunch. It is closely related to the regressive form of Zeno's dichotomy paradox. Our discussion appeared in his column in December of that year. It is astounding that 2,500 years after Zeno first posed his paradoxes a new one should appear.[1]

2. During the 1970s, I was deeply engaged in controversies regarding the nature of scientific explanation. According to the received view of that time, explanations are deductive or inductive arguments, but causation plays no essential role in them. I was convinced that many explanations, if not all, are intrinsically causal in nature. Unfortunately, the philosophers who held this view had no adequate theory of causality. I tried to remedy this defect. Going back to David Hume's eighteenth-century critique of causal connections, I came to the conclusion that there are causal processes that connect causes to their effects. I believed that such processes *transmit causal influence* from one spacetime locale to another. The problem was to analyze the concept of causal transmission.

To solve this problem I appealed to the "at-at" theory of motion that Bertrand Russell had employed to deal with Zeno's arrow paradox (see page 23 below). To make my case, I had to distinguish genuine causal processes from pseudo-processes. A pulse of light, for example, is a causal process. A moving shadow is a pseudo-process. If a pulse of white light is "marked" by passing through a red filter, the light pulse becomes red and remains red without any additional intervention. The mark is *transmitted* because it continues to be present in the pulse without any further external intervention. It is *at* the appropriate place in the process *at* the right time. In contrast, the shape of a moving shadow can be modified by an irregularity in the surface on which it is cast, but the change in shape vanishes as soon as the shadow passes the irregularity. The modification is not transmitted.[2]

I have modified my views on causality and explanation

---

[1]See (Salmon, 1975, pp. 48–52; 1980, ibid.) for a full discussion of this problem.
[2]The "at-at" theory was originally published in (Salmon, 1977).

since 1977; nevertheless, the "at-at" theory is still an essential part. Zeno's arrow paradox thus plays a key role—via Russell's analysis—in the current literature on causality and explanation. It remains an integral part of the theories of causation and explanation I consider fundamentally sound.[3]

3. Although Russell proclaimed that Weierstrass had, in the nineteenth century, strictly banished all infinitesimals from mathematics, Abraham Robinson (1966) reintroduced them in the twentieth-century domain of mathematics known as *nonstandard analysis*. These infinitesimals are *not* subject to the criticisms rightly leveled against those of the earlier type. In 1970, I wondered whether another treatment of Zeno's paradoxes could be carried out with these resources. Since that time, several such studies have appeared. Here are two examples.

(i) Michael J. White (1982) provided a treatment of the arrow paradox using nonstandard analysis with its infinitesimals. A classical scholar, White also applied these resources to the interpretation of ancient writings on Zeno. However, this resolution—though extremely interesting in itself—does not appear to me to improve on Russell's approach via the "at-at" theory. Nevertheless, White's analysis is available to those who are unwilling to accept Russell's "at-at" theory of motion.

(ii) Brian Skyrms (1983) takes Zeno's paradox of plurality, which Grünbaum interpreted as a geometrical paradox (see pages 12–16 below), as the point of departure for a rich discussion of measure theory. Grünbaum, Skyrms, and I agree that this paradox is the most fundamental of all. Still, it has received nowhere near the amount of attention given to the four more famous paradoxes. Skyrms's paper is divided into two parts. In the first, "Zeno to Epicurus," he discusses ancient treatments—including those of Aristotle, of course. In the second, "Post Cantor," he offers a sophisticated view of modern measure theory.[4] Whereas Grünbaum used one plau-

---

[3]See (Salmon, 1998, especially Essay 1) for more recent developments.
[4]Georg Cantor is the founder of the modern theory of infinite numbers.

sible theory of measure to resolve the paradox (an approach I was quite willing to accept), Skyrms looks at a variety of approaches, including one based on nonstandard analysis.

Skyrms's closing remark could be the theme of this book: "Perhaps enough has been said to show that the truly deep issues first raised by Zeno still deserve to engage our interest" (1983, page 250). To facilitate further study of these problems, the Bibliography is updated with the addition of Section IV, Supplementary Sources, whose size also dramatizes the current high level of interest in these problems. I am truly grateful to Hackett Publishing Company for aiding in the continuation of this extraordinary enterprise that spans two and a half millennia.

W. C. S.
September, 2000

CONTENTS

Resolution of the Paradox

ABNER SHIMONY

A PHILOSOPHICAL PUPPET PLAY

Dramatis personae: Zeno, Pupil, Lion

Scene: The school of Zeno at Elea.

Pup. Master! There is a lion in the streets!

Zen. Very good. You have learned your lesson in geography well. The fifteenth meridian, as measured from Greenwich, coincides with the high road from the Temple of Poseidon to the Agora—but you must not forget that it is an imaginary line.

Pup. Oh no, Master! I must humbly disagree. It is a *real* lion, a *menagerie* lion, and it is coming toward the school!

Zen. My boy, in spite of your proficiency at geography, which is commendable in its way—albeit essentially the art of the surveyor and hence separated by the hair of the theodolite from the craft of a slave—you are deficient in philosophy. That which is real cannot be imaginary, and that which is imaginary cannot be real. Being is, and non-being is not, as my revered teacher Parmenides demonstrated first, last, and continually, and as I have attempted to convey to you.

Pup. Forgive me, Master. In my haste and excitement, themselves expressions of passion unworthy of you and of our school, I have spoken obscurely. Into the gulf be-

1

tween the thought and the word, which, as you have taught us, is the trap set by non-being, I have again fallen. What I meant to say is that a lion has escaped from the zoo, and with deliberate speed it is rushing in the direction of the school and soon will be here!

The lion appears in the distance.

Zen. O my boy, my boy! It pains me to contemplate the impenetrability of the human intellect and its incommensurability with the truth. Furthermore, I now recognize that a thirty-year novitiate is too brief—*sub specie aeternitatis*—and must be extended to forty years, before the apprenticeship proper can begin. A real lion, perhaps; but really running, impossible; and really arriving here, absurd!

Pup. Master . . .

Zen. In order to run from the zoological garden to the Eleatic school, the lion would first have to traverse half the distance.

The lion traverses half the distance.

Zen. But there is a first half of that half, and a first half of *that* half, and yet again a first half of *that* half to be traversed. And so the halves would of necessity regress to the first syllable of recorded time—nay, they would recede yet earlier than the first syllable. To have traveled but a minute part of the interval from the zoological garden to the school, the lion would have been obliged to embark upon his travels *infinitely long ago.*

The lion bursts into the schoolyard.

Pup. O Master, run, run! He is upon us!

Zen. And thus, by *reductio ad absurdum,* we have proved that the lion could never have *begun* the course, the mere fantasy of which has so unworthily filled you with panic.

The pupil climbs an Ionic column, while the lion devours Zeno.

Pup. My mind is in a daze. Could there be a flaw in the Master's argument?

WESLEY C. SALMON

Introduction

The paradoxes of Zeno of Elea are objects of beauty and charm, and sources of intense intellectual excitement. Using everyday occurrences, such as a footrace or the flight of an arrow, Zeno shows that simple considerations lead to profound difficulties. In his attempt to demonstrate the impossibility of plurality, motion, and change, he points to problems lying at the very heart of our concepts of space, time, motion, continuity, and infinity. Since these concepts play fundamental roles in philosophy, mathematics, and physics, the implications of the paradoxes are far-reaching indeed. It is perhaps amusing to be confronted by a simple argument which purports to demonstrate the unreality of something as obviously real as motion; it is deeply intriguing to find that the resolution of the paradox requires the subtlety of modern physics, mathematics, and philosophy. It is difficult to think of any other problem in science or philosophy which can be stated so simply and whose resolution carries one so far or so deep. Bertrand Russell was hardly exaggerating when he said, "Zeno's arguments, in some form, have afforded grounds for almost all theories of space and time and infinity which have been constructed from his time to our own."[1]

---

[1] Bertrand Russell, "The Problem of Infinity Considered Historically," in *Our Knowledge of the External World* [100], reprinted below, p. 54.

Bracketed numerals in the footnotes throughout the book refer to the numbered entries in the Bibliography. For all titles in the footnotes which are listed also in the Bibliography, full publication information will be found only in the Bibliography.

THE HISTORICAL ZENO[2]

Precious little is known about Zeno of Elea. His fame derives mainly from four paradoxes of motion attributed to him by Aristotle. None of Zeno's writings has survived, but a few passages in other authors are purported to be direct quotations. At best, we have less than two hundred of Zeno's own words, and the paradoxes of motion are not included in this corpus.

It is known that Zeno lived in the fifth century B.C., and that he was a devoted disciple of Parmenides. Parmenides maintained that reality is one, immutable, and unchanging; all plurality, change, and motion are mere illusions of the senses. Zeno, according to Plato's testimony, propounded a series of arguments designed to show the absurdity of the views of those who made fun of Parmenides.[3] Zeno was no mere sophist whose sole aim was to confound by verbal trickery, nor was he a skeptic who denied the possibility of all knowledge. He seriously accepted the Parmenidean view, and posed his paradoxes as real difficulties for those who held a different metaphysic. Whether his arguments were directed specifically against the Pythagoreans, against some other particular philosophical school, or more generally against any view that affirmed plurality is still the subject of historical debate.[4]

In addition to his paradoxes of motion, several other arguments of Zeno have come down to us, the most important being a paradox of plurality. Since the denial of plurality is the central thesis of Parmenides, it is likely that this paradox plays an even more fundamental role for Zeno than the more famous paradoxes of motion. Moreover, regardless of Zeno's estimate of the relative importance of

[2] Part I of the Bibliography provides historical references. Gregory Vlastos, "Zeno of Elea" [28], is an excellent introductory survey; H. D. P. Lee, *Zeno of Elea* [2], is more detailed and gives the ancient source materials.

[3] Plato, *The Parmenides*.

[4] Florian Cajori, "The Purpose of Zeno's Arguments on Motion" [23], surveys various opinions concerning the direction of Zeno's attack. The issue is also discussed in Owen, "Zeno and the Mathematicians," reprinted below.

the two kinds of paradoxes, we shall see that the paradox of plurality is logically more basic than the paradoxes of motion.

Aristotle credits Zeno with the invention of dialectic, a method frequently exemplified in Greek philosophy (but related only indirectly to dialectic as conceived by Hegel and Marx). The Greek dialectical method involves a dialogue between two speakers, one of whom propounds and defends a thesis while the other attempts to reduce it to absurdity by deriving a contradiction, a method familiar from the Platonic dialogues. Dialectic involves extensive use of the argument by *reductio ad absurdum.* Although this form of argument had probably been discovered by mathematicians somewhat earlier than Zeno, he quite possibly imported the technique into philosophy and gave it a central place in philosophical method. This accomplishment secures for Zeno an important position in the early history of logic.[5]

Zeno's paradoxes have been the object of extensive historical research especially in the last hundred years. Due to the scantiness of material, various interpretations and reconstructions are possible. On some reconstructions Zeno is guilty of elementary logical and mathematical errors, while on others he displays extraordinary logical and mathematical acumen. Vlastos attributes to Zeno "crudities and blunders,"[6] and Booth claims that "Zeno's arguments . . . involved elementary fallacies; they were not uttered with that full and marvelous understanding which some scholars have attributed to him."[7] Russell, on the other hand, says that Zeno "invented four arguments, all immeasurably subtle and profound. . . ."[8] While there may be serious

---

[5] I. M. Bocheński, *Ancient Formal Logic* [36], and *A History of Formal Logic* [37], and William and Martha Kneale, *The Development of Logic* [38], discuss Zeno's significance in the history of logic.

[6] Vlastos, "Zeno" [27], p. 28.

[7] N. B. Booth, "Zeno's Paradoxes" [21], p. 201.

[8] Bertrand Russell, *The Principles of Mathematics* [102], p. 347.

doubt about the subtlety and profundity of the arguments
Zeno actually propounded, there can be no doubt that
subtle and profound problems have arisen from the consideration of his paradoxes.

THE ARGUMENTS

The orientation of this book is systematic rather than historical. Zeno's paradoxes have interested philosophers of
all periods, but until the middle of the nineteenth century
the paradoxes were almost always regarded as mere sophisms which could be removed with little trouble.[9] In the
last hundred years, however, they have been taken very
seriously, and in the twentieth century have become the
subject of vigorous philosophical discussion. This controversy, still continuing in the professional journals, testifies
to the fact that Zeno has raised issues still very much alive.
The articles selected for inclusion in this book represent
attempts to deal with these issues; they are concerned only
incidentally with the historicity of the arguments. There is
this much historical justice in the approach: if Zeno is not
the father of these problems, he certainly is their grand-
father.

We shall be concerned with five of Zeno's arguments,
namely, the four famous paradoxes of motion and a "paradox of plurality" (which we shall construe as a geometrical
paradox). Since we do not have any text which even pre-
tends to quote Zeno directly on the four paradoxes of
motion, we shall have to be content with paraphrases. Our
primary source is Aristotle, who makes it quite clear that
he is not quoting Zeno. Since Russell presents (below) a
standard version of the paradoxes of motion, I shall simply
attempt to make as clear as possible the gist of each.

1) *Achilles and the Tortoise* (page 50 below). Imagine

---

[9] Florian Cajori, "The History of Zeno's Arguments on Motion" [22], provides a comprehensive history of the discussions of Zeno's paradoxes from
antiquity to the early part of the twentieth century.

that Achilles, the fleetest of Greek warriors, is to run a footrace against a tortoise. It is only fair to give the tortoise a head start. Under these circumstances, Zeno argues, Achilles can never catch up with the tortoise, no matter how fast he runs. In order to overtake the tortoise, Achilles must run from his starting point A to the tortoise's original starting point T_0 (see Figure 1). While he is doing that, the tortoise will have moved ahead to T_1. Now Achilles must reach the point T_1. While Achilles is covering this new distance, the tortoise moves still farther to T_2.

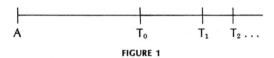

FIGURE 1

Again, Achilles must reach this new position of the tortoise. And so it continues; whenever Achilles arrives at a point where the tortoise *was*, the tortoise has already moved a bit ahead. Achilles can narrow the gap between him and the tortoise, but he can never actually catch up with him. This is the most famous of all of Zeno's paradoxes. It is sometimes known simply as "The Achilles."

2) *The Dichotomy.* This paradox comes in two forms. According to the first, Achilles cannot get to the end of any racecourse, tortoise or no tortoise; indeed, he cannot finish covering any finite distance (page 48 below). Thus he cannot even reach the original starting point T_0 of the tortoise in the previous paradox. Zeno argues as follows. Before the runner can cover the whole distance he must cover the first half of it (see Figure 2).

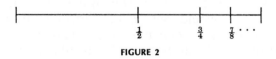

FIGURE 2

Then he must cover the first half of the remaining distance, and so on. In other words, he must first run one-half, then an additional one-fourth, then an additional one-eighth, etc., always remaining somewhat short of his goal. Hence, Zeno concludes, he can never reach it. This form of the paradox has very nearly the same force as "Achilles and the Tortoise," the only difference being that in "The Dichotomy" the goal is stationary, while in "Achilles and the Tortoise" it moves, but at a speed much less than that of Achilles.

The second form of "The Dichotomy" attempts to show, worse yet, that the runner cannot even get started (page 48 below). Before he can complete the full distance, he must run half of it (see Figure 3). But before he can complete

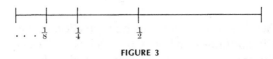

FIGURE 3

the first half, he must run half of that, namely, the first quarter. Before he can complete the first quarter, he must run the first eighth. And so on. In order to cover any distance no matter how short, Zeno concludes, the runner must already have completed an infinite number of runs. Since the sequence of runs he must already have completed has the form of a regression,

$$\ldots \tfrac{1}{16}, \tfrac{1}{8}, \tfrac{1}{4}, \tfrac{1}{2},$$

it has no first member, and hence, the runner cannot even get started.

3) *The Arrow* (page 50 below). In this paradox, Zeno argues that an arrow in flight is always at rest. At any given instant, he claims, the arrow is where it is, occupying a portion of space equal to itself. During the instant it cannot move, for that would require the instant to have parts, and an instant is *by definition* a minimal and indivisible element of time. If the arrow did move during the instant

it would have to be in one place at one part of the instant, and in a different place at another part of the instant. Moreover, for the arrow to move during the instant would require that during the instant it must occupy a space larger than itself, for otherwise it has no room to move. As Russell says, "It is never moving, but in some miraculous way the change of position has to occur *between* the instants, that is to say, not at any time whatever" (page 51 below). This paradox is more difficult to understand than "Achilles and the Tortoise" or either form of "The Dichotomy," but another remark by Russell is apt: "The more the difficulty is meditated, the more real it becomes" (page 51).

4) *The Stadium* (pages 51–53 below). Consider three rows of objects, A, B, and C, arranged as indicated in the first position of Figure 4. Then, while row A remains at rest, rows B and C move in opposite directions until all three rows are lined up as shown in the second position. In the process, C_1 passes twice as many B's as A's; it lines up with the first A to its left, but with the second B to its left. According to Aristotle, Zeno concluded that "double the time is equal to half."

	First Position				Second Position	
	A_1	A_2	A_3		A_1 A_2 A_3	
B_1	B_2	B_3			B_1 B_2 B_3	
	C_1	C_2	C_3		C_1 C_2 C_3	

FIGURE 4

Some such conclusion would be warranted if we assume that the time it takes for C to pass to the next B is the same as the time it takes to pass to the next A, but this assumption seems patently false. It appears that Zeno had no appreciation of relative speed, assuming that the speed of C relative to B is the same as the speed of C relative to A. If that were the only foundation for the paradox we would have no reason to be interested in it, except perhaps as a historical curiosity. It turns out, however, as both Russell

(pages 53–54) and Owen (page 148) show, that there is
an interpretation of this paradox which gives it serious import.

Suppose, as people occasionally do, that space and
time are atomistic in character, being composed of space-
atoms and time-atoms of nonzero size, rather than being
composed of points and instants whose size is zero.[10] Under
these circumstances, motion would consist in taking up
different discrete locations at different discrete instants.
Now, if we suppose that the A's are not moving, but the B's
move to the right at the rate of one place per instant while
the C's move to the left at the same speed, some of the C's
get past some of the B's without ever passing them. C_1
begins at the right of B_2 and it ends up at the left of B_2, but
there is no instant at which it lines up with B_2; consequently,
there is no time at which they pass each other—it never
happens.

It has been suggested, and Owen elaborates this theme,
that Zeno's arguments fit into an overall pattern.[11] "Achilles
and the Tortoise" and "The Dichotomy" are designed to refute the doctrine that space and time are continuous, while
"The Arrow" and "The Stadium" are intended to refute the
view that space and time have an atomic structure. Thus,
it has been argued, Zeno tries to cut off all possible avenues
of escape from the conclusion that space, time, and motion
are not real but illusory.

The paradox of plurality is much less famous than the
four paradoxes of motion. Since we have what purports to
be a direct quotation from Zeno, by Simplicius (6th century
A.D., a full millenium later than Zeno), we will present it
here. Simplicius was a commentator on Aristotle who probably had at least a digest or summary of Zeno's work at his
disposal. The statements are obscure and open to various

---

[10] E.g., J. O. Wisdom, "Achilles on a Physical Racecourse," reprinted
below.
[11] "Zeno and the Mathematicians," reprinted below.

interpretations.[12] The two passages are separated, but seem to be parts of a single argument.

> In his [Zeno's] book, in which many arguments are put forward, he shows in each that a man who says that there is a plurality is stating something self-contradictory. One of these arguments is that in which he shows that, if there is a plurality, things are both large and small, so large as to be infinite in magnitude, so small as to have no magnitude at all. And in this argument he shows that what has neither magnitude nor thickness nor mass does not exist at all. For, he argues, if it were added to something else, it would not increase its size; for a null magnitude is incapable, when added, of yielding an increase in magnitude. And thus it follows that what was added was nothing. But if, when it is subtracted from another thing, that thing is no less; and again, if, when it is added to another thing, that thing does not increase, it is evident that both what was added and what was subtracted were nothing.[13]
>
> . . . .
>
> The infinity of magnitude he showed previously by the same process of reasoning. For, having first shown that "if what is had not magnitude, it would not exist at all," he proceeds: "But, if it is, then each one must necessarily have some magnitude and thickness and must be at a certain distance from another. And the same reasoning holds good of the one beyond: for it also will have magnitude and there will be a successor to it. It is the same to say this once and to say it always: for no such part will be the last nor out of relation to another. So, if there is a plurality, they must be both large and small. So small as to have no magnitude, so large as to be infinite."[14]

The force of this argument is geometrical; it deals with the extended continuum. If extended things exist, Zeno argues, they must be composed of parts; thus there is a plurality of parts. Further, these parts must themselves have parts. Since the process of subdivision is indefinitely repeat-

[12] Owen's discussion is extremely helpful; see pp. 142–144 below.
[13] Lee, *Zeno of Elea* [2], p. 19. Reprinted by permission.
[14] *Ibid.*, p. 21. Reprinted by permission.

able, there must be an infinity of parts. The atomic constitution of matter has no bearing upon this argument. It is not necessary that the parts in question be physically separable from one another; it is sufficient that they be conceptually distinguishable. Even if there are atoms (or subatomic particles) which cannot be split, still there are spatial extensions of which we can distinguish different parts. Two difficulties arise. First, the ultimate parts must have no magnitude, for if they have magnitude they can be further subdivided. But an extended object cannot be composed of parts which have no magnitude, for no matter how many of them are put together, the result will have no magnitude: by adding zeros together, you get nothing but zero. Thus, the second difficulty arises. The parts must have magnitude. But the addition of an infinite number of magnitudes, all greater than zero, will yield an infinite magnitude. Hence, extended objects, if they exist, are "so small as to have no magnitude, (and) so large as to be infinite."[15]

This argument has been criticized on the ground that an infinite number of terms, each of which is greater than zero, may form a convergent series and have a finite sum. The retort is inapplicable. It is a necessary (but not sufficient) condition of convergence that there be no smallest term. In the paradox of plurality, the ultimate parts of which an extension is composed cannot form a convergent series. If one ultimate part were of greater magnitude than another, the former would not be ultimate, for it would admit of further subdivision. The process of subdivision described in the paradox can be carried out everywhere.[16] When we are speaking of ultimate parts there is no meaningful way of assigning unequal magnitudes to them, and thus the sum of such parts cannot be the sum of a convergent series unless all of the terms are zero. It must be the sum of equal (possibly zero) magnitudes. An infinite series, all of whose terms

---

[15] Lee, *ibid.*, p. 21.
[16] Zeno himself probably made precisely this point. See Lee, *ibid.*, pp. 12–13 (fragment 2); p. 22.

are equal and greater than zero, is divergent and has no finite sum. An infinite series, all of whose terms are zero, converges to zero.

In the face of this paradox it is not surprising that philosophers from Aristotle to the present have denied that the continuum is composed of points. Unfortunately for this view, the calculus, and *ipso facto* a vast part of modern mathematical physics, is logically founded upon a conception of the continuum according to which it is an ordered set of unextended points. Grünbaum alone, among the authors who have dealt with Zeno's paradoxes, has addressed himself to precisely this argument. His answer is far from elementary, involving as it does Cantor's theory of (super-denumerable) infinite aggregates, modern topology, and measure theory.[17]

The paradox of plurality applies, *mutatis mutandis*, to any continuum of point-like elements. Thus, it deals with the temporal continuum as well as the various spatial continua. This paradox, consequently, underlies the paradoxes of motion. Motion may be described in mathematical terms as a functional relation between space and time. The function ranges over the elements of the temporal continuum and its values are the elements of the spatial continuum. The paradox of plurality calls into question the consistency of our conceptions of these continua. The paradoxes of motion raise further questions about the nature of this function, in particular, its status as a continuous function; but the paradoxes of motion cannot be resolved if the paradox of plurality is unresolved.

[17] "Zeno's Metrical Paradox of Extension," reprinted below, contains this answer. According to Cantor's theory, there are infinite aggregates of different sizes. Infinite aggregates having the same number of members as the set of all positive integers are called "denumerable"; any set containing a larger number of members is super-denumerable. The set of all integers, positive or negative, is denumerable; so is the set of all rational numbers. The set of all real numbers, rational or irrational, is larger than the foregoing sets and hence super-denumerable; so is the set of all points in a geometrical continuum such as a line segment or an area. See the Appendix for fuller explanations of these basic concepts of set theory.

It would be a mistake to suppose that Zeno's paradoxes are fully resolved if it is possible to give a logically consistent characterization of the continuum. There is, in addition to the logical question, also a semantical one. Zeno's paradoxes deal with *physical* extension, *physical* duration, *physical* process, and *physical* motion. These problems are not answered merely by developing a consistent system of pure mathematics. It is also necessary to show how the abstract mathematical system can be used for the description of concrete physical reality. Whitehead, for one, does not claim Cantor's theory of the continuum is inconsistent; he does claim that it is inadequate for the description of physical process (pages 17–19 below). Black and Wisdom (see below) make the same claim, but for different reasons. Unlike Whitehead, though, they decline to draw far-reaching metaphysical conclusions.

ZENO'S PARADOXES AND MODERN METAPHYSICS

Although few philosophers have supposed that Zeno's paradoxes validly prove the unreality of plurality, motion, and change, the absolute idealism of the late nineteenth and early twentieth centuries does bear strong resemblance to the Parmenidean view, both in its conclusions and in its arguments. F. H. Bradley, while making no explicit mention of Zeno, uses thoroughly Eleatic arguments to support the conclusions that space and time, motion and change, are unreal. "Time, like space, has most evidently proved not to be real, but a contradictory appearance."[18] "The problem of change defies solution, so long as change is not degraded to the rank of mere appearance."[19] It is this resemblance that prompted Russell to remark how little orthodox metaphysics had progressed since Parmenides.[20]

The vast majority of philosophers, convinced that the

[18] F. H. Bradley, *Appearance and Reality* [42], p. 36.
[19] *Ibid.*, p. 41.
[20] Bertrand Russell, *Our Knowledge of the External World* [100], p. 180.

reality of motion and change is more compelling than any argument to prove their unreality, have found in Zeno's arguments only a challenge to show where they go wrong. This attitude by no means trivializes Zeno's arguments, for erroneous arguments can be profound, and the analysis of such arguments may be vastly illuminating. Trivialization occurs only if the analysis reveals foolish mistakes.

In a similar spirit, some recent philosophers, though unwilling to accept Zeno's entire conclusion, have found warrant in the paradoxes for profound logical or metaphysical doctrines. Dialecticians (in the modern sense) from Hegel onward have taken these arguments to support their view that reality contains inherent contradictions.[21] Dialectical logic rejects the logical laws of contradiction and excluded middle, and some philosophers have taken this way to resolve Zeno's paradoxes. Robin refers to "the absolute conception of the principle of contradiction" as "the vice of Eleaticism,"[22] and the eminent physicist Sir James Jeans, in a moment of philosophizing, claims that the fallacy of the Achilles paradox ". . . lies in the supposition that quantities can be sharply divided into finite and non-finite—in other words, the law of the excluded middle."[23]

William James, Alfred North Whitehead, and Henri Bergson, three of the most influential metaphysicians of the twentieth century, have held that Zeno's paradoxes, while not proving the impossibility of motion, do validly show that the mathematical account of continuity is inadequate for the description of temporal processes. James and Whitehead have seen in these paradoxes a proof that temporal processes are discontinuous. Whitehead writes:

> . . . if we admit that 'something becomes,' it is easy, by
> employing Zeno's method, to prove that there can be no

[21] G. W. F. Hegel, *Lectures on the History of Philosophy* [43], pp. 261–278. But see also Adam Schaff, "Marxist Dialectics and the Principle of Contradiction" [46].

[22] Léon Robin, *Greek Thought and the Origins of the Scientific Spirit* [7], p. 95.

[23] Sir James Jeans, *Physics and Philosophy* [45], p. 94.

continuity of becoming. There is a becoming of continuity, but no continuity of becoming. The actual occasions are the creatures which become, and they constitute a continuously extensive world. In other words, extensiveness becomes, but 'becoming' is not itself extensive.

Thus, the ultimate metaphysical truth is atomism.[24] Whitehead maintains that the physical world is an extended spatiotemporal continuum, but he believes that it comes into existence in chunks. These pieces come into being as whole entities or not at all. In retrospect they can be conceptually subdivided into parts—even into infinitely many parts—but the parts do not represent entities that can come to be by themselves. An act of becoming is an indivisible unit; if you subdivide it in any way the resulting parts are not smaller acts of becoming. This is what Whitehead means by saying that ". . . in every act of becoming there is the becoming of something with temporal extension; but . . . the act itself is not extensive. . . ."[25] After remarking that some allowance must be made for the inadequacy of mathematical knowledge at the time of Zeno, he claims that the paradoxes have a valid core. He details the argument as follows:

> The argument, so far as it is valid, elicits a contradiction from the two premises: (i) that in a becoming something (*res vera*) becomes, and (ii) that every act of becoming is divisible into earlier and later sections which are themselves acts of becoming. Consider, for example, an act of becoming during one second. The act is divisible into two acts, one during the earlier half of the second, the other during the later half of the second. Thus that which becomes during the whole second presupposes that which becomes during the first half-second. Analogously, that which becomes during the first half-second presupposes that which becomes during the first quarter-second, and so on indefinitely. Thus if we consider the process of becoming up to the beginning of the second in question, and ask what then becomes, no answer can be given. For, whatever creature

---

[24] Alfred North Whitehead, *Process and Reality* [48], p. 53. Reprinted by permission.
[25] *Ibid.*, p. 107.

we indicate presupposes an earlier creature which became after the beginning of the second and antecedently to the earlier creature. Therefore there is nothing which becomes, so as to effect a transition into the second in question.

The difficulty is not evaded by assuming that something becomes at each non-extensive instant of time. For at the beginning of the second of time there is no next instant at which something can become.

Zeno in his 'Arrow in Its Flight' seems to have had an obscure grasp of this argument. But the introduction of motion brings in irrelevant details. The true difficulty is to understand how the arrow survives the lapse of time.[26]

Bergson, in contrast with James and Whitehead, admits that there is real continuity of becoming, but he takes the paradoxes of Zeno to prove that the intellect is incapable of understanding motion and change. In his celebrated "cinematographic" characterization of ordinary knowledge he maintains that the usual approach to a physical process consists in accumulating a series of static descriptions of its successive states, much as a motion picture consists of a large number of still pictures. By stringing these static representations together, Bergson argues, we can never come to grips with movement and change themselves. We find ourselves committed to the absurdity ". . . that movement is made of immobilities" (page 63 below). It is only by entering into the process and perceiving it directly that we can genuinely understand physical becoming. Such insight cannot be achieved by mathematical analysis or by logical reasoning; metaphysical intuition is the only way. "Philosophy perceived this," he says, "as soon as it opened its eyes. The arguments of Zeno of Elea, although formulated with a very different intention, have no other meaning" (page 63).

The arguments of Bergson have been subjected to searching criticism by Russell,[27] while Grünbaum has provided

---

[26] *Ibid.,* p. 106. Reprinted by permission.
[27] Bertrand Russell, "The Philosophy of Bergson" [101].

excellent critical discussions of Bergson, James, and Whitehead.[28] Although these analyses show, I believe, that Zeno's
paradoxes do not validly establish any such metaphysical
conclusions, an extremely important point emerges. The perceptual continuum and perceived becoming exhibit a structure radically different from that of the mathematical
continuum. Experience does seem, as James and Whitehead
emphasize, to have an atomistic character. If physical change
could be understood only in terms of the structure of the
perceptual continuum, then the mathematical continuum
would be incapable of providing an adequate description
of physical processes. In particular, if we set the epistemological requirement that physical continuity must be constructed from physical points which are explicitly definable
in terms of observables, then it will be impossible to endow
the physical continuum with the properties of the mathematical continuum. In our discussion of "Zeno's Paradoxes
and Modern Physics," we shall see, however, that no such
rigid requirement needs to be imposed.

ZENO'S PARADOXES AND MODERN MATHEMATICS

In the nineteenth century, the logical foundations of the
calculus were laid, just about two centuries after Newton
and Leibniz discovered what is known as the fundamental
theorem.[29] The first part of the job was done by Cauchy
who, in the earlier half of the century, clarified the concepts of functions, limits, and continuity, at the same time
showing how the concepts of derivatives, differentials, anti-
derivatives, and definite integrals could be based upon
them.[30] The chief defect in his work—a striking logical gap

---

[28] Adolf Grünbaum, "Relativity and the Atomicity of Becoming" [73], and
Modern Science and Zeno's Paradoxes [72].

[29] Carl B. Boyer, *The History of the Calculus and its Conceptual Development* [31], gives a comprehensive historical account of the development of the
calculus and its foundations.

[30] Richard Courant and Herbert Robbins, *What Is Mathematics?* [133], provides a sound elementary explanation of these fundamental concepts.

—was his failure to establish the real number system, including the irrationals. The second part of the job, remedying this defect, was accomplished in the latter half of the century by Dedekind, Weierstrass, and Cantor. The completed work found the calculus arithmetized and freed from a foundation in intuitions of space and motion. It involved the construction of a linear continuum of real numbers identical in structure to the geometrical straight line. In this way, the isomorphism between geometry and arithmetic presupposed by analytic geometry was actually secured. The new foundations banished infinitesimals, as infinitely small quantities, from the calculus, and led to the development of a theory of infinite aggregates and an arithmetic of transfinite numbers.[31]

Until these foundations had been laid, certain logical and mathematical questions concerning Zeno's paradoxes could not be given satisfactory answers. For example, Zeno believed that there was no such thing as a definite infinite cardinal number.[32] It was only with the work of Cantor that the notion of an actually infinite aggregate was shown to be sensible and self-consistent, and that the existence of differing infinite cardinal numbers was established. The smallest infinite sets are called "denumerable"; larger ones are called "super-denumerable."

[31] The Appendix of this volume presents a few of the most pertinent facts of set theory; in addition, there are several excellent introductions to this area. Hans Hahn, "Infinity" [125], is brief and clear. Bertrand Russell, *Introduction to Mathematical Philosophy* [129], is lengthier and more detailed, but quite intelligible to the non-mathematical reader. Edward V. Huntington, *The Continuum and Other Types of Serial Order* [126], and Raymond L. Wilder, *Introduction to the Foundations of Mathematics* [131], provide brief, clear accounts, which are nevertheless longer and more detailed than the article by Hahn. Abraham A. Fraenkel, *Abstract Set Theory* [124], is very clear and very thorough. E. Kamke, *Theory of Sets* [127], is rather condensed, but excellent for the reader with a little mathematical sophistication. Georg Cantor, *Contributions to the Founding of the Theory of Transfinite Numbers* [123], is Cantor's original work.

[32] One of Zeno's paradoxes rests upon precisely this error. See Russell, "The Problem of Infinity Considered Historically," reprinted below, p. 47, and Lee, *Zeno of Elea* [2], p. 19.

The super-denumerability of the continuum is essential to the theory of measure Grünbaum uses to deal with Zeno's geometrical paradox.[33] It is important to realize, however, that contemporary logicians and mathematicians are not uniformly satisfied with Cantor's conception of higher orders of infinity; indeed, it is explicitly rejected by intuitionistic philosophers of mathematics.[34] However, the standard theory of measure employed by Grünbaum is an important component of the parts of contemporary mathematics which have many empirical applications. Zeno's paradox of plurality poses a serious challenge to those who would reject entirely the notion of super-denumerable infinities. The problem is to explain the relation between unextended points and extended lines by providing a theory of measure according to which the measure of an extended continuum is other than zero. Grünbaum does not claim it cannot be done, but he does emphasize the magnitude of the departure from the standard theories.

Before the nineteenth century, there was no clear conception of functions and limits. A function was often regarded as something which moved or flowed; there was considerable controversy about the ability of a function to "reach" its limit. With the modern conception of function and limit, such questions dissolve. The limit is simply a number, the values of the function are numbers, and the limit may or may not be among the values of the function—depending upon the particular function being dealt with. There is no "movement" of the function, so that there is no special mystery about "reaching." Until this point is clarified, "The Achilles" and "The Dichotomy" seem to present extreme difficulties about functions reaching limits; the question of whether Achilles could catch the tortoise

---

[33] "Zeno's Metrical Paradox of Extension," reprinted below.

[34] For an excellent discussion of the various philosophies of mathematics, including a sympathetic presentation of intuitionism, see Stephan Körner, *The Philosophy of Mathematics* [128].

seemed to be the same as the question of whether the function that described his motion could "reach" its limit.

Before Cauchy's definition of the derivative as a certain limit, the derivative was widely regarded as a ratio of infinitesimal quantities. The use of the derivative to represent velocity thus implied that physical motion over a finite distance is compounded out of infinitesimal movements over infinitesimal distances during infinitesimal time spans. To such conceptions, Zeno's paradoxes of plurality, the arrow, and the stadium have direct application. Between the invention of the calculus and the work of Cauchy, the concept of the infinitesimal was highly confused. The infinitesimal was the "ghost of a departed quantity," a zero which is not really a zero.

In the nineteenth century, a more satisfactory definition of functionality was provided. A function is a pairing of elements of two (not necessarily distinct) classes, the domain of the function and its values. On the basis of this definition, if motion is a functional relation between time and position, then motion consists solely of the pairing of times with positions. Motion consists not of traversing an infinitesimal distance in an infinitesimal time; it consists of the occupation of a unique position at each given instant of time. This conception has been appropriately dubbed "the at-at theory of motion." The question, how does an object get from one position to another, does not arise. Thus, Russell was led to remark, "Weierstrass, by strictly banishing all infinitesimals, has at last shown that we live in an unchanging world, and that the arrow, at every moment of its flight, is truly at rest. The only point where Zeno probably erred was in inferring (if he did infer) that, because there is no change, therefore the world must be in the same state at one time as at another. This consequence by no means follows. . . ."[35]

[35] Russell, The Principles of Mathematics [102], p. 347.

In the paradox of the arrow, Zeno has been accused of an (understandable) inability to distinguish between instantaneous motion and instantaneous rest. To avoid Zeno's difficulties, Aristotle simply denied meaning to these concepts.[36] Today we assign a meaning to "instantaneous velocity" (including zero velocity as a special case) through the concept of the derivative. It is important to note, however, that this notion is defined by a limit process, so the value of the velocity at an instant depends logically upon what happens at neighboring instants. Instantaneous velocity is taken as the limit of ratios of space and time increments (average velocities) taken over ever decreasing time intervals; without velocities referred to intervals, in contrast to single instants, instantaneous velocity would have no meaning. Although instantaneous velocity does characterize motion at an instant, it does so by means of implicit reference to what goes on at neighboring times. If we confine attention entirely to what happens at one instant, without considering any other instants, it is impossible to distinguish instantaneous motion and instantaneous rest. We can only say that an object was at a particular place at that moment, but not whether it was moving or at rest. As Russell has emphasized, the value of a function is a constant, and in this sense, Bergson to the contrary notwithstanding, motion *is* compounded out of immobilities. In calling this view an absurdity, Bergson has committed the classical fallacy of composition.

The product of nineteenth-century mathematics that has most obvious application to Zeno's paradoxes is the theory of infinite series. Prior to Cauchy, there was no adequate theory of infinite series, no satisfactory definition of the sum of an infinite series, and no criterion of convergence. The eighteenth century saw many efforts to sum divergent series. It was only with nineteenth-century developments in

---

[36] Aristotle, *Physics* VI. 3.

mathematics that the convergent series generated by "The Achilles" and "The Dichotomy" could be handled.

The definition of the sum of an infinite series is a natural extension of the definition of addition of a finite number of terms.[37] Given an infinite series,

$$s_1 + s_2 + s_3 + \ldots$$

we form the sequence of partial sums,

$$S_1 = s_1$$
$$S_2 = s_1 + s_2$$
$$S_3 = s_1 + s_2 + s_3$$

etc.

If the sequence of partial sums,

$$S_1, S_2, S_3, \ldots$$

has a limit, the series is said to be convergent, and the limit of the sequence of partial sums is taken, *by definition*, to be the sum of the series. If the sequence of partial sums has no limit, the series is said to be divergent, and it has no sum. Given this definition of the sum of an infinite series, it becomes perfectly meaningful to say that the infinitely many terms of a convergent series have a finite sum.

Both the first form of "The Dichotomy" and "Achilles and The Tortoise" present us with infinite series to be summed. In particular, in "The Dichotomy" it is shown that to cover the whole racecourse (say it is one mile in length) the runner must cover the following series of nonoverlapping distances:

$$\tfrac{1}{2} + \tfrac{1}{4} + \tfrac{1}{8} + \ldots.$$

Each term of the series is greater than zero, and the sequence of partial sums converges to the limit of one. If Zeno had intended to argue that it is impossible to maintain consistently that the sum of infinitely many positive terms is finite, the foregoing definition shows him wrong.

Writing early in the twentieth century, Peirce remarked of "The Achilles" that ". . . this ridiculous little catch presents

[37] The reader who does not have a clear grasp of the concepts of sequences, series, and limits would do well to consult Courant and Robbins, *What Is Mathematics?* [133], chap. 6.

no difficulty at all to a mind adequately trained in mathematics and logic."[38] I presume his low opinion reflected a
belief that the entire source of the paradox was Zeno's inability to realize that an infinite series could have a finite
sum. There is no reason to suppose Peirce thought more
highly of any other of Zeno's paradoxes.

We have seen that nineteenth-century mathematics shed
great light upon the difficulties Zeno had raised. But these
developments did not provide a full resolution. The nineteenth century did not provide an adequate theory of
measure and dimension with which to dispose of the geometrical paradox. Moreover, there was no clear realization
in the nineteenth century that something more than a
mathematical definition was needed to resolve paradoxes
of *physical* space, time, and motion. In addition, it is
necessary to show that the mathematical system can be
coordinated with physical reality in such a way as to establish the adequacy of the mathematical results for the description of physical processes. A clear recognition of the
importance of this *semantical* problem is essentially a product of twentieth-century philosophy of science. As we shall
see, Zeno's paradoxes have still provided substantial problems with which mathematically sophisticated twentieth-
century philosophers can grapple.

INFINITY MACHINES

Russell's discussion of Zeno's paradoxes of motion in
"The Problem of Infinity Considered Historically" (reprinted
below) is a modern classic. Written in 1914, it brought together a good deal of the then-recent historical scholarship
on Zeno, and discussed the paradoxes in the light of
the most up-to-date mathematical knowledge available. It
seemed to many scientifically minded philosophers that
Russell had, in this and other writings, cut the ground
completely from under the metaphysical interpretations of

---

[38] Charles Sanders Peirce, *Collected Papers* [94], 6.177.

Zeno's paradoxes by such philosophers as Bergson and Bradley, and had provided something approaching a definitive resolution in the light of modern logic and mathematics.

Philosophers—even scientifically minded philosophers—cannot, it seems, remain permanently satisfied with an answer to a problem. Zeno's paradoxes were scrutinized again and again, not only by philosophers like Whitehead, who believed that profound metaphysical consequences could still be drawn, but also by those whose chief interest was logical analysis of the paradoxes themselves. Some of these philosophers, notably Max Black, found further difficulties lurking in the paradoxes. While fully aware of the salient facts about the summing of infinite series, Black argued that the mathematical definition of the sum of a series does not provide a full resolution of "The Dichotomy" or "The Achilles." Black's provocative article, "Achilles and the Tortoise" (reprinted below), elicited a number of responses, some of which are included in this book: Wisdom[39] cites Black with marked approval, and brings out pointedly the consequences for mathematical physics; Thomson[40] finds a large measure of agreement with Black concerning the nature of the difficulty remaining behind the paradoxes.

In "The Dichotomy" and "The Achilles" the performance of the runner is analyzed into an infinite sequence of tasks;[41] in "The Dichotomy" (first form) the runner must cover the first half, then the next quarter, etc.; in "The Achilles" he must first reach the tortoise's original starting point, then the point the tortoise has reached in the meantime, etc. The crucial problem, according to Black and Thomson, is whether it makes sense to suppose that anyone has completed an infinite sequence of runs. Black puts the matter forcefully and succinctly when he says that the mathe-

[39] "Achilles on a Physical Racecourse."

[40] "Tasks and Super-Tasks."

[41] As Thomson and a number of other writers have shown, considerable care must be exercised in the use of the word "task," and other near relatives such as "act" and "run" (both used as nouns).

matical operation of summing the infinite series will tell
us where and when Achilles will catch the tortoise *if* he can
catch the tortoise at all, but that is a big "if" (page 70
below). There is a fundamental logical difficulty in supposing that he *can* catch the tortoise. Indeed, Black argues, "the
expression, 'infinite series of acts,' is self-contradictory . . ."
(page 72). He describes a number of "infinity machines"
in order to show that it is impossible to say consistently that
the machine has completed an infinite sequence of operations, and *mutatis mutandis,* that the runner has completed
an infinite number of runs.

The simplest and most familiar of the infinity machines is
the desk lamp discussed by Thomson (page 94 below).
This lamp is of a common variety; it has a single push-button
switch on its base. If the lamp is off and you push the switch,
the lamp turns on; if it is on and you push the switch, the
lamp turns off. Now suppose that someone pushes the
switch an infinite number of times; he accomplishes this by
completing the first thrust in one-half minute, the second
in a quarter of a minute, the next in an eighth, etc., much
as the runner in The Dichotomy is supposed to cover the
infinite sequence of distances in decreasing times. Consider the final state of the lamp after the infinite sequence
of switchings. Is the lamp on or off? It cannot be on, for
each time it was on it was switched off. It cannot be off,
for *each* time it was off it was switched on.

The speed of switching that is demanded is, of course,
beyond human capability, but we are concerned with logical
possibilities, not "medical" limitations. Moreover, there is
no use trying to evade the problem by saying that the bulb
would burn out or the switch would wear out. Even if we
cover these eventualities by technological advances, there
remains a *logical* problem in supposing that an infinite sequence of switchings has been achieved. The lamp must be
both on and off, and also, neither on nor off. This is a
thoroughly unsatisfactory state of affairs.

Black and Thomson are *not* maintaining that the runner

cannot complete the race, or that Achilles cannot catch the tortoise. We all know they can, and to argue otherwise would be pointless. Black is arguing that it is improper to describe the feat as "completing an infinite sequence of tasks." Wisdom and Thomson draw similar morals. They are all suggesting that the paradoxes arise because of a mis-description of the situation.

These authors have elicited a fundamental point. We must begin by realizing that no definition, by itself, can provide the answer to a physical problem. Take the simplest possible case, the familiar definition of arithmetical addition for two terms. We find, by experience, that it applies in some situations and not in others. If we have m apples in one basket and n oranges in another, then we will have $m + n$ pieces of fruit if we put them together in one container. (Popular folklore notwithstanding, we obviously can "add" apples and oranges.) However, as is well-known, if we have m quarts of alcohol in one bucket and n quarts of water in another, we will not have $m + n$ quarts of solution if we put them together in the same container. This shows that combining baskets of apples and oranges is a suitable physical counterpart of arithmetical addition, while mixing alcohol and water is not.

The same sort of question arises when we consider applying the (now standard) definition of the sum of an infinite series. Does a given physical situation correspond with a particular mathematical operation, in this case, the operation of summing an infinite series? Black and Wisdom conclude that the running of a race does not correspond with the summing of an infinite series, for the completion of an infinite sequence of tasks is a logical impossibility, and so the running cannot properly be described as completing an infinite sequence of tasks. This conclusion has far-reaching implications for modern science. If Black and Wisdom are correct, the usual scientific description of the race-course as a mathematical continuum which is infinitely divisible is fundamentally incorrect. It may be a useful idealization for some purposes, but Zeno's paradoxes show that the description cannot be literally correct. The inescapable consequence of this view would seem to be that mathematical physics must have a radically different mathematical foundation if it is to deal adequately with physical reality.

Many people may be tempted at this point to say that the mathematical continuity of space, time, and motion are fictions we can profitably dispense with by now. Taking some encouragement from quantum mechanics, they may suggest that a discrete, atomistic conception is more adequate anyhow. Those who embrace this view face three major problems: first, they are open to the charge, elaborated by Grünbaum (pages 174–175, 244–246 below), of misconstruing the evidence from quantum mechanics; second, they must cope with the difficulties posed by "The Arrow" and "The Stadium";[42] and third, they are proposing a major overhaul of modern mathematical physics which has hardly been attempted, let alone achieved.

Not everyone is persuaded by the arguments of Black and Thomson. Benacerraf, in a careful logical analysis of the infinity machines, attempts to show that the alleged contradictions do not arise.[43] Consider Thomson's lamp; the same considerations will apply to any of the infinity machines. Thomson has described a physical switching process that occupies one minute. Given that we begin at t_0 with the lamp off, and given that a switching occurs at $t_1 = \frac{1}{2}$, $t_2 = \frac{3}{4}$, etc., we have a description that tells, for any moment *prior to the time* $T = 1$ (i.e., one minute after t_0), whether the lamp is on or off. For $T = 1$, and subsequent times, it tells us nothing. For any time *prior to* T that the lamp is on, there is a subsequent time *prior to* T that the lamp is off, and conversely. But this does not imply that the lamp is both on and off at T; it says nothing whatever about the state of the lamp at T, so that we can make any supposition we like with-

---

[42] See Russell, pp. 50–54 below; Owen, pp. 148–163 below, and Grünbaum, pp. 244–250 below.

[43] "Tasks, Super-Tasks, and the Modern Eleatics," reprinted below.

out any logical conflict. We have, in effect, a function defined over a half-open interval $0 \leqq t < 1$, and we are asked to infer its value at $t = 1$. Obviously, there is no answer to such a question. If the function approached a limit at $t = 1$, it would be natural to extend the definition of the function by making that limit the value of the function at the endpoint. But the "switching function" describing Thomson's lamp has no such limit, so any extension we might choose would seem arbitrary. In "The Dichotomy" and "The Achilles," by contrast, the "motion function" of the runner *does* approach a limit, and this limit provides a suitably appealing answer to the question about the location of the runner at the conclusion of his sequence of runs.

One cannot escape the feeling, however, that there is a significant and as yet unmentioned difference between the infinite sequence of runs Achilles must make to catch the tortoise and the infinite sequence of switch-pushes envisaged in connection with Thomson's lamp. Grünbaum's discussion of the infinity machines brings out the difference (pages 218–244 below). No one is interested in showing that Achilles can cover an infinite distance in a finite time; in fact, he cannot and we all know it. The problem is to show that he can cover an infinite number of distances that have a finite sum. Clearly, no infinite series of positive distances can have a finite sum unless the terms converge to zero without a positive lower bound. The infinite sequence of runs Achilles must make to catch the tortoise has this character, but the physical motions involved in switching an ordinary desk lamp differ from Achilles' runs in just this respect. To operate the switch, the finger must travel a certain minimal distance (say $\frac{1}{8}$ inch), and the sum of infinitely many such motions of the finger is infinitely large. The same applies to the working parts of the switch. The impossibility in the Thomson lamp example is the impossibility of the finger and the parts of the lamp moving an *infinite* distance in a finite time. Grünbaum shows that the same consideration applies to a number of different infinity machines, including those described by Black. When these machines are modified so as to eliminate motions over infinite distances, their paradoxical aspect vanishes.

Professor Thomson has kindly furnished a reply (included below) to Benacerraf's paper in which he acknowledges for the most part the validity of Benacerraf's criticisms. He maintains, however, that the paradox has not been completely resolved. It is notable that the problems Thomson sees as remaining lead directly into Zeno's paradox of plurality—a paradox which, as I have already suggested, is even more fundamental than the famous paradoxes of motion.

ZENO'S PARADOXES AND MODERN PHYSICS

At just about the time Black touched off the still-continuing discussion of infinity machines (1950), Adolf Grünbaum published two papers of fundamental importance on Zeno's paradoxes. One of these papers—a precursor to "Zeno's Metrical Paradox of Extension"—deals with the purely *mathematical* problem of providing a consistent account of the extended continuum, for instance the geometrical line, according to which it is literally composed of unextended points.[44] It attempts to answer the question of how an extension can be compounded out of elements lacking any extension whatever: How can we "add" together a lot of zeroes and get anything but zero? The other paper is concerned with the *semantical* problems that arise when we consider the application of mathematical systems to physical reality.[45] An example of this latter type of problem has already been discussed in connection with the infinity machines, but the general problem is considerably broader in scope. Grünbaum's article, "Modern Science and Refutation of the Paradoxes of Zeno" (below), provides a brief and elementary discussion of both types of problems and the relations between them. It also serves as an

[44] "A Consistent Conception of the Extended Linear Continuum as an Aggregate of Unextended Elements" [69].
[45] "Relativity and the Atomicity of Becoming" [73].

introduction to the two more substantial pieces by Grün-baum, one of which deals in detail with the purely mathe-matical problem, the other with certain of the semantical problems.

The dual aspect of the problems raised by Zeno's para-doxes results from the fact that, although the use of mathe-matics in the empirical sciences has been of unquestionable value, the statements of pure mathematics themselves do not describe the physical world. Systems of pure mathe-matics, as such, involve primitive terms which have no physical reference whatever, and statements that involve such terms are strictly without descriptive meaning. Pure Euclidean geometry, for instance, does not describe physical space. It is a formal system that involves undefined terms like "point," "congruent," and "intersects." Intuitive inter-pretations of these terms may have guided the construction of the formal system, but such considerations are entirely heuristic and are no part of the mathematical theory itself.[46]

Systems of pure mathematics may be applied to physical reality by providing physical interpretations. *Coordinating definitions* which give empirical referents for some of the key terms are the semantical means by which a physical interpretation is achieved. For example, when a sufficient number of geometrical terms are given meaning in terms of physical measurement, a geometrical system becomes a description of physical space—a description that may be true or false. The interpreted system is no longer merely an abstract system; it becomes an empirical theory in applied mathematics.[47]

It is of fundamental importance to remember that Zeno's paradoxes are arguments concerning *physical* change, *physi-cal* motion, and *physical* plurality. They are—so to speak—

---

[46] Wilder, *Introduction to the Foundations of Mathematics* [131], gives a clear characterization of systems of pure mathematics and their interpretations.

[47] Hans Reichenbach, *The Philosophy of Space and Time* [141], explains the concept of a coordinating definition, and discusses the relations between mathematical formalizations and physical space and time.

paradoxes of applied mathematics. No theory of pure mathematics can fully resolve them. Although it is necessary for the resolution of the paradoxes to provide logically consistent accounts of the continuum, sums of convergent infinite series, mathematical functions, and derivatives, these achievements are by no means sufficient. It is also necessary to show how these mathematical concepts can be used for the description of physical phenomena. We must be able to show how the required coordinating definitions can be supplied, and this is the semantical problem.[48]

The applicability of mathematical concepts to specific types of physical phenomena is not an automatic consequence of their consistency. We have already seen this in connection with the "addition" of apples and oranges in contrast with the "addition" of alcohol and water. Special relativity shows, for another example, that composition of velocities is not an admissible interpretation of standard vector addition. As we saw in our consideration of infinity machines, the question of whether the sum of a convergent series can represent a certain physical "sum" (as in "The Dichotomy" or "The Achilles") goes beyond the question of the consistency of the definition of "the sum of an infinite series."

Whether spatial or temporal manifolds can be described by means of a mathematical continuum is a separate issue over and above the problem of its consistency. This distinction between formal consistency and physical applicability makes it possible for such widely diverse authors as Bergson, Black, Whitehead, and Wisdom to accept Zeno's arguments to the extent of agreeing that the mathematical conception of the continuum, though perhaps consistent, is incompetent to describe actual physical processes. Grünbaum, however, argues not only for the consistency of the mathematical concept of the continuum, but also for its

---

[48] Even Russell was not sufficiently aware of the import of the semantical problem, and this is one respect in which subsequent authors, especially Grünbaum, have improved upon his treatment of Zeno's paradoxes.

physical applicability.[49] In this respect he goes far beyond authors like Peirce who seem to hold that pure mathematical theory can provide a full resolution of Zeno's paradoxes.

An ordering of things—whether they are purely mathematical entities like numbers and points or actual physical entities like places and times—must be given in terms of an ordering relation. Numbers are often ordered by a relation like *greater than*, places by a relation like *to the left of*, and times by a relation like *later than*. As usually understood, the real numbers (including integers, rationals, and irrationals) in their natural order form a mathematical continuum. If we use the real number system to represent time we are assuming that there is an isomorphism between the real numbers and the temporal continuum. This presupposes that instants of time occur corresponding precisely to the real numbers and that the *later than* relation between instants has precisely the same structure as the *greater than* relation between real numbers. One consequence is that instants of time do not have immediately preceding or succeeding instants; between any two instants there are infinitely many others. Another consequence is that there is a super-denumerable infinity of instants, and each instant has zero duration. The same type of situation occurs if the real number system is used to represent points on a line in physical space.

The use of the real number system to represent spatial and temporal magnitudes in physical science is customary. If a physical square has sides one foot long we do not hesitate to say that its diagonal is $\sqrt{2}$ feet long, and that a particle moving uniformly along the diagonal at one foot per second will take $\sqrt{2}$ seconds to traverse the distance.

---

[49] My discussion of "Zeno's Paradoxes and Modern Physics" owes an extremely heavy debt to Grünbaum, "Relativity and the Atomicity of Becoming" [73]. Some of his main points are summarized in "Modern Science and Refutation of the Paradoxes of Zeno," reprinted below, and some are presented more fully in "Modern Science and Zeno's Paradoxes of Motion," also in this anthology.

Furthermore, if a physical object travels from one place to another we suppose that its center of mass occupies a continuum of intervening points at a continuum of corresponding instants. This type of approach is characteristic of modern as well as classical physics; it is firmly entrenched in the very use of the calculus and analytic geometry to describe physical motion and change.

If we assume that the various attacks upon the mathematical consistency of the continuum have been satisfactorily answered, Zeno's paradoxes challenge us to show how it is possible to provide a correlation between the mathematical continuum and any alleged physical continuum. Whitehead and Bergson, for example, have denied the possibility of providing the requisite correlation between the mathematical continuum and physical time. An answer to them must take the form of showing how it is possible to provide a correlation between the *later than* relation among instants of time having zero duration and the *greater than* relation among real numbers. As Whitehead puts it, the fundamental problem of the arrow paradox is to explain "how the arrow survives the lapse of time,"[50] i.e., how an object can endure through a continuum of instants. The problem is made even more vivid when we conceive an enduring physical object like Zeno's arrow to be a continuum of intimately related instantaneous point-events with neither spatial nor temporal extension. Such a continuum of point-events is an important special case of the more general class of causal processes—a class whose members are construed quite generally to be continua of point-events. Whether or not we conceive a particular physical object or a causal process as traversing space, it certainly always has a temporal dimension, so that it involves at least the temporal continuum.

If physical science is to be genuinely empirical, it is usually said, the scientific concepts must somehow be connected

---

[50] Whitehead, *Process and Reality* [48], p. 106; see p. 19 above.

with the objects of experience. However, when we attempt to provide the correspondence between the mathematical continuum and physical reality via coordinating definitions, we encounter two difficulties. First, we are unable to find any unextended elements of experience to serve as correlates of the unextended elements of the continuum. The specious present of experience is not without duration; the smallest area we can perceive is not a mathematical point. Moreover, it is impossible in principle to define unextended points, instants, or events from the elements of experience. In the neighborhood of any point there is a super-denumerable infinity of points too close to be perceptually distinguished. How could we discriminate, in terms of the elements of experience, between two points that are arbitrarily close together, the distance between them being much smaller than the least we can detect?[51]

Second, even if we could provide an interpretation for such notions as points, instants, and events, the relation of *later than* among instants and events does not have the structure of the *later than* relation we experience directly. James and Whitehead have both argued convincingly that the experience of temporal succession is one that relates *extended* elements in such manner that each has an *immediate* successor.[52] These are serious difficulties. Given the apparent unsuitability of the elements of experience, is there any way of providing an empirical interpretation of the mathematical continuum?

The difficulties arise out of what might be described as a too narrowly empirical outlook.[53] If we insist that every

[51] See Russell, *Our Knowledge of the External World* [100], pp. 121ff., for an attempt to supply the required reconstruction. See Grünbaum, "Whitehead's Method of Extensive Abstraction" [74], for a critical evaluation of this construction (borrowed from Whitehead by Russell).

[52] See Whitehead, *Process and Reality* [48], pp. 105–107. This passage contains a relevant quotation from William James, *Some Problems of Philosophy* [44], chap. 10.

[53] Early operationism propounded a narrow empiricism of this type. For a clear presentation and critical analysis, see Carl G. Hempel, "A Logical Ap-

scientific concept be explicitly definable in terms of observables and if we insist that the *later than* relation of physics must have the same structure as the *later than* relation of direct experience, then the situation is hopeless. The necessary coordinating definitions simply cannot be given; the mathematical continuum remains a purely mathematical concept with no physical application. If this situation obtained we would, of course, be obliged to reconstruct mathematical physics from the very beginnings on the basis of a radically new kind of mathematics. But the difficulties can be circumvented. In the first place, we now realize that it is not necessary to provide an explicit correlate in experience for every theoretical concept. A physical interpretation of an abstract theory can often be achieved by providing coordinating definitions for some theoretical terms; the remaining theoretical terms derive meaning from their relations to the interpreted terms.[54] Thus it is not required to provide an explicit reconstruction of point-events from the elements of experience; it is sufficient to provide an interpretation of the concept of a *continuum of point-events*. This interpretation is easy to find; any physical process constitutes an empirical correlate.

In the second place, we must show how the physical *later than* relation can be explicated without dependence upon the phenomenological *later than*. This rather complicated task has been undertaken by Leibniz and many successors; it amounts to a causal theory of time.[55] According

---

praisal of Operationism," *Scientific Monthly*, LXXIX (1954), 215–220; reprinted with revisions in Carl G. Hempel, *Aspects of Scientific Explanation* (New York: The Free Press, 1965).

[54] This process is often called "partial interpretation." See Carl G. Hempel, *Fundamentals of Concept Formation in Empirical Science, International Encyclopedia of Unified Science*, Vol. II, no. 7 (Chicago: University of Chicago Press, 1952), chap. 2, sec. 7.

[55] Carrying out this program is the main purpose of Reichenbach, *The Direction of Time* [140], and Grünbaum, *Philosophical Problems of Space and Time* [139], chaps. 7–8. Pp. 180 and 208 in the latter relate the analysis directly to Zeno's paradoxes.

to this theory there are objective causal relations among physical events; we can detect these relations, and we can distinguish between cause and effect. All of this can be done, it is claimed, on the basis of observable properties of physical events without reference to our intuitive sense of time-direction. On pain of circularity the identification of cause and effect must be made without reference to temporal relations among events.. The physical *later than* relation is then defined by the condition that an effect is later than its cause; as Leibniz has said, "If of two elements which are not simultaneous one comprehends the cause of the other, then the former is considered as *preceding*, the latter as *succeeding*."[56] This type of explication frees the physical *later than* relation from any necessity of sharing structural characteristics of the *later than* relation of immediate experience. Grünbaum summarizes the results as follows:

> Since we have founded the "later than" relation on the relation of causal influence, . . . it now becomes entirely intelligible that influence relations can exist between events in a network of dependence such that the events constitute a linear Cantorean continuum with respect to the relation of "later than"! In this way, the concept of "later than" becomes the key to the temporal order without involving the nextness property.[57]

In subsequent writings, Grünbaum has made significant alterations in his treatment of the relation of *later than*.[58] Instead of attempting to invoke an asymmetrical causal relation directly, he begins with a symmetrical relation of causal connectedness which does not, by itself, distinguish cause

---

[56] G. Leibniz, "Initia rerum mathematicarum metaphysica," *Math. Schriften*, VII, 18. Quoted by Grünbaum in "Relativity and the Atomicity of Becoming" [73], p. 166.

[57] Grünbaum, "Relativity and the Atomicity of Becoming" [73], pp. 168–69. Reprinted by permission.

[58] These changes were motivated by Grünbaum's desire to avoid reliance upon Reichenbach's "mark" method of distinguishing cause from effect, a method Grünbaum regards as inadequate. For a full discussion of the issues involved, see Grünbaum, *Philosophical Problems of Space and Time* [139], chap. 7, and *Modern Science and Zeno's Paradoxes* [72], pp. 56–64.

from effect or earlier from later. This relation can be used,
however, as a foundation for a temporal continuum with
such properties as denseness. Although the relation of causal
connectedness does not endow this continuum with any
asymmetry of earlier and later, the required asymmetry (or
anisotropy, as Grünbaum calls it) can be superimposed on
the basis of further empirical properties of events in the
physical world—especially in terms of thermodynamic considerations involving entropy. These modifications, although
they are of great importance for some aspects of the theory
of time, do not constitute any abandonment of the causal
theory, and they do not in any way invalidate the conclusions drawn with respect to Zeno's paradoxes. In particular,
the original reply to Whitehead still stands:

> Although the events postulated by the theory of relativity
> are without duration, a continuum of them does have posi-
> tive duration, and . . . we can give a physical process as
> a co-ordinating definition for a "continuous set of instants."
> Therefore we are able to say that Whitehead is in error, when
> he writes concerning the issue of becoming during a sec-
> ond of time; "The difficulty is not evaded by assuming that
> something becomes at each non-extensive instant of time.
> For at the beginning of the second of time there is no next
> instant at which something can become."[59] On the theory
> which we have offered, no next instant is required for be-
> coming, and processes of finite durations can be resolved
> consistently into non-extensive events [i.e., processes can
> be postulated to be aggregates of point-events.][60] . . .
> Change consists, in the sense of the theory of aggregates, of
> certain point events and their relations. If these events take
> place, then change does. If the set of events is temporally
> dense, then there is no *first* (*non-degenerate*) sub-interval in
> the continuum. . . . Therefore, there is then no *initial change.*

[59] Whitehead, *Process and Reality* [48], p. 106. See p. 19 above.

[60] It should not be inferred that Grünbaum provides an alternative account of
physical becoming. For his critique of this concept see Grünbaum, *Modern
Science and Zeno's Paradoxes* [72], chap. 1. See also J. J. C. Smart, *Philosophy
and Scientific Realism* [142], chap. 7.

> Our analysis has shown that the theory has no valid reason
> to make provision for such initial change. . . . Events simply
> are or occur . . . but they do not "advance" into a pre-
> existing frame called 'time.' . . . time is a system of relations
> between events, and as events are, so are their relations.
> An event does not move and neither do any of its relations.[61]

In saying above that the major difficulty in applying the
mathematical continuum to the physical world lies in a too
narrowly empirical outlook, there was no suggestion of an
abandonment of empiricism or a compromise with ration-
alism. Modern physics is thoroughly empirical in the only
important sense. Its theories must stand the test of empirical
confirmation or disconfirmation. This does not mean that
every physical concept must be explicitly *defined* in terms
of observables. It requires only that enough coordinating
definitions be provided to connect the abstract theory with
experience to the extent that it becomes subject to empirical
test. The physical theories to which we have referred have
been faced with experiential tests and have been highly
confirmed by them. We need ask no more. The postulation
of physical processes which are analyzable as continua of
point-events is fully justified.

Grünbaum has recently published a monograph, *Modern
Science and Zeno's Paradoxes,*[62] in which he discusses in
great detail the mathematical and physical issues raised by
Zeno's paradoxes. Aside from the treatments of the geometrical paradox, infinity machines, and quantum mechanics
—all of which are included in the selections reprinted below
—he provides detailed consideration of the status of temporal becoming, the nature of the physical relation of *later
than*, and the structure of the perceptual continuum. The
reader who wants to go beyond the contents of this book
in dealing with Zeno's paradoxes would do well to take up
Grünbaum's excellent monograph.

[61] Grünbaum, "Relativity and the Atomicity of Becoming" [73], pp. 171–172.
Reprinted by permission.
[62] [72].

SOME PHILOSOPHICAL MORALS

Zeno's paradoxes pose a compelling temptation for philosophers: few can resist the urge to comment upon them in some fashion. Those with a strong practical bent may try to dispose of such problems by getting up and walking around —much in the manner of Dr. Johnson's famous "refutation" of Berkeley's idealism. Such approaches are, of course, totally irrelevant. Everyone, including Parmenides and Zeno, insists that motion *seems* to occur; the force of the paradoxes rests upon the difficulty of reconciling the appearance of motion with the logical considerations Zeno advances. To reiterate, verbally or by example, that things seem to move does not advance our understanding of the problems in the least.

A word of caution also needs to be offered, I believe, regarding a temptation to go too far in the opposite direction. Parmenides and Zeno sought to prove a priori (as did Bradley some twenty-five centuries later) that motion and change do not occur. Today most philosophers would agree that this is not the sort of problem that can be settled a priori. Whether motion and change occur is a question of fact, and the answer to this question requires empirical evidence. Whitehead, admitting the reality of motion and change, takes Zeno's arguments to show that they occur atomistically rather than continuously. For Whitehead, the discontinuous character of becoming sometimes appears to be an a priori result given only that change and motion occur. Again, it is important to realize that the question of whether motion and change are continuous is an additional factual question over and above the empirical question of their mere occurrence, and this further question requires further empirical evidence.[63] This point should be kept in mind when one attempts to resolve the paradoxes. A resolu-

---

[63] See Grünbaum, "The Falsifiability of a Component of a Theoretical System," in *Mind, Matter, and Method*, eds. P. K. Feyerabend and G. Maxwell (Minneapolis: University of Minnesota Press, 1966), pp. 296–299, for a brief indication of the character of this empirical problem.

tion that proves a priori that motion must be continuous is too strong to be valid. Whereas the foregoing practical dismissal of the paradoxes errs by not providing enough of a resolution, an a priori proof of the continuity of motion would be too much of a resolution to be acceptable.

I should like to conclude with a homely analogy. Zeno's paradoxes have an onion-like quality; as one peels away outer layers by disposing of the more superficial difficulties, new and more profound problems are revealed. For instance, as we show that it is mathematically consistent to suppose that an infinite series of positive terms has a finite sum, the problem of the infinity machines arises. When we show how the infinity machines can be handled, the problem of composing the continuum out of unextended elements appears. When charges concerning the consistency of the continuum are met, the problem of identity of structure between the mathematical continuum and the continuum of physical time confronts us. And so on. Will we ever succeed in stripping away all of the layers and providing a complete resolution of all the difficulties that arise out of Zeno's paradoxes? And if we should succeed, what would be left in the center? In a certain sense, nothing, it would seem. We will not find a metaphysical nutmeat such as Whitehead's atomism, or any other fundamental truth about the nature of reality. However, we should not conclude that nothing of value remains. The layers we have peeled away have in them the elements of a nourishing philosophical broth. The analysis itself, dealing in detail with a host of fundamental problems, is richly rewarding in terms of our understanding of space, time, motion, continuity, and infinity. We would be foolish indeed to conclude that the onion was nothing but skin, and to discard the whole thing as worthless.

It would, of course, be rash to conclude that we had actually arrived at a complete resolution of all problems that come out of Zeno's paradoxes. Each age, from Aristotle on down, seems to find in the paradoxes difficulties that are roughly commensurate with the mathematical, logical, and

philosophical resources then available. When more powerful tools emerge, philosophers seem willing to acknowledge
deeper difficulties that would have proved insurmountable
for more primitive methods. We may have resolutions which
are appropriate to our present level of understanding, but
they may appear quite inadequate when we have advanced
further. The paradoxes do, after all, go to the very heart of
space, time, and motion, and these are profoundly difficult
concepts.

Or, has the onion infinitely many layers? If so, we may be
faced with an infinite sequence of tasks that does defy
completion in a finite time, for the steps become longer,
not shorter, as the difficulties become deeper.

The Problem of Infinity Considered Historically

BERTRAND RUSSELL

Zeno's four arguments against motion were intended to exhibit the contradictions that result from supposing that there is such a thing as change, and thus to support the Parmenidean doctrine that reality is unchanging.[1] Unfortunately, we only know his arguments through Aristotle,[2] who stated them in order to refute them. Those philosophers in the present day who have had their doctrines stated by opponents will realise that a just or adequate presentation of Zeno's position is hardly to be expected from Aristotle; but by some care in interpretation it seems possible to reconstruct the so-called "sophisms" which have been "refuted" by every tyro from that day to this.

Zeno's arguments would seem to be "ad hominem"; that is to say, they seem to assume premises granted by his opponents, and to show that, granting these premises, it is possible to deduce consequences which his opponents must deny. In order to decide whether they are valid arguments or "sophisms," it is necessary to guess at the tacit premises,

From *Our Knowledge of the External World* (New York: W. W. Norton & Company, Inc., 1929), lecture 6, pp. 182–198. Reprinted by permission of George Allen & Unwin Ltd. Footnote numbers have been changed to number consecutively throughout the article.

[1] This interpretation is combated by Milhaud, *Les philosophes-géomètres de la Grèce*, p. 140n., but his reasons do not seem to me convincing. All the interpretations in what follows are open to question, but all have the support of reputable authorities.

[2] *Physics* VI. 9, 239b (R.P. 136–139).

and to decide who was the "homo" at whom they were aimed. Some maintain that they were aimed at the Pythagoreans,[3] while others have held that they were intended to refute the atomists.[4] M. Evellin, on the contrary, holds that they constitute a refutation of infinite divisibility,[5] while M. G. Noël, in the interests of Hegel, maintains that the first two arguments refute infinite divisibility, while the next two refute indivisibles.[6] Amid such a bewildering variety of interpretations, we can at least not complain of any restrictions on our liberty of choice.

The historical questions raised by the above-mentioned discussions are no doubt largely insoluble, owing to the very scanty material from which our evidence is derived. The points which seem fairly clear are the following: (1) that, in spite of MM. Milhaud and Paul Tannery, Zeno is anxious to prove that motion is really impossible, and that he desires to prove this because he follows Parmenides in denying plurality;[7] (2) that the third and fourth arguments proceed on the hypothesis of indivisibles, a hypothesis which, whether adopted by the Pythagoreans or not, was certainly much advocated, as may be seen from the treatise *On Indivisible Lines* attributed to Aristotle. As regards the first two arguments, they would seem to be valid on the hypothesis of indivisibles, and also, without this hypothesis, to be such as would be valid if the traditional contradictions in infinite numbers were insoluble, which they are not.

[3] Cf. Gaston Milhaud, *Les philosophes-géomètres de la Grèce*, p. 140n.; Paul Tannery, *Pour l'histoire de la science hellène*, p. 249; John Burnet, *Early Greek Philosophy* [2nd ed. (London: Adam & Charles Black, 1908)], p. 362.

[4] Cf. R. K. Gaye, "On Aristotle, *Physics*, Z ix" [25], esp. 111. Also Moritz Cantor, *Vorlesungen über Geschichte der Mathematik*, 1st ed., Vol. 1, 1880, p. 168, who, however, subsequently adopted Paul Tannery's opinion, *Vorlesungen*, 3rd ed. (Vol. 1, p. 200).

[5] "Le mouvement et les partisans des indivisibles," *Revue de Métaphysique et de Morale*, Vol. I [1893], pp. 382–395.

[6] "Le mouvement et les arguments de Zénon d'Elée," *Revue de Métaphysique et de Morale*, Vol. I, pp. 107–125.

[7] Cf. M. Brochard, "Les prétendus sophismes de Zénon d'Elée," *Revue de Métaphysique et de Morale*, Vol. I, pp. 209–215.

We may conclude, therefore, that Zeno's polemic is directed against the view that space and time consist of points and instants; and that as against the view that a finite stretch of space or time consists of a finite number of points and instants, his arguments are not sophisms, but perfectly valid.

The conclusion which Zeno wishes us to draw is that plurality is a delusion, and spaces and times are really indivisible. The other conclusion which is possible, namely, that the number of points and instants is infinite, was not tenable so long as the infinite was infected with contradictions. In a fragment which is not one of the four famous arguments against motion, Zeno says:

"If things are a many, they must be just as many as they are, and neither more nor less. Now, if they are as many as they are, they will be finite in number.

"If things are a many, they will be infinite in number; for there will always be other things between them, and others again between these. And so things are infinite in number."[8]

This argument attempts to prove that, if there are many things, the number of them must be both finite and infinite, which is impossible; hence we are to conclude that there is only one thing. But the weak point in the argument is the phrase: "If they are just as many as they are, they will be finite in number." This phrase is not very clear, but it is plain that it assumes the impossibility of definite infinite numbers. Without this assumption, which is now known to be false, the arguments of Zeno, though they suffice (on certain very reasonable assumptions) to dispel the hypothesis of finite indivisibles, do not suffice to prove that motion and change and plurality are impossible. They are not, however, on any view, mere foolish quibbles: they are serious arguments, raising difficulties which it has taken two thousand years to answer, and which even now are fatal to the teachings of most philosophers.

[8] Simplicius, *Phys.* 140, 28d (R.P. 133); Burnet, *op. cit.*, pp. 364–365.

The first of Zeno's arguments is the argument of the race-course, which is paraphrased by Burnet as follows:[9]

"You cannot get to the end of a race-course. You cannot traverse an infinite number of points in a finite time. You must traverse the half of any given distance before you traverse the whole, and the half of that again before you can traverse it. This goes on *ad infinitum,* so that there are an infinite number of points in any given space, and you cannot touch an infinite number one by one in a finite time."[10]

Zeno appeals here, in the first place, to the fact that any distance, however small, can be halved. From this it follows, of course, that there must be an infinite number of points in a line. But, Aristotle represents him as arguing, you cannot touch an infinite number of points *one by one* in a finite time. The words "one by one" are important.

(1) If *all* the points touched are concerned, then, though you pass through them continuously, you do not touch them "one by one." That is to say, after touching one, there

---

[9] *Op. cit.,* p. 367.

[10] Aristotle's words are: "The first is the one on the non-existence of motion on the ground that what is moved must always attain the middle point sooner than the end-point, on which we gave our opinion in the earlier part of our discourse." *Phys.* VI. 9, 939b (R.P. 136). Aristotle seems to refer to *Phys.* VI. 2, 223ab [R.P. 136a]: "All space is continuous, for time and space are divided into the same and equal divisions. . . . Wherefore also Zeno's argument is fallacious, that it is impossible to go through an infinite collection or to touch an infinite collection one by one in a finite time. For there are two senses in which the term 'infinite' is applied both to length and to time, and in fact to all continuous things, either in regard to divisibility, or in regard to the ends. Now it is not possible to touch things infinite in regard to number in a finite time, but it is possible to touch things infinite in regard to divisibility: for time itself also is infinite in this sense. So that in fact we go through an infinite [space], in an infinite [time] and not in a finite [time], and we touch infinite things with infinite things, not with finite things." Philoponus, a sixth-century commentator (R.P. 136a, *Exc. Paris Philop. in Arist. Phys.* 803, 2. Vit.), gives the following illustration: "For if a thing were moved the space of a cubit in one hour, since in every space there are an infinite number of points, the thing moved must needs touch all the points of the space: it will then go through an infinite collection in a finite time, which is impossible."

is not another which you touch next: no two points are next each other, but between any two there are always an infinite number of others, which cannot be enumerated one by one.

(2) If, on the other hand, only the successive middle points are concerned, obtained by always halving what remains of the course, then the points are reached one by one, and, though they are infinite in number, they are in fact all reached in a finite time. His argument to the contrary may be supposed to appeal to the view that a finite time must consist of a finite number of instants, in which case what he says would be perfectly true on the assumption that the possibility of continued dichotomy is undeniable. If, on the other hand, we suppose the argument directed against the partisans of infinite divisibility, we must suppose it to proceed as follows:[11] "The points given by successive halving of the distances still to be traversed are infinite in number, and are reached in succession, each being reached a finite time later than its predecessor; but the sum of an infinite number of finite times must be infinite, and therefore the process will never be completed." It is very possible that this is historically the right interpretation, but in this form the argument is invalid. If half the course takes half a minute, and the next quarter takes a quarter of a minute, and so on, the whole course will take a minute. The apparent force of the argument, on this interpretation, lies solely in the mistaken supposition that there cannot be anything beyond the whole of an infinite series, which can be seen to be false by observing that 1 is beyond the whole of the infinite series $\frac{1}{2}, \frac{3}{4}, \frac{7}{8}, \frac{15}{16}, \ldots$.

The second of Zeno's arguments is the one concerning Achilles and the tortoise, which has achieved more notoriety than the others. It is paraphrased by Burnet as follows:[12]

---

[11] Cf. Mr. C. D. Broad, "Note on Achilles and the Tortoise" [55], pp. 318–319.
[12] *Op. cit.*

"Achilles will never overtake the tortoise. He must first reach the place from which the tortoise started. By that time the tortoise will have got some way ahead. Achilles must then make up that, and again the tortoise will be ahead. He is always coming nearer, but he never makes up to it."[13]

This argument is essentially the same as the previous one. It shows that, if Achilles ever overtakes the tortoise, it must be after an infinite number of instants have elapsed since he started. This is in fact true; but the view that an infinite number of instants make up an infinitely long time is not true, and therefore the conclusion that Achilles will never overtake the tortoise does not follow.

The third argument,[14] that of the arrow, is very interesting. The text has been questioned. Burnet accepts the alterations of Zeller, and paraphrases thus:

"The arrow in flight is at rest. For, if everything is at rest when it occupies a space equal to itself, and what is in flight at any given moment always occupies a space equal to itself, it cannot move."

But according to Prantl, the literal translation of the unemended text of Aristotle's statement of the argument is as follows: "If everything, when it is behaving in a uniform manner, is continually either moving or at rest, but what is moving is always in the *now*, then the moving arrow is motionless." This form of the argument brings out its force more clearly than Burnet's paraphrase.

Here, if not in the first two arguments, the view that a finite part of time consists of a finite series of successive instants seems to be assumed; at any rate the plausibility of the argument seems to depend upon supposing that there are consecutive instants. Throughout an instant, it is said, a

[13] Aristotle's words are: "The second is the so-called Achilles. It consists in this, that the slower will never be overtaken in its course by the quickest, for the pursuer must always come first to the point from which the pursued has just departed, so that the slower must necessarily be always still more or less in advance." *Phys.* VI. 9, 239b (R.P. 138).

[14] *Phys.* VI. 9, 239b (R.P. 138).

moving body is where it is: it cannot move during the instant, for that would require that the instant should have parts. Thus, suppose we consider a period consisting of a thousand instants, and suppose the arrow is in flight throughout this period. At each of the thousand instants, the arrow is where it is, though at the next instant it is somewhere else. It is never moving, but in some miraculous way the change of position has to occur *between* the instants, that is to say, not at any time whatever. This is what M. Bergson calls the cinematographic representation of reality. The more the difficulty is meditated, the more real it becomes. The solution lies in the theory of continuous series: we find it hard to avoid supposing that, when the arrow is in flight, there is a *next* position occupied at the *next* moment; but in fact there is no next position and no next moment, and when once this is imaginatively realised, the difficulty is seen to disappear.

The fourth and last of Zeno's arguments is[15] the argument of the stadium.

The argument as stated by Burnet is as follows:

First Position	Second Position
A	A ....
B ....→	B ....
C ←....	C ....

"Half the time may be equal to double the time. Let us suppose three rows of bodies, one of which (A) is at rest while the other two (B, C) are moving with velocity in opposite directions. By the time they are all in the same part of the course, B will have passed twice as many of the bodies in C as in A. Therefore the time which it takes to pass C is twice as long as the time it takes to pass A. But the time which B and C take to reach the position of A is the same. Therefore double the time is equal to the half."

[15] *Phys.* VI. 9, 293b (R.P. 139).

Gaye[16] devoted an interesting article to the interpretation of this argument. His translation of Aristotle's statement
is as follows:

"The fourth argument is that concerning the two rows of
bodies, each row being composed of an equal number of
bodies of equal size, passing each other on a race-course as
they proceed with equal velocity in opposite directions, the
one row originally occupying the space between the goal
and the middle point of the course, and the other that between the middle point and the starting-post. This, he thinks,
involves the conclusion that half a given time is equal to
double that time. The fallacy of the reasoning lies in the assumption that a body occupies an equal time in passing
with equal velocity a body that is in motion and a body of
equal size that is at rest, an assumption which is false. For
instance (so runs the argument), let A A . . . be the stationary
bodies of equal size, B B . . . the bodies, equal in number and
in size to A A . . . , originally occupying the half of the course
from the starting-post to the middle of the A's, and C C . . .
those originally occupying the other half from the goal to
the middle of the A's, equal in number, size, and velocity,
to B B . . . . Then three consequences follow. First, as the B's
and C's pass one another, the first B reaches the last C at
the same moment at which the first C reaches the last B.
Secondly, at this moment the first C has passed all the A's,
whereas the first B has passed only half the A's and has consequently occupied only half the time occupied by the first
C, since each of the two occupies an equal time in passing
each A. Thirdly, at the same moment all the B's have passed
all the C's: for the first C and the first B will simultaneously
reach the opposite ends of the course, since (so says Zeno)
the time occupied by the first C in passing each of the B's
is equal to that occupied by it in passing each of the A's,
because an equal time is occupied by both the first B and the

---

[16] *Loc. cit.* [25].

first C in passing all the A's. This is the argument: but it presupposes the aforesaid fallacious assumption."

This argument is not quite easy to follow, and it is only valid as against the assumption that a finite time consists of a finite number of instants. We may restate it in different language. Let us suppose three drill-sergeants, A, A', and A'',

First Position				Second Position		
B	B'	B''			B	B'	B''
.	.	.			.	.	.
A	A'	A''		A	A'	A''
.	.	.		.	.	.
C	C'	C''	C	C'	C''
.	.	.	.	.	.

standing in a row, while the two files of soldiers march past them in opposite directions. At the first moment which we consider, the three men B, B', B'' in one row, and the three men C, C', C'' in the other row, are respectively opposite to A, A', and A''. At the very next moment, each row has moved on, and now B and C'' are opposite A'. Thus B and C'' are opposite each other. When, then, did B pass C'? It must have been somewhere between the two moments which we supposed consecutive, and therefore the two moments cannot really have been consecutive. It follows that there must be other moments between any two given moments, and therefore that there must be an infinite number of moments in any given interval of time.

The above difficulty, that B must have passed C' at some time between two consecutive moments, is a genuine one, but is not precisely the difficulty raised by Zeno. What Zeno professes to prove is that "half of a given time is equal to double that time." The most intelligible explanation of the argument known to me is that of Gaye.[17] Since, however, his explanation is not easy to set forth shortly, I will re-state

[17] *Op. cit.* [25], p. 105.

what seems to me to be the logical essence of Zeno's contention. If we suppose that time consists of a series of consecutive instants, and that motion consists in passing through a series of consecutive points, then the fastest possible motion is one which, at each instant, is at a point consecutive to that at which it was at the previous instant. Any slower motion must be one which has intervals of rest interspersed, and any faster motion must wholly omit some points. All this is evident from the fact that we cannot have more than one event for each instant. But now, in the case of our A's and B's and C's, B is opposite a fresh A every instant, and therefore the number of A's passed gives the number of instants since the beginning of the motion. But during the motion B has passed twice as many C's, and yet cannot have passed more than one each instant. Hence the number of instants since the motion began is twice the number of A's passed, though we previously found it was equal to this number. From this result, Zeno's conclusion follows.

Zeno's arguments, in some form, have afforded grounds for almost all the theories of space and time and infinity which have been constructed from his day to our own. We have seen that all his arguments are valid (with certain reasonable hypotheses) on the assumption that finite spaces and times consist of a finite number of points and instants, and that the third and fourth almost certainly in fact proceeded on this assumption, while the first and second, which were perhaps intended to refute the opposite assumption, were in that case fallacious. We may therefore escape from his paradoxes either by maintaining that, though space and time do consist of points and instants, the number of them in any finite interval is infinite; or by denying that space and time consist of points and instants at all; or lastly, by denying the reality of space and time altogether. It would seem that Zeno himself, as a supporter of Parmenides, drew the last of these three possible deductions, at any rate in regard to time. In this a very large number of philosophers have followed him. Many others, like M. Bergson, have preferred to deny that space and time consist of points and instants. Either of these solutions will meet the difficulties in the form in which Zeno raised them. But, as we saw, the difficulties can also be met if infinite numbers are admissible. And on grounds which are independent of space and time, infinite numbers, and series in which no two terms are consecutive, must in any case be admitted. Consider, for example, all the fractions less than 1, arranged in order of magnitude. Between any two of them, there are others, for example, the arithmetical mean of the two. Thus no two fractions are consecutive, and the total number of them is infinite. It will be found that much of what Zeno says as regards the series of points on a line can be equally well applied to the series of fractions. And we cannot deny that there are fractions, so that two of the above ways of escape are closed to us. It follows that, if we are to solve the whole class of difficulties derivable from Zeno's by analogy, we must discover some tenable theory of infinite numbers. What, then, are the difficulties which, until the last thirty years, led philosophers to the belief that infinite numbers are impossible?

The difficulties of infinity are of two kinds, of which the first may be called sham, while the others involve, for their solution, a certain amount of new and not altogether easy thinking. The sham difficulties are those suggested by the etymology, and those suggested by confusion of the mathematical infinite with what philosophers impertinently call the "true" infinite. Etymologically, "infinite" should mean "having no end." But in fact some infinite series have ends, some have not; while some collections are infinite without being serial, and can therefore not properly be regarded as either endless or having ends. The series of instants from any earlier one to any later one (both included) is infinite, but has two ends; the series of instants from the beginning of time to the present moment has one end, but is infinite. Kant, in his first antinomy, seems to hold that it is harder for the past to be infinite than for the future to be so, on the ground that the past is now completed, and that nothing infinite can be completed. It is very difficult to see how he can have imagined that there was any sense in this remark; but it seems most probable that he was thinking of the infinite as the "unended." It is odd that he did not see that the future too has one end at the present, and is precisely on a level with the past. His regarding the two as different in this respect illustrates just that kind of slavery to time which, as we agreed* in speaking of Parmenides, the true philosopher must learn to leave behind him.

The confusions introduced into the notions of philosophers by the so-called "true" infinite are curious. They see that this notion is not the same as the mathematical infinite, but they choose to believe that it is the notion which the mathematicians are vainly trying to reach. They therefore inform the mathematicians, kindly but firmly, that they are mistaken in adhering to the "false" infinite, since plainly the "true" infinite is something quite different. The reply to this is that what they call the "true" infinite is a notion totally irrelevant to the problem of the mathematical infinite, to which it has only a fanciful and verbal analogy. So remote is it that I do not propose to confuse the issue by even mentioning what the "true" infinite is. It is the "false" infinite that concerns us, and we have to show that the epithet "false" is undeserved.

There are, however, certain genuine difficulties in understanding the infinite, certain habits of mind derived from the consideration of finite numbers, and easily extended to infinite numbers under the mistaken notion that they represent logical necessities. For example, every number to which we are accustomed, except 0, has another number immediately before it, from which it results by adding 1; but the first infinite number does not have this property. The numbers before it form an infinite series, containing all the ordinary finite numbers, having no maximum, no last finite number, after which one little step would plunge us

*[Russell, *Our Knowledge of the External World* [100], p. 181.]

into the infinite. If it is assumed that the first infinite number is reached by a succession of small steps, it is easy to show that it is self-contradictory. The first infinite number is, in fact, beyond the whole unending series of finite numbers. "But," it will be said, "there cannot be anything beyond the whole of an unending series." This, we may point out, is the very principle upon which Zeno relies in the arguments of the race-course and the Achilles. Take the race-course: there is the moment when the runner still has half his distance to run, then the moment when he still has a quarter, then when he still has an eighth, and so on in a strictly unending series. Beyond the whole of this series is the moment when he reaches the goal. Thus there certainly can be something beyond the whole of an unending series. But it remains to show that this fact is only what might have been expected.

The difficulty, like most of the vaguer difficulties besetting the mathematical infinite, is derived, I think, from the more or less unconscious operation of the idea of *counting*. If you set to work to count the terms in an infinite collection, you will never have completed your task. Thus, in the case of the runner, if half, three-quarters, seven-eighths, and so on of the course were marked, and the runner was not allowed to pass any of the marks until the umpire said "Now," then Zeno's conclusion would be true in practice, and he would never reach the goal.

But it is not essential to the existence of a collection, or even to knowledge and reasoning concerning it, that we should be able to pass its terms in review one by one. This may be seen in the case of finite collections; we can speak of "mankind" or "the human race," though many of the individuals in this collection are not personally known to us. We can do this because we know of various characteristics which every individual has if he belongs to the collection, and not if he does not. And exactly the same happens in the case of infinite collections: they may be known by their characteristics although their terms cannot be enumerated. In this sense, an unending series may nevertheless form a whole, and there may be new terms beyond the whole of it.

Some purely arithmetical peculiarities of infinite numbers have also caused perplexity. For instance, an infinite number is not increased by adding one to it, or by doubling it. Such peculiarities have seemed to many to contradict logic, but in fact they only contradict confirmed mental habits. The whole difficulty of the subject lies in the necessity of thinking in an unfamiliar way, and in realising that many properties which we have thought inherent in number are in fact peculiar to finite numbers. If this is remembered, the positive theory of infinity . . . will not be found so difficult as it is to those who cling obstinately to the prejudices instilled by the arithmetic which is learnt in childhood.

The Cinemato-graphic View of Becoming

HENRI BERGSON

Now, if we try to characterize more precisely our natural attitude towards Becoming, this is what we find. Becoming is infinitely varied. That which goes from yellow to green is not like that which goes from green to blue: they are different *qualitative* movements. That which goes from flower to fruit is not like that which goes from larva to nymph and from nymph to perfect insect: they are different *evolutionary* movements. The action of eating or of drinking is not like the action of fighting: they are different *extensive* movements. And these three kinds of movement themselves—qualitative, evolutionary, extensive—differ profoundly. The trick of our perception, like that of our intelligence, like that of our language, consists in extracting from these profoundly different becomings the single representation of becoming *in general*, undefined becoming, a mere abstraction which by itself says nothing and of which, indeed, it is very rarely that we think. To this idea, always the same, and always obscure or unconscious, we then join, in each particular case, one or several clear images that represent *states* and which serve to distinguish all becomings

From Henri Bergson, *Creative Evolution*, trans. Arthur Mitchell (New York: Holt, Rinehart and Winston, 1911), chap. 4, pp. 304–311. Copyright 1911, 1939 by Holt, Rinehart and Winston, Inc. Reprinted by permission of Holt, Rinehart and Winston, Inc., and Macmillan & Co. Ltd., London.

from each other. It is this composition of a specified and definite state with change general and undefined that we substitute for the specific change. An infinite multiplicity of becomings variously colored, so to speak, passes before our eyes: we manage so that we see only differences of color, that is to say, differences of state, beneath which there is supposed to flow, hidden from our view, a becoming always and everywhere the same, invariably colorless.

Suppose we wish to portray on a screen a living picture, such as the marching past of a regiment. There is one way in which it might first occur to us to do it. That would be to cut out jointed figures representing the soldiers, to give to each of them the movement of marching, a movement varying from individual to individual although common to the human species, and to throw the whole on the screen. We should need to spend on this little game an enormous amount of work, and even then we should obtain but a very poor result: how could it, at its best, reproduce the suppleness and variety of life? Now, there is another way of proceeding, more easy and at the same time more effective. It is to take a series of snapshots of the passing regiment and to throw these instantaneous views on the screen, so that they replace each other very rapidly. This is what the cinematograph does. With photographs, each of which represents the regiment in a fixed attitude, it reconstitutes the mobility of the regiment marching. It is true that if we had to do with photographs alone, however much we might look at them, we should never see them animated: with immobility set beside immobility, even endlessly, we could never make movement. In order that the pictures may be animated, there must be movement somewhere. The movement does indeed exist here; it is in the apparatus. It is because the film of the cinematograph unrolls, bringing in turn the different photographs of the scene to continue each other, that each actor of the scene recovers his mobility; he strings all his successive attitudes on the invisible movement of the film. The process then consists in extracting from all the movements peculiar to all the figures an impersonal movement abstract and simple, *movement in general,* so to speak: we put this into the apparatus, and we reconstitute the individuality of each particular movement by combining this nameless movement with the personal attitudes. Such is the contrivance of the cinematograph. And such is also that of our knowledge. Instead of attaching ourselves to the inner becoming of things, we place ourselves outside them in order to recompose their becoming artificially. We take snapshots, as it were, of the passing reality, and, as these are characteristic of the reality, we have only to string them on a becoming, abstract, uniform and invisible, situated at the back of the apparatus of knowledge, in order to imitate what there is that is characteristic in this becoming itself. Perception, intellection, language so proceed in general. Whether we would think becoming, or express it, or even perceive it, we hardly do anything else than set going a kind of cinematograph inside us. We may therefore sum up what we have been saying in the conclusion that the *mechanism of our ordinary knowledge is of a cinematographical kind.*

Of the altogether practical character of this operation there is no possible doubt. Each of our acts aims at a certain insertion of our will into the reality. There is, between our body and other bodies, an arrangement like that of the pieces of glass that compose a kaleidoscopic picture. Our activity goes from an arrangement to a re-arrangement, each time no doubt giving the kaleidoscope a new shake, but not interesting itself in the shake, and seeing only the new picture. Our knowledge of the operation of nature must be exactly symmetrical, therefore, with the interest we take in our own operation. In this sense we may say, if we are not abusing this kind of illustration, that *the cinematographical character of our knowledge of things is due to the kaleidoscopic character of our adaptation to them.*

The cinematographical method is therefore the only practical method, since it consists in making the general character of knowledge form itself on that of action, while expecting that the detail of each act should depend in its turn on that of knowledge. In order that action may always be enlightened, intelligence must always be present in it; but intelligence, in order thus to accompany the progress of activity and ensure its direction, must begin by adopting its rhythm. Action is discontinuous, like every pulsation of life; discontinuous, therefore, is knowledge. The mechanism of the faculty of knowing has been constructed on this plan. Essentially practical, can it be of use, such as it is, for speculation? Let us try with it to follow reality in its windings, and see what will happen.

I take of the continuity of a particular becoming a series of views, which I connect together by "becoming in general." But of course I cannot stop there. What is not determinable is not representable: of "becoming in general" I have only a verbal knowledge. As the letter x designates a certain unknown quantity, whatever it may be, so my "becoming in general," always the same, symbolizes here a certain transition of which I have taken some snapshots; of the transition itself it teaches me nothing. Let me then concentrate myself wholly on the transition, and, between any two snapshots, endeavor to realize what is going on. As I apply the same method, I obtain the same result; a third view merely slips in between the two others. I may begin again as often as I will, I may set views alongside of views forever, I shall obtain nothing else. The application of the cinematographical method therefore leads to a perpetual recommencement, during which the mind, never able to satisfy itself and never finding where to rest, persuades itself, no doubt, that it imitates by its instability the very movement of the real. But though, by straining itself to the point of giddiness, it may end by giving itself the illusion of mobility, its operation has not advanced it a step, since it remains as far as ever from its goal. In order to advance with the moving reality, you must replace yourself within it. Install yourself within change, and you will grasp at once both change itself and the successive states in which *it might* at any instant be immobilized. But with these successive states, perceived from without as real and no longer as potential immobilities, you will never reconstitute movement. Call them *qualities, forms, positions,* or *intentions,* as the case may be, multiply the number of them as you will, let the interval between two consecutive states be infinitely small: before the intervening movement you will always experience the disappointment of the child who tries by clapping his hands together to crush the smoke. The movement slips through the interval, because every attempt to reconstitute change out of states implies the absurd proposition, that movement is made of immobilities.

Philosophy perceived this as soon as it opened its eyes. The arguments of Zeno of Elea, although formulated with a very different intention, have no other meaning.

Take the flying arrow. At every moment, says Zeno, it is motionless, for it cannot have time to move, that is, to occupy at least two successive positions, unless at least two moments are allowed it. At a given moment, therefore, it is at rest at a given point. Motionless in each point of its course, it is motionless during all the time that it is moving.

Yes, if we suppose that the arrow can ever *be* in a point of its course. Yes again, if the arrow, which is moving, ever coincides with a position, which is motionless. But the arrow never *is* in any point of its course. The most we can say is that it might be there, in this sense, that it passes there and might stop there. It is true that if it did stop there, it would be at rest there, and at this point it is no longer movement that we should have to do with. The truth is that if the arrow leaves the point A to fall down at the point B, its movement AB is as simple, as indecomposable, in so far as it is movement, as the tension of the bow that shoots it. As the shrapnel, bursting before it falls to the ground, covers the explosive zone with an indivisible danger, so the arrow which goes from A to B displays with a single stroke, although over a certain extent of duration, its indivisible mobility. Suppose an elastic stretched from A to B, could you divide its extension? The course of the arrow is this very extension; it is equally simple and equally undivided. It is a single and unique bound. You fix a point C in the interval passed, and say that at a certain moment the arrow was in C. If it had been there, it would have been stopped there, and you would no longer have had a flight from A to B, but *two* flights, one from A to C and the other from C to B, with an interval of rest. A single movement is entirely, by the hypothesis, a movement between two stops; if there are intermediate stops, it is no longer a single movement. At bottom, the illusion arises from this, that the movement, *once effected,* has laid along its course a motionless trajectory on which we can count as many immobilities as we will. From this we conclude that the movement, *whilst being effected,* lays at each instant beneath it a position with which it coincides. We do not see that the trajectory is created in one stroke, although a certain time is required for it; and that though we can divide at will the trajectory once created, we cannot divide its creation, which is an act in progress and not a thing. To suppose that the moving body *is* at a point of its course is to cut the course in two by a snip of the scissors at this point, and to substitute two trajectories for the single trajectory which we were first considering. It is to distinguish two successive acts where, by the hypothesis, there is only one. In short, it is to attribute to the course itself of the arrow everything that can be said of the interval that the arrow has traversed, that is to say, to admit a *priori* the absurdity that movement coincides with immobility.

We shall not dwell here on the three other arguments of Zeno. We have examined them elsewhere. It is enough to point out that they all consist in applying the movement to the line traversed, and supposing that what is true of the line is true of the movement. The line, for example, may be divided into as many parts as we wish, of any length that we wish, and it is always the same line. From this we conclude that we have the right to suppose the movement articulated as we wish, and that it is always the same movement.

We thus obtain a series of absurdities that all express the same fundamental absurdity. But the possibility of applying the movement *to* the line traversed exists only for an observer who keeping outside the movement and seeing at every instant the possibility of a stop, tries to reconstruct the real movement with these possible immobilities. The absurdity vanishes as soon as we adopt by thought the continuity of the real movement, a continuity of which every one of us is conscious whenever he lifts an arm or advances a step. We feel then indeed that the line passed over between two stops is described with a single indivisible stroke, and that we seek in vain to practice on the movement, which traces the line, divisions corresponding, each to each, with the divisions arbitrarily chosen of the line once it has been traced. The line traversed by the moving body lends itself to any kind of division, because it has no internal organization. But all movement is articulated inwardly. It is either an indivisible bound (which may occupy, nevertheless, a very long duration) or a series of indivisible bounds. Take the articulations of this movement into account, or give up speculating on its nature.

When Achilles pursues the tortoise, each of his steps must be treated as indivisible, and so must each step of the tortoise. After a certain number of steps, Achilles will have overtaken the tortoise. There is nothing more simple. If you insist on dividing the two motions further, distinguish both on the one side and on the other, in the course of Achilles and in that of the tortoise, the *submultiples* of the steps of each of them; but respect the natural articulations of the two courses. As long as you respect them, no difficulty will arise, because you will follow the indications of experience. But Zeno's device is to reconstruct the movement of Achilles according to a law arbitrarily chosen. Achilles with a first step is supposed to arrive at the point where the tortoise was, with a second step at the point which it has moved to while he was making the first, and so on. In this case, Achilles would always have a new step to take. But obviously, to overtake the tortoise, he goes about it in quite another way. The movement considered by Zeno would only be the equivalent of the movement of Achilles if we could treat the movement as we treat the interval passed through, decomposable and recomposable at will. Once you subscribe to this first absurdity, all the others follow.[1]

---

[1] That is, we do not consider the sophism of Zeno refuted by the fact that the geometrical progression $a(1+ \frac{1}{n} + \frac{1}{n^2} + \frac{1}{n^3} + \ldots$, etc.)—in which a designates the initial distance between Achilles and the tortoise, and n the relation of their respective velocities—has a finite sum if n is greater than 1. On this point we may refer to the arguments of F. Evellin, which we regard as conclusive (see Evellin, *Infini et quantité*, Paris, 1880, pp. 63–97; cf. *Revue philosophique*, XI, 1881, pp. 564–568). The truth is that mathematics, as we have tried to show in a former work, deals and can deal only with lengths. It has therefore had to seek devices, first, to transfer to the movement, which is not a length, the divisibility of the line passed over, and then to reconcile with experience the idea (contrary to experience and full of absurdities) of a movement that is a length, that is, of a movement *placed upon* its trajectory and arbitrarily decomposable like it.

Achilles and the Tortoise

MAX BLACK

1. Suppose Achilles runs ten times as fast as the tortoise and gives him a hundred yards start. In order to win the race Achilles must first make up for his initial handicap by running a hundred yards; but when he has done this and has reached the point where the tortoise started, the animal has had time to advance ten yards. While Achilles runs these ten yards, the tortoise gets one yard ahead; when Achilles has run this yard, the tortoise is a tenth of a yard ahead; and so on, without end. Achilles never catches the tortoise, because the tortoise always holds a lead, however small.

This is approximately the form in which the so-called "Achilles" paradox has come down to us. Aristotle, who is our primary source for this and the other paradoxes attributed to Zeno, summarises the argument as follows: "In a race the quickest runner can never overtake the slowest, since the pursuer must first reach the point whence the pursued started, so that the slower must always hold a lead" (*Physics*, 239b).[1]

Max Black, "Achilles and the Tortoise," *Analysis*, XI (1950–51), 91–101. Reprinted by permission of the author, and the editor and publisher of *Analysis*. Footnotes have been renumbered to run consecutively throughout the article.

---

[1] Aristotle's solution seems to be based upon a distinction between two meanings of 'infinite'—(i) as meaning "infinite in extent," (ii) as meaning "infinitely divisible." "For there are two senses in which length and time and generally anything continuous are called 'infinite': they are called so either in respect of divisibility or in respect of their extremities. So while a thing in a finite time cannot come in contact with things quantitatively infinite, it can come in contact with things infinite in respect of divisibility; for in this sense the time itself is also infinite . . . ." *Physics*, 233a. This type of answer has been

2. It would be a waste of time to prove, by independent argument, that Achilles will pass the tortoise. Everybody. knows this already, and the puzzle arises because the conclusion of Zeno's argument is known to be absurd. We must try to find out, if we can, exactly what mistake is committed in this argument.[2]

3. A plausible answer that has been repeatedly offered[3] takes the line that "this paradox of Zeno is based upon a mathematical fallacy" (A. N. Whitehead, *Process and Reality* [48], p. 107).

Consider the lengths that Achilles has to cover, according to our version of the paradox. They are, successively, a hundred yards, ten yards, one yard, a tenth of a yard, and so on. So the total number of yards he must travel in order to catch the tortoise is

$$100 + 10 + 1 + \tfrac{1}{10} + \dots .$$

This is a convergent geometrical series whose sum can be expressed in decimal notation as 111. $\dot{1}$, that is to say exactly $111\tfrac{1}{9}$. When Achilles has run this number of yards, he will be

popular (cf. e.g. J. S. Mill, *System of Logic*, 5th ed., 389–390). Several writers object that infinite divisibility of the line implies its actually having an infinite number of elements—and so leaves the puzzle unresolved. But see H. R. King, "Aristotle and the Paradoxes of Zeno" [82].

For references to the vast literature on this and the other arguments of Zeno, see F. Cajori, "The History of Zeno's Arguments on Motion" [22].

[2] It has sometimes been held, e.g. by Paul Tannery in *Revue Philosophique* 20 (1885), that Zeno's arguments were sound. "Tannery's explanation of the four arguments, particularly of the 'Arrow' and 'Stade' raises these paradoxes from childish arguments to arguments with conclusions which follow with compelling force . . . it exhibits Zeno as a logician of the first rank." Cajori, *ibid.* [22], p. 6.

Cf. Russell's remark that the arguments of Zeno "are not, however, on any view, mere foolish quibbles: they are serious arguments, raising difficulties which it has taken two thousand years to answer, and which even now are fatal to the teachings of most philosophers" [above, p. 47].

[3] In addition to the reference to Whitehead, see for instance Descartes (letter to Clerselier, Adam and Tannery ed. of *Works* [13 vols., Paris: Cerf, 1897–1913], IV, 445–447), and Peirce (*Collected Papers* [94], 6.177–8, p. 122). Peirce says ". . . this silly little catch presents no difficulty at all to a mind adequately trained in mathematics and in logic . . ." (6.177).

dead level with his competitor; and at any time thereafter he will be actually ahead.

A similar argument applies to the time needed for Achilles to catch the tortoise. If we suppose that Achilles can run a hundred yards in ten seconds, the number of seconds he needs in order to catch up is

$$10 + 1 + \tfrac{1}{10} + \tfrac{1}{100} + \ldots .$$

This, too, is a convergent geometrical series, whose sum is expressed in decimal notation as 11.$\dot{1}$, that is to say exactly 11$\tfrac{1}{9}$. This, as we should expect, is one tenth of the number we previously obtained.

We can check the calculation without using infinite series at all. The relative velocity with which Achilles overtakes the tortoise is nine yards per second. Now the number of seconds needed to cancel the initial gap of a hundred yards at a relative velocity of pursuit of nine yards per second is 100 divided by 9 or 11$\tfrac{1}{9}$. This is exactly the number we previously obtained by summing the geometrical series representing the times needed by Achilles. During this time, moreover, since Achilles is actually travelling at ten yards per second, the actual distance he travels is 10 × 11$\tfrac{1}{9}$, or 111$\tfrac{1}{9}$, as before. Thus we have confirmed our first calculation by an argument not involving the summation of infinite series.

4. According to this type of solution, the fallacy in Zeno's argument is due to the use of the words "never" and "always." Given the premise that "the pursuer must first reach the point whence the pursued started," it does *not* follow, as alleged, that the quickest runner "never" overtakes the slower: Achilles does catch the tortoise at some time—that is to say at a time exactly 11$\tfrac{1}{9}$ seconds from the start. It is wrong to say that the tortoise is "always" in front: there is a place—a place exactly 111$\tfrac{1}{9}$ yards from Achilles' starting point—where the two are dead level. Our calculations have showed this, and Zeno failed to see that only a finite time and finite space are needed for the infinite series of steps that Achilles is called upon to make.

5. This kind of mathematical solution has behind it the authority of Descartes and Peirce and Whitehead[4]—to mention no lesser names—yet I cannot see that it goes to the heart of the matter. It tells us, correctly, when and where Achilles and the tortoise will meet, *if* they meet; but it fails to show that Zeno was wrong in claiming they *could not* meet.

Let us be clear about what is meant by the assertion that the sum of the infinite series

$$100 + 10 + 1 + \tfrac{1}{10} + \tfrac{1}{100} + \ldots$$

is $111\frac{1}{9}$. It does not mean, as the naive might suppose, that mathematicians have succeeded in adding together an infinite number of terms. As Frege pointed out in a similar connection,[5] this remarkable feat would require an infinite supply of paper, an infinite quantity of ink, and an infinite amount of time. If we had to add all the terms together, we could never prove that the series had a finite sum. To say that the sum of the series is $111\frac{1}{9}$ is to say that if enough terms of the series are taken, the difference between the sum of that *finite number* of terms and the number $111\frac{1}{9}$ becomes, and stays, as small as we please. (Or to put it another way: Let n be any number less than $111\frac{1}{9}$. We can always find a finite number of terms of the series whose sum will be less than $111\frac{1}{9}$ but greater than n.)

Since this is all that is meant by saying that the infinite series has a sum, it follows that the "summation" of all the terms of an infinite series is not the same thing as the summation of a finite set of numbers. In one case we can get the answers by working out a finite number of additions; in the other case we *must* "perform a limit operation," that is to say, prove that there is a number whose difference from the sum of the initial members of the series can be made to remain as small as we please.

6. Now let us apply this to the race. The series of distances

[4] See the last footnote.
[5] *Grundgesetze der Arithmetik*, II (1903), §124. Or see my translation in *Philosophical Review* 59 (1950), 332.

traversed by Achilles is convergent. This means that if Achilles takes enough steps whose sizes are given by the series 100 yards, 10 yards, 1 yard, $\frac{1}{10}$ yard, etc. the distance *still to go* to the meeting point eventually becomes, and stays, as small as we please. After the first step he still has $11\frac{1}{9}$ yards to go; after the second, only $1\frac{1}{9}$ yard; after the third, no more than $\frac{1}{9}$ yard; and so on. The distance still to go is reduced by ten at each move.

But the distance, however much reduced, still remains to be covered; and after each step there are infinitely many steps still to be taken. The logical difficulty is that Achilles seems called upon to perform *an infinite series of tasks;* and it does not help to be told that the tasks become easier and easier, or need progressively less and less time in the doing. Achilles may get nearer to the place and time of his rendezvous, but his task remains just as hard, for he still has to perform what seems to be logically impossible. It is just as hard to draw a very small square circle as it is to draw an enormous one: we might say both tasks are infinitely hard. The logical difficulty is not in the extent of the distance Achilles has to cover but in the apparent impossibility of his travelling any distance whatsoever. I think Zeno had enough mathematical knowledge to understand that if Achilles could run $111\frac{1}{9}$ yards—that is to say, keep going for $11\frac{1}{9}$ seconds —he would indeed have caught the tortoise. The difficulty is to understand how Achilles could arrive anywhere at all without first having performed an infinite series of acts.

7. The nature of the difficulty is made plainer by a second argument of Zeno, known as the "Dichotomy" which, according to Aristotle, is "the same in principle" (*Physics,* 239b). In order to get from one point to another, Achilles must first reach a third point midway between the two; similarly, in order to reach this third point he must first reach a fourth point; to reach this point he must first reach another point; and so on, without end. To reach *any* point, he must first reach a nearer one. So, in order to get moving, Achilles must already have performed an infinite series of

acts—must, as it were, have travelled along the series of points from the infinitely distant and *open* "end."[6] This is an even more astounding feat than the one he accomplishes in winning the race against the tortoise.

The two arguments are complementary: the "Achilles" shows that the runner cannot reach any place, even if he gets started; while the "Dichotomy" shows that he cannot get started, i.e. cannot leave any place he has reached.

8. Mathematicians have sometimes said that the difficulty of conceiving the performance of an infinite series of tasks is factitious. All it shows, they say, is the weakness of human imagination and the folly of the attempt to make a mental image of mathematical relationships.[7] The line really does have infinitely many points, and there is no logical impediment to Achilles' making an infinite number of steps in a finite time. I will try to show that this way of thinking about the race is untenable.

9. I am going to argue that the expression, "infinite series of acts," is self-contradictory, and that failure to see this arises from confusing a series of acts with a series of numbers generated by some mathematical law. (By an "act" I mean something marked off from its surroundings by having a definite beginning and end.)

In order to establish this by means of an illustration I shall try to make plain some of the absurd consequences of talking about "counting an infinite number of marbles." And in order to do this I shall find it convenient to talk about counting an infinite number of marbles as if I sup-

---

[6] This, at any rate, is the usual interpretation, though I cannot see that Aristotle was thinking of anything more than an argument resembling the "Achilles" in all respects except that of the ratio in which the distance is divided. For the contrary view see, for instance, Sir Thomas Heath, *Mathematics in Aristotle* [14], pp. 135–136.

[7] "La perception sensible n'embrasse que le fini; l'imagination atteint encore les infiniment grands et les infiniment petits, tant qu'ils restent finis; mais elle n'atteint ni l'infini, limite des infiniment grands, ni le zéro, limite des infiniment petits: ces deux etats extrémes de la grandeur sont de pures idées, accessibles à la seule raison." L. Couturat, *De l'infini mathématique* (1896), 562.

posed it was sensible to talk in this way. But I want it to be understood all the time that I do not think it sensible to talk in this way, and that my aim in so talking is to show how absurd this way of talking is. Counting may seem a very special kind of "act" to choose, but I hope to be able to show that the same considerations will apply to an infinite series of any kinds of acts.

10. Suppose we want to find out the number of things in a given collection, presumably identified by some description. Unless the things are mathematical or logical entities it will be impossible to deduce the size of the collection from the description alone; and somebody will have to do the work of taking a census. Of course he can do this without having any idea of how large the collection will turn out to be: his instructions may simply take the form, "Start counting and keep on until there is nothing left in the collection to count." This implies that there will be a point at which there will be "nothing left to count," so that the census-taker will then know his task to have been completed.

Now suppose we can know that the collection is infinite. If, knowing this, we were to say "Start counting and continue until there is nothing left to count" we should be practicing a deception. For our census-taker would be led to suppose that sooner or later there would be nothing left to count, while all the time we would know this supposition to be false. An old recipe for catching guinea pigs is to put salt on their tails. Since they have no tails, this is no recipe at all. To avoid deception we should have said, in the case of the infinite collection, "Start counting and *never* stop." This should be enough to tell an intelligent census-taker that the collection is infinite, so that there is no sense in trying to count it.

If somebody says to me "Count all the blades of grass in Hyde Park" I might retort "It's too difficult; I haven't enough time." But if some cosmic bully were to say "Here is an infinite collection; go ahead and count it," only logical confusion could lead me to mutter "Too difficult; not enough time." The trouble is that, no matter what I do, the result of all my work will not and cannot count as compliance with the instructions. If somebody commands me to obey a certain "instruction," and is then obliging enough to add that nothing that I can do will count as compliance with that instruction, only confusion could lead me to suppose that any task had been set.

11. Some writers, however, have said that the difficulty of counting an infinite collection is just a matter of *lack of time*.[8] If only we could count faster and faster, the whole job could be done in a finite time; there would still never be a time at which we were ending, but there would be a time at which we already would have ended the count. It is not necessary to finish counting; it is sufficient that the counting shall have been finished.

Very well. Since the task is too much for human capacity, let us imagine a machine that can do it. Let us suppose that upon our left a narrow tray stretches into the distance as far as the most powerful telescope can follow; and that this tray or slot is full of marbles. Here, at the middle, where the line of marbles begins, there stands a kind of mechanical scoop; and to the right, a second, but empty tray, stretching away into the distance beyond the farthest reach of vision. Now the machine is started. During the first minute of its operation, it seizes a marble and transfers it to the empty tray; then it rests a minute. In the next half-minute the machine seizes a second marble on the left, transfers it, and rests half-a-minute. The third marble is moved in a quarter of a minute, with a corresponding pause; the next in one eighth of a minute; and so until the movements are so fast that all we can see is a grey blur. But at the end of exactly four minutes the machine comes to a halt, and we now see that the left-hand tray that was full seems to be empty,

---

[8] "Quand vous dites qu'une collection infinie ne pourra jamais être numérotée tout entière, il ne s'agit pas là d'une impossibilité intrinsèque et logique, mais d'une impossibilité pratique et matérielle: c'est tout simplement une question de temps." L. Couturat, *ibid.*, 462.

while the right-hand tray that was empty seems full of marbles.

Let us call this an *infinity machine*. And since it is the first of several to be described let us give it the name "Alpha."

12. I hope nobody will object that the wear and tear on such a machine would be too severe; or that it would be too hard to construct! We are dealing with the logical coherence of ideas, not with the practicability of mechanical devices. If we can conceive of such a machine without contradiction, that will be enough; and believers in the "actual infinite" will have been vindicated.

13. An obvious difficulty in conceiving of an infinity machine is this. How are we supposed to know that there are infinitely many marbles in the left-hand tray at the outset? Or, for that matter, that there are infinitely many on the right when the machine has stopped? Everything we can observe of Alpha's operations (and no matter how much we slow it down!) is consistent with there having been involved only a very large, though still finite, number of marbles.

14. Now there is a simple and instructive way of making certain that the machine shall have infinitely many marbles to count. Let there be only *one* marble in the left-hand tray to begin with, and let some device always return *that same marble* while the machine is resting. Let us give the name "Beta" to a machine that works in this way. From the standpoint of the machine, as it were, the task has not changed. The difficulty of performance remains exactly the same whether the task, as in Alpha's case, is to transfer an infinite series of qualitatively similar but different marbles; or whether the task, as in Beta's case, is constantly to transfer the *same* marble that is immediately returned to its original position. Imagine Alpha and Beta both at work side by side on their respective tasks: every time the one moves, so does the other; if one succeeds in its task, so must the other; and if it is impossible for either to succeed, it is impossible for *each*.

15. The introduction of our second machine, Beta, shows clearly that the infinite count really is impossible. For the single marble is always returned, and each move of the machine accomplished nothing. A man given the task of filling three holes by means of two pegs can always fill the third hole by transferring one of the pegs; but this automatically creates another empty place, and it won't help in the least to run through this futile series of operations faster and faster. (We don't get any nearer to the end of the rainbow by running faster). Now our machine, Beta, is in just this predicament: the very act of transferring the marble from left to right immediately causes it to be returned again; the operation is self-defeating and it is logically impossible for its end to be achieved. Now if this is true for Beta, it must be true also for Alpha, as we have already seen.

16. When Hercules tried to cut off the heads of Hydra, two heads immediately grew where one had been removed. It is rumoured that the affair has been incorrectly reported: Zeus, the all powerful, took pity on Hercules and eased his labor. It was decreed that only *one* head should replace the head that had been cut off and that Hercules should have the magical power to slash faster and faster in geometrical progression. If this is what really happened, had Hercules any cause to be grateful? Not a bit. Since the head that was sliced off immediately grew back again, Hercules was getting nowhere, and might just as well have kept his sword in its scabbard.

17. Somebody may still be inclined to say that nevertheless when the machine Beta finally comes to rest (at the end of the four minutes of its operation) the single marble might after all be found in the right-hand tray, and this, if it happened, would *prove* that the machine's task had been accomplished. However, it is easy to show that this suggestion will not work.

I said, before, that "some device" always restored the marble to its original position in the left-hand tray. Now the most natural device to use for this purpose is another machine—Gamma, say—working like Beta but *from right to left*. Let it be arranged that no sooner does Beta move the marble from left to right than Gamma moves it back again. The successive working periods and pauses of Gamma are then equal in length to those of Beta, except that Gamma is working while Beta is resting, and vice versa. The task of Gamma, moreover, is exactly parallel to that of Beta, that is, to transfer the marble an infinite number of times from one side to the other. If the result of the whole four minutes' operation by the first machine is to transfer the marble from left to right, the result of the whole four minutes' operation by the second machine must be to transfer the marble from right to left. But there is only one marble and it must end somewhere! Hence neither machine can accomplish its task, and our description of the infinity machines involves a contradiction.

18. These considerations show, if I am not mistaken, that the outcome of the infinity machine's work is independent of what the machine is supposed to have done antecedently. The marble might end up on the right, on the left, or nowhere. When Hercules ended his slashing, Zeus had to decide whether the head should still be in position or whether, after all, Hercules' strenuous efforts to do the impossible should be rewarded.

Hercules might have argued that every time a head appeared, he had cut it off, so no head ought to remain; but the Hydra could have retorted, with equal force, that after a head had been removed another had always appeared in its place, so a head ought to remain in position. The two contentions cancel one another and neither would provide a ground for Zeus's decision.

Even Zeus, however, could not abrogate the continuity of space and motion; and this, if I am not mistaken, is the source of the contradiction in our description of the machine Beta. The motion of the marble is represented, graphically, by a curve with an infinite number of oscillations, the rapidity of the oscillations increasing constantly as approach is made to the time at which the machine comes to rest. Now to say that motion is continuous is to deny that any real motion can be represented by a curve of this character. Yet every machine that performed an infinite series of acts in a finite time would have to include a part that oscillated "infinitely fast," as it were, in this impossible fashion. For the beginning of every spatio-temporal act is marked by a change in the velocity or in some other magnitude characterizing the agent.

19. It might be thought that the waiting-intervals in the operations of the three infinity machines so far described have been essential to the argument. And it might be objected that the steps Achilles takes are performed consecutively and without intervening pauses. I will now show that the pauses are not essential.

Consider for this purpose two machines, Delta and Epsilon, say, that begin to work with a single marble each, but in opposite directions. Let Delta start with the marble *a* and Epsilon with the marble *b*. Now suppose the following sequence of operations: while Delta transfers marble *a* from left to right in one minute, Epsilon transfers marble *b* from right to left; then Delta moves *b* from left to right in half a minute while Epsilon returns *a* from right to left during the same time; and so on, indefinitely, with each operation taking half the time of its predecessor. During the time that either machine is transporting a marble, its partner is placing the other marble in position for the next move.[9] Once again, the total tasks of Delta and Epsilon are exactly parallel: if the first is to succeed, both marbles must end on the right, but if the second is to succeed, both must end on the left. Hence neither can succeed, and there is a contradiction in our description of the machines.

20. Nor will it help to have a machine—Phi, say—transferring marbles that become progressively smaller in geo-

---

[9] An alternative arrangement would be to have three similar machines constantly circulating three marbles.

metrical progression.[10] For, by an argument already used, we can suppose that while Phi is performing its operations, one of the machines already described is going through its paces at the same rates and at the same times. If Phi could complete its task, Alpha, Beta, Gamma, Delta and Epsilon would have to be able to complete their respective tasks. And we have already seen that this is not possible. The size of the successive tasks has nothing to do with the logical impossibility of performing an infinite series of operations. Indeed it should be clear by this time that the logical possibility of the existence of any one of the machines depends upon the logical possibility of the existence of all of them or, indeed, of any machine that could count an infinite number of objects. If the idea of the existence of any one of them is self-contradictory, the same must be true for each of them. The various descriptions of these different hypothetical devices simply make it easier for us to see that one and all are logically impossible. And though a good deal more needs to be said about this, I hope I have said enough to show why I think this notion of counting an infinite collection is self-contradictory.

21. If we now reconsider for a moment the arguments that have been used in connection with our six infinity machines, we can easily see that no use was made of the respects in which counting differs from any other series of acts. Counting differs from other series of acts by the conventional assignment of numerals to each stage of the count, and it differs in other respects, too. But every series of acts is like counting in requiring the successive doing of things, each having a beginning and end in space or time. And this is all that was used or needed in our arguments. Since our arguments in no way depended upon the specific peculiarities of counting they would apply, as I said at the outset, to any infinite series of acts.

22. And now let us return to Achilles. If it really were

[10] Somebody might say that if the marble moved by Beta eventually shrunk to nothing there would be no problem about its final location! [See Paul Benacerraf, "Tasks, Super-Tasks, and the Modern Eleatics," reprinted below.]

necessary for him to perform an infinite number of acts or, as Aristotle says "to pass over or severally to come in contact with infinite things" (*Physics*, 233a), it would indeed be logically impossible for him to pass the tortoise. But all the things he really does are finite in number; a finite number of steps, heart beats, deep breaths, cries of defiance, and so on. The track on which he runs has a finite number of pebbles, grains of earth, and blades of grass,[11] each of which in turn has a finite, though enormous number of atoms. For all of these are things that have a beginning and end in space or time. But if anybody says we must imagine that the atoms themselves occupy space and so are divisible "in thought," he is no longer talking about spatio-temporal things. To divide a thing "in thought" is merely to halve the numerical interval which we have assigned to it. Or else it is to suppose what is in fact physically impossible beyond a certain point, the actual separation of the physical thing into discrete parts. We can of course choose to say that we shall represent a distance by a numerical interval, and that every part of that numerical interval shall also count as representing a distance; then it will be true a priori that there are infinitely many "distances." But the class of what will then be called "distances" will be a series of pairs of numbers, not an infinite series of spatio-temporal things. The infinity of this series is then a feature of one way in which we find it useful to *describe* the physical reality; to suppose that therefore Achilles has to *do* an infinite number of things would be as absurd as to suppose that because I can attach two numbers to an egg I must make some special effort to hold its halves together.

23. To summarise: I have tried to show that the popular mathematical refutation of Zeno's paradoxes will not do, because it simply assumes that Achilles can perform an

---

[11] Cf. Peirce: "I do not think that if each pebble were broken into a million pieces the difficulty of getting over the road would necessarily have been increased; and I don't see why it should if one of these millions—or all of them— had been multiplied into an infinity." *Op. cit.* [94], 6.182.

infinite series of acts. By using the illustration of what would be involved in counting an infinite number of marbles, I have tried to show that the notion of an infinite series of acts is self-contradictory. For any material thing, whether machine or person, that set out to do an infinite number of acts would be committed to performing a motion that was discontinuous and therefore impossible. But Achilles is not called upon to do the logically impossible; the illusion that he must do so is created by our failure to hold separate the finite number of real things that the runner has to accomplish and the infinite series of numbers by which we describe what he actually does. We create the illusion of the infinite tasks by the kind of mathematics that we use to describe space, time, and motion.

Achilles on a Physical Racecourse

J. O. WISDOM

§1. Professor Max Black has recently given an account of the fallacy in Zeno's paradoxes of the "Achilles" and the "Dichotomy."[1] His analysis, it seems to me, makes a contribution to what is needed but is incomplete. His account is in part essentially the same as, and in part different from, one that I had put forward;[2] and this in its turn was very similar to one offered by Weiss slightly earlier.[3] I now wish to take the opportunity of adding a little to these accounts and of clarifying certain points. Discussion may be confined to the "Achilles."

Zeno's premiss is this: "For Achilles to catch the tortoise, he must run to the tortoise's initial place; then the tortoise will have advanced to a second place, so that Achilles must run on to the tortoise's second place; and so on." We shall have occasion to refer to the phrase "and so on" in this premiss. Now Achilles' point-to-point run may be described by an infinite geometric series; if Achilles runs twice as

J. O. Wisdom, "Achilles on a Physical Racecourse," *Analysis*, XII (1951–52), 67–72. Reprinted by permission of the author, and the editor and publisher of *Analysis*. Footnotes have been renumbered to number consecutively throughout the article.

[1] Max Black, "Achilles and the Tortoise" [reprinted above].

[2] J. O. Wisdom, "Why Achilles Does Not Fail to Catch the Tortoise" [122].

[3] Paul Weiss, *Reality* (Princeton: University Press, 1938), pp. 237–241. I should like to take the opportunity of expressing regret that in my earlier paper I made no mention of the very similar ideas published slightly earlier by Professor Weiss in his book *Reality*, which I had not then come across.

fast as the tortoise and the tortoise has a start of unit distance, then, ignoring the tortoise, the premiss is: "Achilles' distance is $1 + \frac{1}{2} + \frac{1}{4} +$ etc." where "distance" means the distance from starting-point to goal. It is indifferent which form of the premiss we use. The conclusion is: "Achilles never catches the tortoise."

To resolve the paradox, we must show either that the inference is invalid or that the premiss is false. Black, Weiss, and I have all worked upon the second alternative. In fact, I hope to show incidentally that the inference is *valid* and therefore that the first alternative will not work.

Black and I both introduce the subject by pointing out that what matters is not to prove that Achilles must reach the tortoise but to find out where Zeno's argument breaks down. And we both criticise the mathematical solution on the same grounds.[4] This solution is that the infinite geometric series representing the distance traversed by Achilles has a 'sum' and that if we calculate this we find it makes Achilles abreast the tortoise. The criticism is that such a 'sum' is a mathematical limit that is not attained by finding the sum of a finite number of terms however much this is increased, i.e. is not attained by any amount of counting and adding. Starting from this, Black's argument is briefly as follows:—

(1) Adding up an infinite number of terms of the geometric series, which represents the course of Achilles, is equivalent to performing "an infinite series of tasks."[5] (2) Black next aims at showing that this is impossible because self-contradictory. It is like "counting an infinite number of marbles,"[6] which amounts to counting without ever stopping. (3) He describes a number of machines, by means of which he shows with great clarity that the difficulty of counting an infinite number of marbles is not due to lack of time and that such counting is self-contradictory. Hence,

---

[4] Black [above, p. 70]; Wisdom, *op. cit.* [122], pp. 61, 70–71. Weiss probably had the same point in mind (*ibid.*, p. 240) but he did not make it explicit.

[5] Black [above, p. 71].

[6] *Ibid.* [above, p. 72].

if Achilles really had to perform an infinite number of tasks, it would be logically impossible for him to reach the tortoise. (4) In fact Achilles performs only a finite number of tasks, such as steps. (5) The illusion that Achilles must perform an infinite number of tasks arises from the kind of mathematics used to describe space, time, and motion, because the mathematical description describes a distance as the sum of an infinite number of lengths, and this supposes matter to be endlessly divided which is "physically impossible beyond a certain point."[7]

By interpreting Zeno's premiss as equivalent to requiring Achilles to perform an infinite series of tasks, Black has in (1) surely not only expressed the matter very graphically but put it in a way that enables him in (2) and (3) to prove that the premiss is self-contradictory. This had been generally accepted (though not by certain mathematicians who made faulty use of the theory of limits); but, on account of its providing one way by which we can approach the resolution of the paradox, a simple proof of it is welcome.

The main body of Black's paper, then, proves that the premiss is self-contradictory, because it involves an infinite number of tasks. The question that arises, however, is whether this result alone is enough to dispose of the paradox. From the earlier part of his paper this would seem to be Black's view; but his concluding remarks (4) and (5) throw doubt on it. Black does not elaborate these remarks, and it is just here that the problem of the paradox opens up.

§2. To prove that the premiss is self-contradictory does not by itself show that the conclusion is false. Indeed the self-contradiction even plays into Zeno's hands, in a way that was not open to him with the logic of his day, for from a self-contradictory premiss all inferences are valid. Thus his conclusion that Achilles never catches the tortoise is validly derived.[8] (Likewise, of course, another conclusion

---

[7] *Ibid.* [above, p. 80].

[8] It is therefore useless to tackle the paradox by trying to show, as several writers cited by Black have attempted to do, that the inference is invalid.

that Achilles *does* catch the tortoise also follows, but this is not interesting.) The conclusion is not, of course, *proved*, even though validly derived, unless the premiss is true; but Zeno's argument assumes that it *is* true (it is the plausibility of this assumption that is fundamental to the paradox, for despite self-contradiction the premiss may still appear quite correctly to describe a physical race). In order to avoid the conclusion, we must deny that the premiss does in fact represent Achilles' course—deny that the mathematical description is a correct description of physical distance.

We note that the denial of the premiss is necessarily true, and therefore that Achilles' distance cannot be represented by the infinite geometric series (i.e. that the 'and so on' is unjustified). That is to say, a physical distance cannot be split up into an infinity of points corresponding to the mathematical points described by an infinite geometric series. Achilles can, of course, go to where the tortoise was, and then go to where the tortoise next arrived, and this can be repeated a number of times, but somewhere or other it can no longer be repeated—the 'and so on' is not justified—i.e. there comes a position where the description of Achilles, as running to where the tortoise was, no longer applies to a physical race. This was one of the main points I was concerned to make in my earlier paper, and it seems to be part at least of what Black had in mind in his brief account of (4) and (5).

§3. But, to dispel the paradox completely, it is not enough to know that the infinite geometric series cannot for logical reasons describe a distance in a physical race; it is not enough to know that Achilles is being asked to complete an infinite series of tasks or to count an infinite number of marbles and to say that he should not be called upon to carry out such a demand. It is not enough for the following reasons. To say that the demand is impossible implies that Achilles cannot catch the tortoise if he runs as prescribed by the premiss. Hence, at this point, Black's contribution in effect supports Zeno's conclusion. Moreover the plausibility of the premiss lies in just this, that it seems reasonable to ask Achilles to carry out the infinite number of tasks stated in the premiss.

To find the source of the plausibility we may begin by noting that the premiss is not expressed in the most explicit way. The premiss "Achilles' distance is $1 + \frac{1}{2} + \frac{1}{4} +$ etc." contains no contradiction if "Achilles' distance" is short for "Achilles' *mathematical* distance."[9]

But the premiss really is "Achilles' *physical* distance is $1 + \frac{1}{2} + \frac{1}{4} +$ etc." It is this that is self-contradictory. In other words "Achilles' distance is $1 + \frac{1}{2} + \frac{1}{4} +$ etc." and "Achilles' distance is physical" are contradictory. How can this be seen in a simple way, so as to dispel the plausibility of the paradox?

In a physical race, what can we do in the way of marking points on Achilles' distance corresponding to the terms of the infinite geometric series? We may mark many such points. But they are physical points and are therefore unlike mathematical points that have no size. Physical points always have some size. Hence there arises the difficulty of packing an infinite number of them into a finite distance. Even if we make the points extremely small, this cannot be done. Even though we make them as small as we please,[10]

---

[9] In a mathematical world, containing mathematical points corresponding to rational numbers and nothing else, there is no question of Achilles' having an infinite number of tasks to perform, because Achilles is now a mathematical variable, and such a variable does not *move* from one value to another and therefore does not get stuck at the 'and so on.' Hence the premiss is inapplicable in such a world. And Achilles cannot run on a racecourse consisting of mathematical points.

[10] Weiss used the idea of minimal sizes that could not be subdivided. He held this on empirical grounds, namely that there appears to be a minimal size in nature, i.e. the size of the electron. And in my earlier paper I put it forward that we cannot meaningfully speak of points below a certain minimal size. This type of approach, however, seems to be unjustifiable. Moreover it is not needed; the paradox can be resolved without assuming a minimal size. Put otherwise, we do not have to assume the finite divisibility of matter to resolve the paradox. Even if matter is infinitely divisible, the foregoing solution holds; for the points, in terms of which the paradox is stated, must be assigned a size, and therefore (despite our power to assign a smaller size indefinitely if we choose) we cannot pack more than a finite number of them into a finite distance.

they still, so long as they are physical and thus greater than zero, cannot be packed into a finite distance. And, if they are reduced to zero, they are no longer physical, but mathematical and no longer relevant. Nor can any device of 'infinitesimals' enable us to pack in an infinite number of them: 'infinitesimals,' 'vanishing quantities,' 'ghosts of departing quantities' of whatever minuteness greater than zero can always be amassed in too great numbers to be packed into a finite distance.

This, I think, is the easiest way of seeing that Zeno's premiss cannot characterise a physical race: the 'and so on' is inapplicable because somewhere two neighbouring physical points will touch each other and it will be impossible to subdivide the distance between them without altering the assigned size of the points.

These considerations obviously apply equally to the "Dichotomy."

All this may or may not be what Black had in mind in (4) and (5); be that as it may, it seems to me to be needed for the complete resolution of the paradox. Black's argument, then, focussed attention on an important self-contradiction but he did not go on to use it. If I may put it so, he attended to Zeno's argument rather than to Zeno's paradox.

§4. *Summary and Conclusion.* The idea that the limit of an infinite series is attainable is a mistake. If a physical action is interpreted by means of an infinite series, then the completion of the action is self-contradictory. Nonetheless, though Zeno's premiss is self-contradictory, it retains plausibility.[11] The self-contradiction must convince us that an infinite mathematical series cannot describe a physical distance, but we do not eliminate the paradox until we have seen in what way it fails as a description. To see this we draw attention to a contradiction between physical distance and mathematical distance given by an infinite mathematical series. This contradiction is brought out when we show that

---

[11] This is perhaps one of the reasons why dialectical philosophers could believe that the physical world could be correctly and adequately described by self-contradictory categories.

a physical distance can consist of only a finite number of physical points, i.e. points that have some size however small greater than zero. Hence the premiss fails to describe a physical distance at some place in the 'and so on': the physical description comes to an end when we have mentioned all of a finite number of points, but the mathematical description by an infinite series goes on without stopping.

The peculiarity of the paradox lies in this, that the premiss, which is false and even self-contradictory, gives a very strong impression of being true.

Looking back over the order of the steps taken, we see that first the premiss was shown to be inapplicable (because self-contradictory) and second the explanation of this was found to lie in facts about physical points. But the most straightforward resolution would begin with these empirical considerations, after which we should go on to show that the premiss was inapplicable (because empirically false). In this way we could state the resolution in the simplest possible terms, divested of allusion to subsidiary considerations, using only the idea of a physical point. It could be put as follows: *A physical point, unlike a mathematical point, has some size, though this may be as small as we please. But, however small a physical point, since it has some size greater than zero, an infinity of them cannot be packed into a finite distance. In particular an infinity of physical points cannot be packed to correspond to the mathematical points described by an infinite geometric series. Hence an infinite geometric series is inapplicable to a physical distance. I.e. a physical race cannot be described by repeated bisection, or Zeno's premiss is false.*

JAMES THOMSON

Tasks and Super-Tasks

"To complete any journey you must complete an infinite number of journeys. For to arrive from A to B you must first go from A to A', the mid-point of A and B, and thence to A'', the mid-point of A' and B, and so on. But it is logically absurd that someone should have completed all of an infinite number of journeys, just as it is logically absurd that someone should have completed all of an infinite number of tasks. Therefore it is absurd to suppose that anyone has ever completed any journey."

The argument says that to complete a journey you must do something that is impossible and hence that you can't complete a journey.

It may seem that this argument is valid; and then, since the conclusion is absurd, we must deny one of the premises. But which? Each has a certain plausibility. To some, it is more plausible that you can't complete an infinite number of journeys than that you must. These people infer the falsity of the first premiss from the truth of the second premiss and the falsity of the conclusion. To others it is more plausible that you must complete an infinite number of journeys than that you can't. These people infer the falsity of the second premiss from the truth of the first premiss and the falsity of the conclusion. The first party says "You couldn't, but you don't need to"; the second party says "You must, but you can."

James Thomson, "Tasks and Super-Tasks," *Analysis*, XV (1954–55), 1–13. Reprinted by permission of the author, and the editor and publisher of *Analysis*. Footnotes have been renumbered to number consecutively throughout the article.

This division was neatly illustrated in some recent numbers of *Analysis*. Professor Max Black[1] argued that the expression 'an infinite number of acts' was self-contradictory,
and thus affirmed the second premiss. Unfortunately, he
was not entirely convincing in his rejection of the first
premiss. Messrs. Richard Taylor[2] and J. Watling[3] rejected
Professor Black's arguments for the second premiss, and at
least part of their reason for doing so was that they were
impressed by the plausibility of the first premiss. Unfortunately, they were not entirely convincing in their rejection of the second.

Luckily we need not take sides in this dispute. For the
argument stated above is not valid. It commits the fallacy
of equivocation. There is an element of truth in each of the
premisses; what the elements of truth are, it is the purpose
of this paper to explain.

Let us begin by considering the second premiss. Is it conceivable that someone should have completed an infinite
number of tasks? Do we know what this would be like?
Let us say, for brevity, that a man who has completed all of
an infinite number of tasks (of some given kind) has completed a super-task (of some associated kind). Then, do we
know what a super-task is? Do we have this concept?

It is necessary here to avoid a common confusion. It is
not in question whether we understand the sentence: The
operation so-and-so can be performed infinitely often. On
the contrary, it is quite certain that we do. But to say that
some operation can be performed infinitely often is not to
say that a super-operation can be performed.

Suppose (A) that every lump of chocolate can be cut in
two, and (B) that the result of cutting a lump of chocolate in
two is always that you get two lumps of chocolate. It follows
that every lump of chocolate is infinitely divisible. Now I

---

[1] "Achilles and the Tortoise" [reprinted above].

[2] "Mr. Black on Temporal Paradoxes" [108].

[3] "The Sum of an Infinite Series" [117].

suppose that one of the assumptions A and B is false. For either a molecule of chocolate is a lump of chocolate, and then A is false, or it is not, in which case the result of cutting some lump of chocolate in two is not a lump of chocolate, and then B is false. But the conjunction of A and B is certainly consistent, and so it is certainly conceivable that a lump be infinitely divisible. But to say that a lump is infinitely divisible is just to say that it can be cut into any number of parts. Since there is an infinite number of numbers, we could say: there is an infinite number of numbers of parts into which the lump can be divided. And this is not to say that it can be divided into an infinite number of parts. If something is infinitely divisible, and you are to say into how many parts it shall be divided, you have $\aleph_0$ alternatives from which to choose. This is not to say that $\aleph_0$ is one of them.

And if something is infinitely divisible, then the operation of halving it or halving some part of it can be performed infinitely often. This is not to say that the operation *can have been* performed infinitely often.

The confusion that is possible here is really quite gross, but it does have a certain seductiveness. Where each of an infinite number of things can be done, e.g. bisecting, trisecting, etc. ad inf., it is natural and correct to say: *You can perform an infinite number of operations.* (Cf. "You can do it seven different ways.") But it is also natural, though incorrect, to want to take the italicised sentence as saying that there is some *one* operation you can perform whose performance is completed when and only when every one of an infinite set of operations has been performed. (A super-operation.) This is perhaps natural because, or partly because, of an apparent analogy. If I say "It is possible to swim the Channel" I cannot go on to deny that it is conceivable that someone *should have* swum the Channel. But this analogy is only apparent. To say that it is possible to swim the Channel is to say that there is some one thing that can be done. When we say that you can perform an infinite number of operations we are not saying that there is some one ("infinite") operation you can do, but that the *set* of operations ("finite" operations) which lie within your power is an infinite set. Roughly speaking: to speak of an infinity of possibilities is not to speak of the possibility of infinity.

So far I have just been saying that a certain inference is invalid. Suppose that we are considering a certain set of tasks—ordinary everyday tasks—and that we have assigned numbers to them so that we can speak of Task 1, Task 2, etc. Then: given that for every n Task n is possible, we cannot straightway infer that some task not mentioned in the premiss is possible, viz. that task whose performance is completed when and only when for every n Task n has been performed. I have not been saying (so far) that the conclusion of the argument may not be true. But it seems extremely likely, so far as I can see, that the people who have supposed that super-tasks are possible of performance (e.g. Messrs. Taylor and Watling) have supposed so just because they have unthinkingly accepted this argument as valid. People have, I think, confused saying (1) it is conceivable that each of an infinity of tasks be possible (practically possible) of performance, with saying (2) that it is conceivable that all of an infinite number of tasks should have been performed. They have supposed that (1) entails (2). A reason for thinking that some writers have made this mistake is as follows. To suppose that (1) entails (2) is of course to suppose that anyone who denies (2) is committed to denying (1). Now to deny (1) is to be committed to holding, what is quite absurd, (3) that for any given kind of task there is a positive integer k such that it is conceivable that k tasks of the given kind have been performed, but inconceivable, logically absurd, that $k + 1$ of them should have been performed. But no-one would hold (3) to be true unless he had confused logical possibility with physical possibility. And we do find that those who wish to assert (2) are constantly accusing their opponents of just this confusion. They seem to think that all they have to do to render (2) plausible is to clear away any confusions that prevent people from accepting (1). (See the cited papers by Messrs. Taylor and Watling, *passim*.)[4]

I must now mention two other reasons which have led people to suppose it obvious that super-tasks are possible of performance. The first is this. It certainly makes sense to speak of someone having performed a number of tasks. But infinite numbers are numbers; therefore it must make sense to speak of someone having performed an infinite number of tasks. But this perhaps is not so much a reason for holding anything as a reason for not thinking about it. The second is a suggestion of Russell's. Russell suggested[5] that a man's skill in performing operations of some kind might increase so fast that he was able to perform each of an infinite sequence of operations after the first in half the time he had required for its predecessor. Then the time required for all of the infinite sequence of tasks would be only twice that required for the first. On the strength of this Russell said that the performance of all of an infinite sequence of tasks was only medically impossible. This suggestion is both accepted and used by both Taylor and Watling.

Russell has the air of one who explains how something that you might think hard is really quite easy. ("Look, you do it *this* way.") But our difficulty with the notion of a super-task is not this kind of difficulty. Does Russell really show us what it would be like to have performed a super-task? Does he explain the concept? To me, at least, it seems that he does not even see the difficulty. It is certainly conceivable that there be an infinite sequence of improvements each of which might be effected in a man's skill. For

---

[4] See also Mr. Taylor's criticism [109] of J. O. Wisdom's paper, "Achilles on a Physical Racecourse" [reprinted above]. I am inclined to think that Dr. Wisdom really does deny (1) and that he supposes that he is committed to this course because he wishes to deny (2).

[5] "The Limits of Empiricism," *Proceedings of the Aristotelian Society*, 1935–36 [N.S. XXXVI, p. 131].

any number n we can imagine that a man is first able to perform just n tasks of some kind in (say) two minutes, and then, after practice, drugs, or meditation is able to perform $n+1$ of them in two minutes. But this is just not to say that we can imagine that someone has effected all the improvements each of which might be effected. If Russell thought it was he was making the mistake already called attention to. And otherwise his suggestion does not help. For the thing said to be possible, and to explain how a super-task is possible, are the things to be explained. If we have no difficulties with "He has effected all of an infinite number of improvements" we are not likely to be puzzled by "He has performed an infinite number of tasks."

It may be that Russell had in mind only this. If we can conceive a machine doing something—e.g. calling out or writing down numbers—at a certain rate, let us call that rate *conceivable*. Then, there is obviously no upper bound to the sequence of conceivable rates. For any number n we can imagine a machine that calls out or writes down the first n numbers in just $2 - \frac{1}{2^{n-1}}$ minutes. But this again is not to say that we can imagine a machine that calls out or writes down all the numerals in just 2 minutes. An infinity of possible machines is not the possibility of an infinity-machine. To suppose otherwise would again be the fallacy referred to.

So far I have only been trying to show that the reasons one might have for supposing super-tasks possible of performance are not very good ones. Now, are there any reasons for supposing that super-tasks are not possible of performance? I think there are.

There are certain reading lamps that have a button in the base. If the lamp is off and you press the button the lamp goes on, and if the lamp is on and you press the button the lamp goes off. So if the lamp was originally off, and you pressed the button an odd number of times, the lamp is on, and if you pressed the button an even number of times the lamp is off. Suppose now that the lamp is off, and I succeed in pressing the button an infinite number of times, perhaps making one jab in one minute, another jab in the next half minute, and so on, according to Russell's recipe. After I have completed the whole infinite sequence of jabs, i.e. at the end of the two minutes, is the lamp on or off? It seems impossible to answer this question. It cannot be on, because I did not ever turn it on without at once turning it off. It cannot be off, because I did in the first place turn it on, and thereafter I never turned it off without at once turning it on. But the lamp must be either on or off. This is a contradiction.

This type of argument refutes also the possibility of a machine built according to Russell's prescription that say writes down in two minutes every integer in the decimal expansion of π. For if such a machine is (logically) possible so presumably is one that records the parity, 0 or 1, of the integers written down by the original machine as it produces them. Suppose the parity machine has a dial on which either 0 or 1 appears. Then, what appears on the dial after the first machine has run through all the integers in the expansion of π?

Now what exactly do these arguments come to? Say that the reading lamp has either of two light-values, 0 ("off") and 1 ("on"). To switch the lamp on is then to add 1 to its value and to switch it off is to subtract 1 from its value. Then the question whether the lamp is on or off after the infinite number of switchings have been performed is a question about the value of the lamp after an infinite number of alternating additions and subtractions of 1 to and from its value, i.e. is the question: What is the sum of the infinite divergent sequence

$$+1, -1, +1, \ldots?$$

Now mathematicians do say that this sequence has a sum; they say that its sum is $\frac{1}{2}$.[6] And this answer does not help

---

[6] Hardy, *Divergent Series* [Oxford: Clarendon Press, 1949], chap. 1. There is an excellent account of the discussions this series has provoked in Dr. Waismann's *Introduction to Mathematical Thinking* [New York: Frederick Ungar Publishing Co., 1951], chap. 10.

us, since we attach no sense here to saying that the lamp is half on. I take this to mean that there is no established method for deciding *what* is done when a super-task is done. And this at least shows that the concept of a super-task has not been *explained*. We cannot be expected to *pick up* this idea, just because we have the idea of a task or tasks having been performed and because we are acquainted with transfinite numbers.

As far as I can see the argument given above about the reading lamp is virtually equivalent to one of Professor Black's arguments.[7] These arguments were however rejected by Taylor and Watling, who said that Black assumed the point at issue by supposing that if any number of tasks have been performed some task of those performed was performed last. This assumption is, they say, exactly the assumption that if any number of tasks have been performed a finite number only have been performed. On the one hand it is not clear to me that Black actually *used* this assumption (clearly he believed it to be true, because it was what he was arguing for) and on the other hand it is clear that the question of a 'last task' is a little more complicated than Watling and Taylor supposed, just because some infinite sequences really do have last terms as well as first ones. (Thus if you could mention all the positive integers in two minutes in the way that Russell suggests you could also mention them all except 32 in two minutes; you would then have performed a super-task, but not the super-task of mentioning all the numbers; but to complete this one you would have only to mention 32, and this would be your last task.) But in any case it should be clear that no assumption about a last task is made in the lamp argument. If the button has been jabbed an infinite number of times in the way described then there was no last jab and we cannot ask whether the last jab was a switching on or a switching off. But we did not ask about a last jab; we asked

[7] *Op. cit.*, para. 17 [p. 76 above].

about the net or total result of the whole infinite sequence of jabs, and this would seem to be a fair question.

. . . .

But now, it may be said, surely it is sometimes possible to complete an infinite number of tasks. For to complete a journey is to complete a task, the task of getting from somewhere to somewhere else. And a man who completes any journey completes an infinite number of journeys. If he travels from 0 to 1, he travels from 0 to $\frac{1}{2}$, from $\frac{1}{2}$ to $\frac{3}{4}$, and so on ad inf., so when he arrives at 1 he has completed an infinite number of tasks. This is virtually the first premiss in the original argument, and it certainly seems both to be true and to contradict the previous result. I think it is true but does not contradict the impossibility of super-tasks.

Let Z be the set of points along the racecourse

$$0, \tfrac{1}{2}, \tfrac{3}{4}, \ldots$$

where 0 is the starting point, 1 the finishing point; suppose these on our left and our right respectively. Notice that Z is open on the right; there is no Z-point to the right of every other Z-point. Z is convergent but its limit-point 1 is not in Z. A point that is neither a Z-point nor to the left of any Z-point I shall call a point external to Z. In particular, 1 is external to Z.

Those who support the first premiss say that all you have to do to get to 1 is to occupy every Z-point from left to right in turn. Or rather they are committed to saying this; for they do say that to get to 1 it is sufficient to run all the distances in the sequence of distances $\frac{1}{2}, \frac{1}{4}, \ldots$; but to occupy every Z-point is to run every one of these distances, since each distance has a right-hand end-point in Z, and, conversely, every Z-point is the right-hand end of one of these distances. But put this way, in terms of points rather than distances, should not their thesis seem odd? For to have arrived at 1 you must have occupied or passed over 1. But 1 is not a Z-point. 1 is not the end-point of any of the distances: first half, third quarter. . . .

Further: suppose someone could have occupied every

Z-point without having occupied any point external to Z. Where would he be? Not at any Z-point, for then there would be an unoccupied Z-point to the right. Not, for the same reason, between Z-points. And, ex hypothesi, not at any point external to Z. But these possibilities are exhaustive. The absurdity of having occupied all the Z-points without having occupied any point external to Z is exactly like the absurdity of having pressed the lamp-switch an infinite number of times or of having made all of an infinite number of additions.

But of course those who say that to finish your journey all you have to do is to run each of an infinite number of distances do not say in so many words that it is possible to have done what was just said to be impossible. And obviously it is possible to have occupied all the Z-points; you do this by starting off for 1 and making sure you get there. You then occupy a point external to Z; but you have occupied all the Z-points too. Now if you are given a set of tasks, and if it is impossible for you to have performed all the tasks set unless you perform a task not set or not explicitly set, should you not suppose that you are to do something you were not explicitly told to do? (If you are wearing shoes and socks and you are told to take off your socks should you not suppose that you are to take off your shoes?) So if you are told to occupy all the Z-points should you not at once proceed to 1?

But the shoes-and-socks analogy is not quite correct. To arrive at 1 you do not have to occupy all the Z-points and then do something else. If you have completed all the journeys that have end-points in Z, there is no further distance to run before arriving at 1. Arriving is not running a last distance. On the contrary, your arriving at 1 is your completing the whole journey and thus is your having completed all the infinite number of journeys (in the only sense in which this is possible). Occupying all the Z-points in turn does not get you to some point short of 1; it does not get you, in particular, to a point *next to* 1. Either occupying all the Z-points *is* getting to 1, or it is *nothing*. And this is, perhaps, obscurely noticed by those who support the first premiss. They say, "*all* you need to do is. . . ." And though it would be permissible to interpret the 'all' as saying that you need not occupy any point external to Z it could also be interpreted as saying that arriving at 1 is not completing a last journey of those specified.

There is then something odd in the claim that to arrive at 1 you need only occupy all the Z-points. Take it narrowly and it is nonsense. But if we take it charitably, is it not something of a joke? For when the order "Run an infinite number of journeys!" is so explained as to be intelligible, it is seen to be the order "Run!" And indeed how could one run any distance without being at some point midway between point of departure and destination? If running to catch a bus is performing a super-task, then this super-task is, for some people at some times, *medically* possible. But *this* super-task is just a task.

If an infinite number of things are to be done, they must be done in some or other order. The order in which they are done imposes an ordering on the set of things to be done. Hence to the performance of an infinite set of tasks we assign not a transfinite cardinal but a transfinite ordinal. What is shown by the example of the lamp-switch and by the impossibility of occupying all Z-points without occupying any point external to Z is that it is impossible to have performed every task in a sequence of tasks of type ω (no last task). Now the man who runs from 0 to 1 and so passes over every Z-point may be said to have run every one of an unending sequence of distances, a sequence of type ω. But the proof that he does depends on a statement about arriving at points. Further it is completing a journey that is completing a task, and completing a journey is arriving at a point. And the sequence of points that he arrives at (or is said here to arrive at) is not a sequence of type ω but a sequence of type $\omega + 1$ (last task, no penultimate task), the sequence of the points

$$0, \tfrac{1}{2}, \ldots, 1$$

in Z's closure. So when we explain in what sense a man who completes a journey completes an infinite number of journeys, and thus explain in what sense the first premiss is true, we thereby explain that what is said to be possible by the first premiss is not what is said to be impossible by the second.

The objection to super-tasks was that we could not say what would be done if a super-task were done. This objection does not apply in the case of the runner; we can say, he was at 0 and now is at 1. But if it is sometimes possible to have performed all of an infinite sequence of tasks of type $\omega + 1$, why is it not possible to mention all the positive integers except 32 in two minutes, by Russell's prescription, and then mention 32 last? This would be performing a sequence of tasks of type $\omega + 1$. Well, here it would seem reasonable to ask about the state of a parity-machine[8] at the end of the first two minutes, i.e. immediately before the last number was mentioned. But it is obviously unreasonable to ask where the runner was when he was at the point immediately preceding his destination.

There are two points I would like to make in conclusion. There may be a certain reluctance to admitting that one does complete an infinite number of journeys in completing one journey. This reluctance would appear strongly if someone said that the concept of an open point-set like Z was *not applicable to* 'physical reality.' Such a reluctance might be lessened by the following consideration. Let Operation 1 be the operation of proceeding from 0 to the midpoint of 0 and 1. Let Operation 2 be the operation of performing Operation 1 and then proceeding from the point where you are to the midpoint of that point and 1. And in general let Operation n be the operation of performing Operation $n-1$

[8] See above, p. 95.

and etc. Then Z is the set of points you can get to by performing an operation of the kind described. And obviously none of the operations described gets you to the point 1, hence we should expect Z not to contain its own limit-point and so to be open. Now we just cannot say a *priori* that we shall *never* have occasion to mention point-sets like Z; one might well want to consider the set of points you can get to by performing operations of this kind. So it is just wrong to say that the concept of an open point-set like Z has no application to 'physical reality' (which is I think what Black and Wisdom are saying). But on the other hand the implicit use of the concept in the first premiss of the Zenoesque argument *is* a misleading one, and this is just what the second premiss calls attention to. Roughly speaking the argument forces us to consider the *applications* of the concept of infinity. (E.g. contrast the ways in which it occurs in the propositions I called (1) and (2) at the beginning of this paper.)[9]

Secondly, it may be helpful to indicate the way in which the topic of this discussion is related to the 'mathematical solution' of the paradox, referred to by all three of the writers I have quoted. People used to raise this topic by asking "*How is it possible* for a man to run all of an infinite number of distances?" Now either they thought, or Whitehead and others thought they thought, that the difficulty of running an infinite number of distances was like the difficulty of getting to a place an infinite number of miles away. Hence Whitehead emphasised that the sequence

$$1, \tfrac{1}{2}, \tfrac{1}{4}, \ldots$$

was convergent and had a finite sum. He also thereby pointed out a play on the word 'never'; the sequence never reaches 0, the sequence of partial sums never reaches 2. (The sequence does not contain its limit; but it is con-

---

[9] I think it is partly this contrast that those people have in mind who claim to distinguish between the concept of a potential infinite and the concept of an actual infinite. But there are not here two concepts but two applications of one concept.

vergent, the limit exists.)[10] But though this is necessary it does not resolve all the hesitations one might feel about the premiss of the paradox. What I have been trying to show is that these hesitations are not merely frivolous, and that insofar as they spring from misunderstandings these misunderstandings are shared by those who support the 'mathematical solution.'

[10] This is clearly explained by Mr. Taylor, op. cit. [109].

Tasks, Super-Tasks, and the Modern Eleatics*

PAUL BENACERRAF

Many years ago Zeno of Elea raised some questions concerning the possibility of motion. He presented arguments designed to show that motion was impossible: that any claim that motion had really taken place was self-contradictory. I don't believe that anyone holds this view today—which proves that some things eventually become evident, even to philosophers. So I won't try to show that motion is really possible.

However, the difficulties Zeno raised were far from silly. They were grounded in legitimate problems concerning space and time, and, although what he claimed to have shown seems to be false, there is far from universal agreement on just what was wrong with his arguments. The debate has lasted these several thousand years. Most likely, it

Paul Benacerraf, "Tasks, Super-Tasks, and the Modern Eleatics," *Journal of Philosophy*, LIX (1962), 765–784. Reprinted, with minor emendations by the author, by permission of the author, and the editor of the *Journal of Philosophy*.

---

*Read to the Philosophy Department Seminar at Princeton University, April 12, 1961. I would like particularly to thank Gregory Vlastos and Ian Hacking for having stimulated my interest in these questions and for their many valuable suggestions and criticisms during the writing of this paper.

will last several thousand more—which proves that some things don't eventually become evident, even to philosophers. I am not entering the arena to do battle on this issue. My purpose is much more modest: I wish to discuss another question, which Zeno may or may not have raised, but which his recent commentators have certainly raised in their analyses of his arguments. I shall limit my discussion to issues raised by James Thomson in his remarkable and stimulating paper "Tasks and Super-Tasks,"[1] basing my own remarks on his treatment of these issues and letting him represent what I take to be a number of widely held views. In this way, I shall manage to be unfair both to Thomson (by scrutinizing his remarks more closely than perhaps they were meant to be) and to those who are in substantial agreement with him (by slighting their individual views where it might conceivably make some difference to the general position).

The Zenonian argument that Thomson discusses goes as follows:

> To complete any journey you must complete an infinite number of journeys. For to arrive from A to B you must first go from A to A', the mid-point of A and B, and thence to A'', the mid-point of A' and B, and so on. But it is logically absurd that someone should have completed all of an infinite number of journeys, just as it is logically absurd that someone should have completed all of an infinite number of tasks. Therefore it is absurd that anyone has ever completed any journey [p. 89 above].

Thomson argues that, whereas previous disputants concerning the proper analysis of this argument divide into two schools: those who deny the first premise and those who deny the second, both schools granting the validity of the argument, the proper analysis shows that the argument is invalid, that it commits the fallacy of equivocation. The ex-

---

[1] [Reprinted above.] Subsequent references to this article will appear in the text and will be by page number.

pression 'completing an infinite number of journeys' can be taken in two ways. If it is taken in one way, the first premise is false and the second true; in the other, the first premise is true and the second false. No way of interpreting it renders *both* premises true.[2]

Very briefly, the two ways are these. If we have made a continuous uninterrupted journey from A to B we can be said to have covered all the stretches described in the first premise; that is, our motion *can be analyzed as* covering in turn AA', A'A'', etc. If there is at least one of these stretches that we haven't covered, then we haven't completed our journey. In this sense, the first premise is true; but in this sense also, the *second* premise is false: completing infinitely many journeys takes no more effort than completing one; to say of someone that he has completed an infinite number of journeys (in *this* sense) is just to describe in a different (and possibly somewhat peculiar) way the act he performed in completing the single continuous journey from A to B. No absurdity is involved with the feat. If, however, we think of "completing an infinite number of journeys" as completing an infinite number of physically distinct acts, each with a beginning and an end, and with, say, a pause of finite duration between any two, then according to Thomson the second premise is true: it *is* logically absurd that one should have completed an infinite number of journeys. But, of course, under this interpretation the first premise is obviously false: one need not complete an infinite number of journeys of this kind in order to complete a single one.

Thomson does two things. First, he considers the second premise under this last interpretation and argues in two

---

[2] This fact alone, of course, does not establish the formal invalidity of the argument. At best it shows that the argument could not be used to establish its conclusion. If the phrase in question is indeed ambiguous, then one not averse to arguing sophistically could well employ the argument in a debate and then, if pushed, admit that one of his premises was false. He would thereby maintain the purity of his logic, if not of his soul.

stages that it must be true—that it is logically impossible to complete an infinite number of journeys or to perform an infinite number of tasks (a "super-task"). He argues that some reasons why people might have thought this possible are bad reasons, and then offers arguments to prove that the concept of "having performed an infinite number of tasks or acts" is a self-contradictory one. The second part of his paper is devoted to showing why, under the first interpretation of 'completing an infinite number of journeys,' the second premise turns out to be false, but might appear to some to be true. It should now be obvious why I have called Thomson and Thomsonites "modern Eleatics." Whereas Zeno tried to show that performing a single task was impossible, his twentieth-century emendators are content to retreat to the position that, although single tasks might be all right, we mustn't have too many of them. As I have already stated, I shall not discuss the correctness of this analysis of the Zenonian argument. But I shall discuss Thomson's arguments to the effect that it is logically impossible to perform an infinite number of tasks.[3] In a final section I shall make some general remarks concerning the possibility of proving or disproving the logical impossibility of performing infinitely many acts or tasks.

I

Thomson's first argument, concerning the lamp, is short, imaginative, and compelling. It appears to demonstrate that "completing a super-task" is a self-contradictory concept. Let me reproduce it here:

[3] In fairness to Thomson, I must add that he is not univocal in the conclusions that he draws from his arguments. He alternates between concluding that super-tasks are a logical impossibility and that "the concept of super-task has not been *explained*" [96], that "talk of super-tasks is *senseless*" [p. 9 in original; omitted in this reprinting]. (In both cases the italics are Thomson's.) Perhaps he does not distinguish between the two, or perhaps he thinks that to show that a contradiction arises from supposing that a super-task has been performed establishes the senselessness of such talk. So far as I can tell, he is not explicit on this point. I shall try to say something about this distinction in the last part of this paper.

There are certain reading lamps that have a button in the base. If the lamp is off and you press the button the lamp goes on, and if the lamp is on and you press the button, the lamp goes off. So if the lamp was originally off, and you pressed the button an odd number of times, the lamp is on, and if you pressed the button an even number of times the lamp is off. Suppose now that the lamp is off, and I succeed in pressing the button an infinite number of times, perhaps making one jab in one minute, another jab in the next half minute, and so on. . . . After I have completed the whole infinite sequence of jabs, i.e. at the end of the two minutes, is the lamp on or off? . . . It cannot be on, because I did not ever turn it on without at once turning it off. It cannot be off, because I did in the first place turn it on, and thereafter I never turned it off without at once turning it on. But the lamp must be either on or off. This is a contradiction [pp. 94–95].

Rarely are we presented with an argument so neat and convincing. This one has only one flaw. It is formally invalid. Let us see why. Consider the following two descriptions:

A. Aladdin starts at t_0 and performs the super-task in question just as Thomson does. Let t_1 be the first instant after he has completed the whole infinite sequence of jabs— the instant about which Thomson asks "Is the lamp on or off?"—and let the lamp be *on* at t_1.

B. Bernard starts at t_0 and performs the super-task in question (on another lamp) just as Aladdin does, and let Bernard's lamp be *off* at t_1.

I submit that *neither* description is self-contradictory, or, more cautiously, that Thomson's argument shows neither description to be self-contradictory (although possibly some other argument might).

According to Thomson, Aladdin's lamp cannot be on at t_1 because Aladdin turned it off after each time he turned it on. *But this is true only of instants before t_1!* From this it follows only that there is no time *between* t_0 and t_1 at which the lamp was on and which was not followed by a time *also before* t_1 at which it was off. Nothing whatever has been said about the lamp *at t_1 or later*. And similarly with Bernard's lamp. The only reasons Thomson gives for supposing that *his* lamp will not be off at t_1 are ones which hold only for times *before* t_1. The explanation is quite simply that Thomson's instructions do not cover the state of the lamp at t_1, although they *do* tell us what will be its state at every instant *between* t_0 and t_1 (including t_0).[4] Certainly, the lamp must be on or off at t_1 (provided that it hasn't gone up in a metaphysical puff of smoke in the interval), but nothing we are told implies which it is to be. The arguments to the effect that it can't be either just have no bearing on the case. To suppose that they *do* is to suppose that a description of the physical state of the lamp at t_1 (with respect to the property of being on or off) is a *logical* consequence of a description of its state (with respect to the same property) at times prior to t_1. I don't know whether this is true or not, and in section II I shall briefly investigate some matters that bear on this issue. But, true or not, the argument is invalid without the addition of a premise to that effect. This will emerge even more clearly if we consider a parallel argument. Imagine someone telling us:

There are two kinds of numbers, fair and foul, and every number <1 is one or the other. Consider the infinite converging sequence $\frac{1}{2}, \frac{1}{4}, \frac{1}{8}, \frac{1}{16}, \frac{1}{32} \ldots$. Its first member is foul, its second member fair, its third member foul, its fourth fair, etc., alternating in such a way that $\frac{1}{2^n}$ is foul if n is odd and fair if n is even, for all positive integers n. What about the limit of the sequence? It is, of course, not in the sequence; but is it foul or fair? It can't be foul, because after every foul there was a fair; and it can't be fair, because we started with a foul and thereafter there was not a fair that was not immediately followed by a foul. But it must be one or the other, for every number <1 is either fair or foul. This is a contradiction.

Of course not. The answer is simply that we haven't been

---

[4] Provided, of course, that we have been diligent in following them and that nothing happens to the lamp between jabs.

told how to classify the limit number. The instructions cover the sequence and the sequence only. Nothing was said about any number not in the sequence. The same is true in the case of the lamp. Thomson tells us nothing about the state of the lamp at t_1. Consequently Aladdin's and Bernard's results were perfectly possible outcomes—at least insofar as the argument under discussion is concerned. No magic was necessary to overcome it. And indeed, Thomson himself was not far from the truth, for in a sentence that I omitted (between "Is the lamp on or off?" and "It cannot be on") he says: "It seems impossible to answer this question" [95]. Quite so. It *is* impossible, on the information given. But a contradiction arises only if the instructions are complete in the following sense: that they have been followed entails either that the lamp is on at t_1 or that it is off at t_1. They are not.

We can now see that what is correct and convincing about Thomson's argument can be put in this way:

> There are certain reading lamps that have a button in the base. If the lamp is off and you press the button the lamp goes on, and if the lamp is on and you press the button the lamp goes off. So if the lamp was originally off and you pressed the button an odd number of times the lamp is on, and if you pressed the button an even number of times the lamp is off. Suppose now that the lamp is off and I succeed in pressing the button an infinite number of times, perhaps making one jab in one minute, another jab in the next half minute, and so on. Does having followed these instructions entail either that at the end of the two minutes the lamp is on or that at the end of the two minutes the lamp is off? It doesn't entail that it is on because in following them I did not ever turn it on without at once turning it off. It doesn't entail that it is off because in following them I did in the first place turn it on, and thereafter I never turned it off without at once turning it on.

But if we now continue the argument with "But it must entail one or the other," we are struck with the obvious falsity of the remark; whereas the continuation "But the lamp must be either on or off," is striking by its obvious irrelevance.

Thomson has a further, parallel argument to the effect that a machine could not exist that would write down in two minutes the sequence of integers that constitutes the decimal expansion of π. Briefly reconstructed, it is this. Call one such machine "Albert." If Albert could exist, so, presumably, could Bosco, a machine which records whether the integer written down by Albert is odd or even (by showing either '0' or '1' on its dial: '0' if the integer in question is even, '1' if it is odd). Then "What appears on the (Bosco's) dial after the first machine has run through all the integers in the decimal expansion of π?" is the rhetorical question. Poor Bosco. Is he supposed to be confused? Or just tired? Bosco has only been told what to do in case Albert presents him with an integer. He has no will of his own, no initiative. Had he been told: "After you are through with Albert's integers start on Cuthbert's" (Cuthbert works out the decimal expansion of $\sqrt{2}$ in two minutes), Bosco's dial would show '1' as soon as he started on Cuthbert's problem. And had we been told that these were his instructions, we should know that he shows '1' as soon as he starts. Thomson's argument "proves too much." It "proves" the nonexistence of any function f satisfying the following conditions:

1. If x is the yth integer in the decimal expansion of π and x is odd, then $f(x,y) = 1$; and

2. If x is the yth integer in the decimal expansion of π and x is even, then $f(x,y) = 0$.

It "proves" it by arguing that the question "What is the value of $f(x,\omega)$?" has no answer.* Of course it has no answer. f is defined only over finite ordinals in its second-argument place. But that hardly proves that f is self-contradictory or

---

*[Any set ordered as a progression, i.e., having the same order as the natural numbers in their natural order, is said to have order type ω; ω is the first transfinite ordinal number. See the Appendix for further explanations of this terminology.—Ed.]

nonexistent. There is no ωth integer in the decimal expansion of π.

But Thomson has a third argument, which we must meet. In effect it is his own analysis of *why* the "contradiction" arises in the case of the lamp (and in the other parallel cases). If his explanation is correct, then indeed there is something wrong with our argument that a contradiction does not arise. Let me quote him again:

> Now what exactly do these arguments come to? Say that the reading lamp has either of two light-values, 0 ("off") and 1 ("on"). To switch the lamp on is then to add 1 to its value and to switch it off is to subtract 1 from its value. Then the question whether the lamp is on or off after the infinite number of switchings have been performed is a question about the value of the lamp after an infinite number of alternating additions and subtractions of 1 to and from its value, i.e. is the question: What is the sum of the infinite divergent sequence $+1, -1, +1, \ldots$? Now mathematicians do say that this sequence has a sum; they say that its sum is $\frac{1}{2}$. And this answer does not help us, since we attach no sense here to saying that the lamp is half on [pp. 95–96].

This too is convincing. It appears that Thomson has found the mathematical analogue of these cases, that *it* is perfectly self-consistent, and that the "contradiction" in the case of the physical example carries into the mathematical example —not *as* a contradiction, but as something that has no physical analogue (for *logical* reasons: it makes no sense here to speak of the lamp as being half on). And indeed this appears to work. If the initial value was 0, then the value of the lamp after n switchings is the sum of the first n terms of the series. Consequently the value of the lamp after *all* the switchings is the sum of *all* the terms, or $\frac{1}{2}$. But if the value of the lamp at t_1 is *always* the value of the lamp at t_0 plus the sum of the values corresponding to the sequence of switchings, this represents a contradiction, since there are only two possible values for the lamp: 0 and 1. This is a different "proof" of the self-contradictoriness of the concept of "super-task." Thomson doesn't explicitly present it as such (he presents it as his analysis of what "went wrong"), but he accepts every one of its assumptions (as he must if his explanation is to make sense).

Thomson then argues that this shows that there is no established method for deciding what is done when a super-task is done. But the argument shows no such thing. (For the sake of brevity and convenience, I shall call the sum of the first n terms of a given series—for positive finite n—its "partial$_n$ sum.") True, for each n the value of the lamp after n switchings is accurately represented by its partial$_n$ sum; but what reason is there to believe that its value after all the switchings will be accurately represented by the sum of all the terms, i.e., by the limit of the partial$_n$ sums?

To make this clear, let me say a bit more about fair and foul numbers. So far we know that $\frac{1}{2^n}$ is foul if n is odd and fair if n is even. In fact, the following is also true: if k is odd and $<2^n$, then $\frac{k}{2^n}$ is foul if n is odd and fair if n is even. But now it is easily verified that, although each member of the infinite sequence of partial$_n$ sums corresponding to the convergent sequence $\frac{1}{2}$, $\frac{1}{4}$, $\frac{1}{8}$, . . . is either fair or foul, the *limit* of this sequence of sums cannot be said to be either. Someone might say:

> You see, although I said nothing about it when this example first came up, 0 is really fair. Adding the first term in the series to it yields a foul: $\frac{1}{2}$. Adding the next term yields a fair: $\frac{3}{4}$, and the next, a foul: $\frac{7}{8}$. In general, adding the nth term changes the value of the partial$_n$ sum from fair to foul or foul to fair. We might even say that the value of the series at the nth term is the value of the partial$_n$ sum, for every n. Surely it must follow that the value of the series after *all* the terms must be the value of the sum of the whole series: the limit of the series of partial$_n$ sums. But the sum of the whole series is 1. Is 1 fair or foul? It makes no sense to say of 1 either that it is or that it isn't. I take this to mean that there is no established method for deciding *what* it would be for there to exist an infinite series of rationals.

Of course not. There is no reason to expect that, just because all the *partial$_n$* sums have a given property ("representing the value of the series at *n*"), the sum of the *whole* series must have that property. The concept of the value of the series *has not been defined* for series whose sum ≥ 1.

For the lamp, there is, similarly, no reason to expect the sum of the infinite series $+1, -1, +1, -1, \ldots$ to represent the "value" of the lamp after the hypothesized infinite series of switchings. To be sure, every partial$_n$ sum represents its value after *n* switchings, just as in the fair-foul case every partial$_n$ sum represents the "value" of the series after *n* terms. But just as the fact that 1 cannot be said to represent a (fair-foul) value does not show that there cannot exist an infinite series of rationals, so the fact that $\frac{1}{2}$ cannot be said to represent a (lamp) value does not show that there cannot be an infinite series of lamp-switchings. All that *either* shows is that defining the concept of "value" for partial$_n$ sums does not *ipso facto* define it for sums of *infinite* series.

So far as the first two of these attempts to prove the (logical) impossibility of super-tasks are concerned, I think it is clear what went amiss. In each case a super-task was defined. But during the course of the argument a question was asked about what could be described as the result of performing a *super-duper-task*. (If a super-task is a task sequence of order type ω, then a *super-duper task* is the result of tacking an extra—ωth—task at the end of a super-task.) Since the definition of the super-task specifies nothing about such an ωth task, it is no wonder that the question goes begging for an answer. Thomson apparently believes that to describe a super-task would *ipso facto* be to describe some corresponding super-duper-task, that there could be no such thing as a super-task *tout court*: if there were anything so big as a super-task, it would have to be at least one task bigger. This would account for the fact that, in each one of his arguments, although what he describes is only a super-task, the question he asks presupposes that the description given is determinate with respect to what would be the outcome of some corresponding super-duper-task. This is a suggestion worth considering.

What would make such a view appear plausible is the picture we have of running the racecourse. Thomson defines the set Z of points on the course as the following series: $0, \frac{1}{2}, \frac{3}{4}, \frac{7}{8}, \ldots$ He argues that, if we consider 0 the starting point and 1 the end point, it is impossible to run through the entire Z-series without reaching a point outside of Z, namely 1. In this case to go from 0 to 1 is, of course, not to perform a super-task. It is to perform the ordinary task of making a continuous run from one point to another. The argument goes:

> . . . suppose someone could have occupied every Z-point without having occupied any point external to Z. Where would he be? Not at any Z-point, for then there would be an unoccupied Z-point to the right. Not, for the same reason, between Z-points. And, ex hypothesi, not at any point external to Z. But these possibilities are exhaustive [pp. 97–98].

If ordered to run so as to occupy every point in the Z-series, we cannot obey without also occupying 1. It is logically impossible to do otherwise. Let us assume that this is right, as it appears to be. But Thomson continues:

> The absurdity of having occupied all the Z-points without having occupied any point external to Z is exactly like the absurdity of having pressed the lamp-switch an infinite number of times . . . [p. 98].

Even supposing that the argument of the racecourse is valid (and we shall return to this), this last point *appears* to be mistaken. If the analogy is exact, then his sentence cries out for completion by a corresponding "without . . ." clause. As I shall try to show, that Thomson thinks there is an exact analogy between these two cases explains what misled him in the lamp argument.

If we complete a super-task in a finite time interval (how else?), there must come a time at which we are no longer performing any task belonging to the super-task. To expire beforehand is to leave some member of the set of tasks undone. Similarly, if we run from 0 to 1, there must come a time at which we are no longer occupying any point in the Z-series. In the latter case, we have two parallel sequences of order type $\omega + 1$: the sequence of members of the Z-series, plus 1 at the end, on the one hand, and the corresponding moments of time on the other. In the case of the lamp, we have a sequence of order type ω, the lamp-switchings, and a sequence of order type $\omega + 1$, the moments at which they take place *plus* the first moment after we're through, which must inexorably come. The passage under discussion indicates that Thomson must believe that, just as we cannot go through all the Z-points without reaching a point outside of Z, the description of the lamp super-task is self-contradictory because it fails to provide an answer to his question about the state of the lamp at the ωth moment, about the outcome of an ωth act had there been one. *But there need not be an ωth act of the relevant kind!* For all we have been told, we can, if we please, light up a cigarette or heave a sigh or quietly expire or what have you at the ωth moment. The analogy apparently fails. And the reason why is that, whereas the members of the Z-series are *abstracted* from a presupposed existing set of points (the line 0 to 1 inclusive), the tasks that constitute the super-task are, as it were, generated serially as we need them; there is not even an apparent logical necessity connected with the existence of a task of the relevant kind to fill the ωth spot in the parallel time series, although there *might* seem to be such a necessity concerning the points on the line.

In the racecourse, covering all the Z-points at least partially determines where you are: you cannot cover them all and remain in the Z-set. If the absurdity of performing a super-task is to be exactly like the absurdity of running through all the Z-points without reaching 1, it must be because there must be an ωth task whose performance is *logically* entailed by the performance of the tasks that properly belong to the super-task.[5] The arguments all aim at showing that such a task could not have been performed and, hence, that the super-task whose existence would have entailed its performance could not itself have been performed. But now, let us return to the racecourse argument, for this too is invalid although, admittedly, much less clearly so.

Imagine that the runner has run through all the members of Z. Now Thomson asks: "Where would he be?" Suppose that we answered "Nowhere." Suppose that in fact the runner was none other than Aladdin's genie, that he had been told to occupy all the Z-points and then vanish (without having occupied 1). Would this strain his magical powers to the breaking point? Let us see.

Of course, we cannot refute the view *just* by pointing out that the genie could cease to exist after having occupied all the points in Z, that he needn't be *anywhere*. To be sure, that shows something wrong with *this* argument, but it is open to the quick retort:

> All right then, at what point does he vanish? For if he vanishes he must vanish *at some point;* there must be some point that is the last point he occupied before vanishing. Call this *p*. Now, *p* lies between two members of Z, or else it lies to the right of every member of Z (we shall disregard points to the left of 0 as well as points to the right of 1). If the first, then there is a member of Z to the right of *p*, which has, therefore, not been occupied. If the second, then *p* = 1 and the genie reached 1. But these possibilities are exhaustive (granted our restrictions). Therefore, even if the

---

[5] I am not attributing to Thomson the explicit belief that if a super-task has been performed then a super-duper-task has been performed: that the performer cannot as a matter of logic put on the brakes in time. I use this merely as a rhetorical device to point up what Thomson *does* appear to believe but fails to argue for, namely, that the statement that a super-task has been performed together with a description of the task logically implies a statement describing the state of the system at the ωth moment with respect to the relevant property. I suppose that another way to put this assumption is to say that to achieve the implied result a super-duper-task *need not* be performed—the super-task will do.

genie vanished, he either failed to cover all the Z-points or he occupied 1.

Let us be stubborn. Consider the following case.

Let t_0 be the time at which the genie started from 0, and where applicable, for each i let t_i be the time at which he is at i. The question then becomes: Does this imply that at t_1 he occupies 1? I argue no; my imaginary adversary argues yes. If the genie has carried out my instructions, at t_1 he cannot be at 1, because at t_1 he is no more. To be sure, he vanishes *at* a point: 1. But what does this mean? In particular, does this mean that 1 is *the last point he occupied?* Of course not. There need not be any last point he occupied—any more than there need be a *first* point he *didn't* occupy (although there *must* be one or the other). To disappear at a point is neutral with respect to the question of "having occupied" that point. There is no necessity either way. 'He disappeared at 1' could mean either that 1 is the last point he occupied *or* that 1 is the first point he didn't occupy, just as to have disappeared at t_1 could involve *either* that t_1 was his last moment on earth *or* that t_1 was earth's first moment without him. *Which* we say is a function of how we choose to regard trajectories and time intervals.

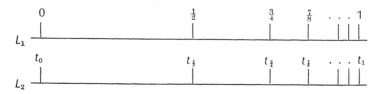

To illustrate, we draw two lines L_1 and L_2. These two lines represent, respectively, the racecourse and the corresponding time scale defined above. We may view each line in two different ways, corresponding to the ways in which each point may be seen as dividing its line into two disjoint and jointly exhaustive sets of points: any point may be seen as dividing its line either into (a) the sets of points to the right of and including it, and the set of points to the left of it; or into (b) the set of points to the right of it and the set of points to the left of and including it. That is, we may assimilate each point to its right-hand segment (a) or to its left-hand segment (b). Which we choose is entirely arbitrary, but (*modulo* the assumption that any run covers a line segment) it determines how we answer the question: "Given that he disappeared at 1, did he occupy 1?" Those who assimilate each point to its left-hand segment (method b) will say that he did and that t_1 was his last moment on earth. On this account earth had no first moment without him, and there was no first point he didn't occupy. Similarly, if we choose method a, then the genie is said not to have occupied 1, although he disappeared at 1, and there is a first point he didn't occupy and a first moment earth was without him: t_1. What we *cannot* do, given the correspondence we have established between the points on L_1 and L_2, is to regard these lines each in a different way. This would lead us to say, for example, that there was a last point he covered on his trajectory (namely 1), but that he was not on earth at t_1. Since t_1 was defined as the time at which he occupied 1 (if he occupies 1, otherwise the time at which he would have occupied 1, had he done so), this is a contradiction. We are inclined to regard the racecourse (L_1) according to method b, whereas, for each of the two methods, there are circumstances where it is clearly more natural to regard the time series in *that* way rather than in the other. But we are at liberty to view it as we like. Normally it makes no difference, but in *this* case *how* we view it makes the *only* difference. My imaginary opponent assumes that if the genie vanished at a point there must be a *last* point he occupied. This holds only if method b of viewing the line is *mandatory*. We have seen that it is not. But wait:

> You agree that it is natural to regard the racecourse as I have regarded it, but you claim that it is possible to regard it otherwise. But is it really? Can you describe a case that it would be reasonable to regard as one in which all the points to the left of 1 have been covered, but not 1 itself. If not,

then all your argument comes to naught, for a possibility
that has no conceivable description is not a real possibility.
I accept the challenge (though not necessarily the implied
view). Let me tell you more about our genie:

Ours is a reluctant genie. He shrinks from the thought of
reaching 1. In fact, being a rational genie, he shows his
repugnance against reaching 1 by shrinking so that the
ratio of his height at any point to his height at the beginning
of the race is always equal to the ratio of the unrun portion
of the course to the whole course. He is full grown at 0,
half-shrunk at $\frac{1}{2}$; only $\frac{1}{4}$ of him is left at $\frac{3}{4}$, etc. His instructions are to continue in this way *and* to disappear at 1.
Clearly, now, he occupied every point to the left of 1 (I
can tell you exactly when and how tall he was at that point),
but he did not occupy 1 (if he followed instructions, there
was nothing left of him at 1). Of course, if we *must* say that
he vanished at a point, it must be at 1 that we must say that
he vanished, but in this case, there is no temptation whatever
to say that he occupied 1. He couldn't have. There wasn't
enough left of him. Note that it does not follow from the
description of the shrinking alone that he never occupies 1.
We could describe his shrinking by saying quite generally
(this is not quite general since it gives his height only at
the rational points) that he is $\frac{1}{2^n}$th his original size when he
is at $\frac{2^n-1}{2^n}$. From this nothing follows about his size *at* 1.
This is perfectly consistent with his appearing at 1 full blown.
If, furthermore, he is instructed to *vanish* at 1, then indeed
he will, for he is obedient (and also very reluctant to reach
1). The difference between this case and the vanishing genie
as originally described (before we said anything about his
shrinking) is that, in the former case, it would appear to
take some effort on his part to vanish at 1, and we might be
reluctant to think that he can do it, whereas here, having
got started downhill, as it were, it would take quite an effort
to reappear full blown at 1. But, of course, although this

difference explains our reluctance in each case to use a particular description, in neither case does it make it impossible to use the "less natural" description.

So, even if he vanished at 1, he need not have occupied 1. Therefore, he could have occupied every Z-point without occupying any point external to Z.

To recapitulate, then. I have argued in this section that Thomson's arguments fail to establish the logical impossibility of super-tasks and that what misleads him in each case is what he takes to be an analogy between performing a super-task and running the racecourse. He feels that, in the latter case, you cannot occupy every Z-point without occupying some ωth point, not in Z—that this is a logical impossibility. Similarly, every putative proof of the impossibility of super-tasks takes the following form:

1. Assume that a super-task has been performed.
2. Consider what happens at the ωth moment:
    a. In the case of the lamp: Is it on or off?
        By one argument, it can't be either, but it *must* be one or the other; by the other argument, it would have to be half on and half off, which presumably it can't be.
    b. In poor Bosco's case: Does '0' or '1' appear on his dial?
        Supposedly *neither* can, but one or the other must.

It has been my contention that the analogy Thomson claims to find does not exist, but that another one *does;* he has failed to establish the impossibility in question even in the case of the racecourse.

The reason why his argument fails in the *latter* case is that he does not show that to occupy all the points in an infinite convergent series of points *logically* entails occupying the limit point. *For all that he has said,* it is perfectly possible to cross over into another dimension or pass into Genieland or simply cease to exist. It has not been shown that the existential compulsion we feel which drags us from one moment to the next is a *logical* one—but *this too* must be shown in proving that to occupy all the Z-points, the runner must occupy a point outside of Z.

The reason why the analogy between super-tasks and the racecourse might seem not to hold is this: even if we viewed the race in a manner more appropriate (though, I insist, not mandatory) to the nonshrinking Genie, i.e., even if we said that in disappearing at 1 he had to occupy 1, there would still be no corresponding necessity concerning the state of the lamp or the state of Bosco. In the racecourse we are dealing with a sequence of points abstracted from a continuum of points. The limit point exists, and we have a choice of saying that the genie occupied it or that he didn't. In the case of super-tasks, there is no assumption of an underlying continuum. The sequence of *points* has a limit: 1. But what reason is there to suppose that the sequence of *tasks* "has a limit," that a task of the corresponding kind is performed at the ωth moment, turning our ordinary super-task into a super-duper-task? None has been given. So, it has not been shown that "the absurdity of having occupied all the Z-points without having occupied any point external to Z is exactly like the absurdity of having pressed the lamp-switch an infinite number of times," except possibly vacuously.

II

What conclusions are we to draw from this rather heady mixture of genies, machines, lamps, and fair and foul numbers? In particular, has it been shown that super-tasks are really possible—that, in Russell's words, they are at most *medically* and not logically impossible? Of course not. In a part of his paper that I did not discuss, Thomson very nicely destroys the arguments of those who claim to prove that super-tasks are logically possible; had there been time I should have examined them. In the preceding section I tried to do the same for Thomson's own neo-Eleatic arguments. I think it should be clear that, just as Thomson did not establish the impossibility of super-tasks by destroying the arguments of their defenders, I did not establish their *possibility* by pointing out gaps in his.

I am not quite sure what constitutes proving that something is logically possible. I think I *do* know, at least in part, what it is to prove that something is logically *impossible*. It is this: if we call an *explicit contradiction* the conjunction of some statement with its negation, then to prove that some statement S is self-contradictory—that what it asserts to be the case is logically impossible—is to prove that S logically implies an explicit contradiction. This is, if you like, a simple-minded but roughly accurate account of disproof by *reductio ad absurdum*. Even a cursory examination of Thomson's arguments will show that this is precisely what he sets out to do for the statement that a super-task has been performed. In each case the argument seemed to require an additional premise connecting the state of the machine or lamp or what have you at the ωth moment with its state at some previous instant or set of instants. The clearest example is that of the lamp, where we can derive a contradiction only by explicitly assuming as an additional premise that a statement describing the state of the lamp (with respect to being on or off) *after* all the switchings is a *logical* consequence of the statements describing its state during the performance of the super-task.

But consider the following dialogue:

He: Well, if that's all we need, why not add it as a new premise? Then we'll have a valid argument with S (the statement we're trying to prove contradictory) as premise and an explicit contradiction as conclusion. Isn't that what we want?

I: No, it isn't. We need more. That would show only that the conjunction of S with our new premise is self-contradictory. That's not much help, since the fault may lie with the new premise or, for that matter, with neither in particular but only with their (possibly illicit) logical relation to each other.

He: But suppose the new premise is *true*. We've validly derived a contradiction from S by assuming only true auxiliary premises. Surely *that* proves S to be self-contradictory!

I: No. Let S be 'The hat is on the cat,' and suppose that in fact the cat is hatless. Then S in conjunction with the true statement, 'The hat isn't on the cat,' implies a contradiction.

He: All right, then. Suppose that this additional premise is not only true, but *obviously* true. Isn't S contradictory if in conjunction with obvious truths it logically implies an explicit contradiction? And it's obviously true that the state of the lamp at *t* is a consequence of its state before *t*.

I: No. At best this would show that it was obviously impossible to perform the particular super-task in question. But I grant at the outset that it's obviously impossible. What right-thinking man would not? For one thing, the parts would soon be worn to a frazzle—as would Aladdin and Bernard.

He: So its being obviously true won't do. Suppose I add the requirement that the additional premise be necessary. Wouldn't something that implies an explicit contradiction when conjoined with necessary premises *have* to be self-contradictory?

I: Again no. It would have to be self-contradictory only if the necessity of the premise involved were *logical* necessity, only if the negation of the auxiliary premise were itself self-contradictory. (This is of course not a vicious circle, nor even a circle at all, since it is possible to establish some statements as self-contradictory without appeal to any auxiliary assumptions whatever.) The only auxiliary premises permitted in a demonstration that a statement is self-contradictory are *analytic* ones—ones true by virtue of the meanings of their constituent parts.

He: If the additional premise concerning the state of the lamp is analytic, then Thomson has in fact succeeded in showing that at least *this* super-task is a logical impossibility. All your counters have gone to naught.

I: No, if the suppressed premise is analytic, then indeed the statement that the lamp has been switched on and off an infinite number of times is self-contradictory—but Thomson hasn't shown it. To achieve his Eleatic purpose, he must not only derive an explicit contradiction from the statement that a super-task has been performed, using only analytic auxiliary assumptions along the way, but he must also *show* that his assumptions *are* analytic.[6] Were this not so, and were he right about the self-contradictoriness of the concept of super-task, then he could make a mockery of the proof by presenting the following one:

> a. A super-task has been performed.
> b. No super-task has been performed.

Therefore: c. $p \cdot -p$

Ex hypothesi (for us) a is self-contradictory. b is therefore analytic, and c follows from the conjunction of a and b. This would be too easy.

In the above dialogue I try to give a rough idea of what I think is missing from Thomson's "proofs." A "swindle" has taken place, and we have been the victims. Somehow, all was going along swimmingly, and suddenly we find ourselves drowning in contradiction with no idea of how we got there. We are told that the concept of a super-task is to blame, but we are not told *what* about it has such dire consequences. We are sufficiently sophisticated mathematically to know that the concept of infinity is not at fault (or if it is, a lot more than the future of super-tasks is at stake). But what then? What *could* he do that he has failed to do?

I said that he had to *show* that the auxiliary premises were analytic. But how does one show that? How does one *show* that a statement owes its truth solely to meanings (if that is the same question)? Obviously there are problems. The key issues in the philosophy of language are involved in the discussion of this point. Perhaps there is no answer to my question. Perhaps the concepts involved are too confused. If so, then so much the worse for Mr. Thomson and his co-neo-Eleatics, for I think that their only hope lies here. If analyticity construed as truth by virtue of meanings collapses, then so

---

[6] Upon reconsideration at the time of reprinting, this condition seems too strong, though some such condition is evidently required.

does the enterprise of showing that the concept of super-task is self-contradictory—for that is merely the other side of the same coin. So I will assume that something sensible can be said about this.

To show that the concept of super-task is self-contradictory, it must be shown that there is something self-contradictory in the concept of a completed infinite series of tasks. There are three possibilities. The first, which I discard at the outset in *this* discussion, although it is an interesting question in its own right, is that the concept of the infinite is itself self-contradictory. The second, which I also discard, for obvious reasons, is that the concept of a completed sequence of tasks is by itself self-contradictory. The last is that somehow the conjunction of the two has this property, whereas neither has it separately. This is the most promising. In order to show this, it would suffice, for example, to show that it is part of the meaning of 'task' that nothing can be called a task that does not take some time to perform *and* that there is a lower bound on the length of time allowable for the performance of a single task.

Similarly, to show that super-tasks are not logically impossible, it would suffice to show that a correct analysis of each of the concepts involved permits their conjunction without explicit contradiction. In defense of Thomson, his arguments would have sufficed for his purposes had they not needed supplementation with an additional premise. This should make us suspect that there exists no such easy proof that super-tasks are a logical impossibility—just as there is no easy proof that they are logically possible. In fact, I strongly suspect that whatever conditions a proper analysis would associate with the concept of a completed series of tasks would fail to preclude the series' being infinite. And furthermore, there is probably no set of conditions that we can (nontrivially) state and show to be includable in a correct statement of the meaning of the expressions in question whose satisfaction would lead us to conclude that a super-task had been performed. I don't mean that we don't understand the meaning of the expression 'completed infinite sequence of tasks,' for we grasp its syntactic structure and understand the meanings of its component parts. I mean only that there is no circumstance that we could imagine and describe in which we would be justified in saying that an infinite sequence of tasks had been completed. It is probably this fact that accounts for Thomson's vacillation (cf. my footnote 3) between the conclusion that super-tasks are logically impossible and that "the concept of super-task has not been explained," "that talk of super-tasks is *senseless.*" Indeed this is a peculiar state of affairs, but similar cases are not hard to find. A thinking robot is such a case. We know much about what it is to think, and we know much about what robots are, but we are not able to describe something that we should be justified in calling a thinking robot. Similarly, there is much we can say about tasks and about infinite sequences, but there is nothing we can describe that it would be reasonable to call a completed infinite sequence of tasks. Possibly someday someone will find such a description. I am not arguing that it could never be done. I am only pointing here to what I take to be a difference between a concept like that of a super-task and that of a man eight feet tall. We may never have seen an instance of the latter, just as presumably we have never witnessed an instance of the former. But the one strains our imagination to the breaking point, whereas the other does not. This is an important difference, but it does not show either that the concept in question is self-contradictory or that it is no concept at all, that the expression is without meaning.

I want to insist here that logic has not stepped in just because our imaginations fail us; something is not logically impossible just because we cannot imagine what it would be like for it to be the case. Our shrinking genie is very much to the point. If he is of any clarificatory value at all, it is insofar as we *recognize* that he covers all the Z-points but fails to cover 1, although, before he was described, *we might not have been able to think of anything that would meet that condition.*[7] To describe such a set of circumstances for the first time is what some have misleadingly called "giving an expression a sense" or "giving it a meaning" or "giving it a use," where the implication is that it had no sense or meaning or use before this one was conferred upon it. This is mistaken. The expression has a meaning, a sense, a use. Possibly it didn't have *this* sense or (what is not the same) was not put to *this* use before. Possibly, even, its meaning has changed to some degree—although that would be more drastic. But the picture of a meaningless, senseless, useless phrase that we now endow with a use (and, therefore, possibly a sense and meaning) is a mistaken one. We see that it is mistaken when we see that we have recognized that the shrinking genie covers all the Z-points but fails to occupy 1. For how could we recognize this if (a) Thomson were right and this was a contradictory notion, or (b) my hypothetical opponents (and Thomson's *alter ego*) were right and the expression 'covers all the Z-points but fails to occupy 1' had no sense, meaning, or use? I submit that we have not given it something it had little or none of before: meaning. Rather we have exploited the meaning that it had. I did not *stipulate* that the genie should count as a case in point. I merely described him and then argued that he *does* so count, and my arguments took the form of linking the features of the case described with the conditions associated with 'covering all the Z-points and failing to occupy 1.' It is by virtue of the meaning of that expression that the shrinking genie can be said to have covered all the Z-points but not to have occupied 1. Had I described him differently, e.g., had I said that his height at any (rational) point $\frac{2^n-1}{2^n}$ on the course is $\frac{1}{2^n} + \epsilon$ times his original height (where ϵ is some arbitrarily small quantity), that he should continue shrinking at the same rate after he shrinks to a height of ϵ, and that he should vanish when he

---

[7] The example is, to be sure, far-fetched, imaginary, what you like. But we are talking about language, and it is important to remember that language is an instrument rich enough to describe the far-fetched and fanciful.

reaches a height of $\frac{1}{2}\epsilon$, then it would have been clear that he occupied 1—no matter how small one chose ϵ (his run is a continuous one, so he cannot skip 1).

I suspect that, by and large, it is principally compound expressions that suffer the fate I attribute to 'completed infinite sequence of tasks' and 'thinking robot.' What seems most notable about such compounds is the fact that one component (e.g., 'infinite sequence') draws the conditions connected with its applicability from an area so disparate from that associated with the other components that the criteria normally employed fail to apply. We have what appears to be a conceptual mismatch. Sequences of *tasks* do not exhibit the characteristics of sequences that lend themselves to proofs of infinity. And since there seems to be an upper bound on our ability to discriminate (intervals, say) and none on how finely we cut the task, it appears that we should never be in a position to claim that a super-task had been performed. But even if this is true, it only takes account of one kind of super-task, and, as I argue above, it hardly establishes that even this kind constitutes a logical impossibility.

To look at the matter diachronically and therefore, I think, a little more soundly, we can see our present situation as akin to that of speakers of English, long before electronic computers of the degree of complexity presently commonplace, when confronted with the question of thinking robots (or, for that matter, just plain thoughtless robots, I suspect). They were as unthinkable as thinking stones. Now they are much less so. I am not sure that even then they constituted a logical contradiction. However, I would not resist as violently an account which implied that the expression 'thinking robot' had changed in meaning to some degree in the interim. Viewed as I suggest we view them, questions of meaning are very much questions of degree—in the sense that although relative to one statement of meaning there may be a more or less sharp boundary established, no statement of meaning (viewing things synchronically now) is uniquely correct. Other hypotheses, and therefore other lines may be just as reasonable in the light of the evidence. The statement of the meaning of a word is a hypothesis designed to explain a welter of linguistic facts, and it is a commonplace that where hypotheses are in question many are always possible.

Therefore, I see two obstacles in the way of showing that super-tasks are logically impossible. The first is that relevant conditions associated with the words and the syntactic structure involved must be found to have been deviated from; and it must be argued that these conditions are sufficiently central to be included in any reasonable account of the meaning of the expression. The second is simply my empirical conjecture that there are no such conditions, that in fact the concept of super-task is of the kind I have been describing above, one suffering from the infirmity of *mismatched* conditions. If this is right it would go a long way toward explaining why Thomson is so successful in showing that arguments *for* the performability of super-tasks are inadequate and why nevertheless his own arguments against their possibility suffer the same fate. The modern Eleatics, although faced with an easier task than that which faced Zeno (people aren't performing super-tasks right and left), have yet to perform it.

Comments on Professor Benacerraf's Paper

JAMES THOMSON

Benacerraf's excellent article puts it beyond doubt that much of "Tasks and Super-Tasks" is mistaken. Where the matter rests is less clear; I do not find myself entirely satisfied with Benacerraf's concluding remarks about the nature and difficulties of the problem.

When I wrote "Tasks and Super-Tasks" I thought that the idea of an ω-task[1] being completable was suspect because or to the extent that one could not say what situation would result from its completion. Thus I thought that the ω-task of occupying all of the points 0, $\frac{1}{2}$, $\frac{3}{4}$, . . . in that order along a racecourse was unproblematic, indeed was to be called an ω-task only as a kind of joke, because for a runner to complete it and for him to move from 0 to 1 are demonstrably the same thing. The resulting situation is simply that he occupies 1. By contrast, I thought that there was some conceptual difficulty about the idea of a lamp having been turned on and off infinitely often, because, roughly speaking, of the question about the state of the lamp immediately afterwards. Unfortunately, I tried to make out that there was a difficulty here by arguing that the lamp could not be in either of its two states. This argument was worthless, because (as Benacerraf points out) it ascribed to the crucial time a property that can be ascribed, without circularity, only to

---

[1] To complete an ω-task is to complete each of an ω-sequence of tasks. Thus an ω-task is the kind of task I previously called a super-task, although in fact only ω-tasks were there in question. A $*\omega$-task is an example of a super-task that is not an ω-task.

earlier times. I also said that the difficulty about the lamp was like that of occupying all the points along the racecourse (the Z-points) without occupying their limit, and this too was wrong.

I am now inclined to think[2] that there are no simple knock-down arguments to show that the notion of a completed ω-task is self-contradictory. It remains possible that difficulties do attend the suggestion that an ω-task can be completed, and that some of these are not merely difficulties in imagining something. And, in fact, I still think there is a difficulty, though not a very dramatic one, in the case of the lamp, which I will try to bring out in a more formal setting.

We have a physical system S which is at each moment in one of two states, say A and B. From time to time S changes from the state it is in to the other state. These changes of state are not of course the kinds of change that take time. Rather, at least in the simplest case, S is in one of its states throughout some period up to but not including some time, and then at that time it is in the other state. (Thus we are making a convention that when S changes state there is a first moment of the later state rather than a last moment of the earlier one.) If S is in state X at time t, and if there is no earlier time t' such that S was in X at all times later than t' and earlier than t, I shall say that a *transition* occurs at t.[3] Now let us consider the hypothesis that S underwent an ω-sequence of transitions in some bounded time interval with t_1 as the earliest time later than all the transitions in the sequence. The hypothesis does not prescribe any state for S at t_1. But all the same, S will be in some state at t_1; suppose, then, that state is A. (Of course the situation is symmetrical as between the two states.) The hypothesis implies that a transition occurs at t_1, and it is consistent with the hypothesis that S remains in state A throughout some small

---

[2] Largely as a result of Benacerraf's article.

[3] Thus when S changes from one state to another there is a transition; I use the word 'transition' so as to leave open whether every transition is a change.

interval beginning at t_1; therefore, let us suppose that too.
Now should we say that at t_1 S *changes* into A? To say that
would be to suggest, perhaps even strongly suggest, that at
the time in question S changes into A *from* its other state.
But what is thereby suggested is false. No interval throughout which S is in B has t_1 as its least upper bound, and it
does not help to invoke a momentary (instantaneous) state
of B-ness, because ex hypothesi there are no momentary
states prior to t_1, and at t_1 S is in A. So we must either say
that S can change (or even go) into one of its states without
changing (or going) into it from its other state, or say that S
can undergo a transition into a state without thereby changing into that state. Neither of these conclusions can be called
contradictory, but each of them contradicts something that
it is quite natural to suppose.[4]

I certainly do not want to make too much of this difficulty.
If someone wants to hold out for the possibility of a bounded
ω-sequence of transitions, he will perhaps give us the se-
mantic point about the word 'change.' That is, he will perhaps concede that something like S cannot properly be said
to change into a state unless it changes into that state from
its other state. (At least, as far as I can see, there is no reason
why he should not admit it, so far as *this* issue goes.) Then
he will opt for the second alternative, and say that it is possible for there to be transitions that are not changes (in the
now agreed sense.) It is indeed natural at first to take for
granted that if something like S undergoes a transition at a
time t, then we can, by taking smaller and smaller open
intervals around t, find one in which only that transition
occurs. To adopt this principle as an axiom is in effect to
require that all transitions be changes. And, independently of
anything about the semantics of the word 'change,' it is to
rule out the possibility of a bounded ω-sequence of transi-

---

[4] The way in which the difficulty comes out depends slightly on the convention noted above.

tions. But we can hardly hope to use this principle to argue against the possibility of such a bounded infinity of changes, since we shall be met with the rejoinder that no-one would take the principle as axiomatic unless the possibility of a bounded ω-sequence of transitions had not occurred to him. This rejoinder is not obviously true, but the possibility of making it shows that we have nothing like a knock-down argument. There is another reason too for not wanting to make too much of the difficulty, and I will return to it in a moment.

One reason for mentioning the difficulty is this: if enough people feel a conceptual difficulty about something, that is some reason for thinking that there *is* a difficulty, though not reason for thinking it is a serious or interesting one. It is possible that the difficulty I just tried to isolate is the difficulty that led some people, myself included, to think that the lamp could not have been switched on and off infinitely often. If it is, then that the difficulty is not a dramatic one is a reason for saying just what the difficulty is. There is another reason for mentioning it. Benacerraf suggests that in trying to argue for the impossibility of an ω-task being completed I tacitly replaced the ω-task by an (ω + 1)-task. But if we think in terms of transitions rather than in terms of tasks, this does not seem to be a mistake at all. The reason why the principle I mentioned above rules out the possibility of a bounded ω-sequence of transitions is that it denies that a transition can be a point of accumulation of transitions. If on the other hand we have a bounded ω-sequence of transitions there will have to be a time which is a least upper bound for them. That time will be one at which a transition occurs; the transition then occurring cannot be any in the sequence, hence we have a transition which is a point of accumulation of transitions. It follows that if we have a completed ω-sequence of transitions we ipso facto have a completed (ω+1)-sequence of them. Benacerraf seems to deny this, perhaps because he takes the question about the lamp at t_1

to be a question about an ωth act. As he says, there may be
no ωth act. Indeed not. If the successive transitions of S are
caused by successive acts of an agent, then for the purposes of this *Gedankenexperiment* we want the agent not to
perform an ωth act; it would only get in the way. But then
there is still a last uncaused transition, and it is this that we
want to inquire about. In general, the idea of an ω-task
arises from consideration of a bounded ω-sequence of points
on the real line. If the sequence is not bounded there is not
even the semblance of a likelihood that the task can be completed; if it is bounded, the sequence will have a least upper
bound and there will be some question to ask about the
state of the world or about what happens at some time corresponding to that bound. It seems very obvious that when
people have difficulties about the idea of an ω-task being
completed the difficulties are about such questions. If then
we want to see how real those difficulties are we must let
the questions come up. It does not seem helpful here to
canvas such possibilities as that the lamp disintegrates at
the crucial moment, or that each time we press the switch
it halves in size. Of course such things might happen. But
if we want to trace the consequences of the suggestion that
such and such an ω-task has been completed, we do better
to ignore them. If we are concerned with the thesis that
ω-tasks *are* completable, we are presumably entitled to
ignore them, since presumably no one would want to maintain that it is possible for such a task to be completed only
on condition that no traces of it remain.[5]

I said that there was another reason for not wanting to
make too much of the mild difficulty about S. It is that there
does not seem any good reason to suppose that this difficulty or any difficulty like it is going to attend every suggestion to the effect that some ω-sequence of tasks can be

---

[5] As if someone were to maintain that it is possible that a man should have
computed all the digits in the decimal expansion of π, provided only that he
did it in his head.

completed. (Compare Benacerraf's remark, p. 128 above.) Whether it does will surely depend on the kind of task in question. In fact, it now seems plausible that there are importantly different kinds of ω-tasks, and different orders of difficulty associated with some of them.

If each of a set of tasks can be completed, it is on any view fallacious to conclude from this that all of them can be completed.[6] What I shall now call the *infinitistic thesis*[7] is this: an ω-sequence of tasks can be completed if and only if any finite initial segment of them can be completed. (The 'if' part is what is characteristic of the thesis; the 'only if' part is suggested by the compactness theorem of propositional logic.[8]) Now let us suppose that every piece of cheese can be cut in two and that the result is always two pieces of cheese. Let D be the sequence of acts of which the first is cutting some piece of cheese into two equal parts and of which the $(n + 1)$th is cutting into two equal parts some piece of cheese which resulted from the nth act. Given our assumptions, any finite initial segment of D can be completed, and so (according to the infinitistic thesis) D can be completed. The result is or would be that we have a denumerably infinite set of pieces of cheese of which none is the smallest. I remark that the difficulty that arose about S does not seem to arise here. Some will find a difficulty in the thought that there is no smallest piece of cheese, but that difficulty does not seem the same. Let us in any case waive that difficulty, and consider another sequence M.

M is a sequence of stages. The first stage consists as before in cutting into two equal parts some piece of cheese, and the $(n + 1)$th consists in doing the same thing to each of the 2^n pieces that resulted from the nth stage. Again, given

[6] Suppose that one task is that of eating your cake and another that of keeping it.

[7] Watling and Taylor seemed to advance this thesis.

[8] I.e., if every finite subset of some infinite set X of formulas is consistent, so is X.

our assumptions, any finite initial segment of M can be completed. (Each stage in M requires only finitely many acts of cutting; the total number of acts required up to and including the nth stage is just $2^{n+1}-1$.) It follows that if D can be completed so can M. But what results from completing M? Whatever qualms we may have had about the completability of D, it was at least fairly clear what we got—pieces of cheese. If we require that a piece of cheese have some size, no pieces result from completing M. What does result?

It is easy to see how the difference between D and M comes about. The successive acts in D determine a chain of finite sets $\{\frac{1}{2}\}$, $\{\frac{1}{2}, \frac{3}{4}\}$, . . . , and the successive stages of M likewise determine such a chain: $\{\frac{1}{2}\}$, $\{\frac{1}{4}, \frac{1}{2}, \frac{3}{4}\}$, . . . , where in either case the rationals represent cuts. The D-chain and its union are similar (in the sense of order-type) to the sequence of acts in D, and the M-chain is similar to the sequence of stages in M. But the union of the M-chain is dense.[9] Perhaps by studying this difference one could find a set of assumptions on which, in some non-trivial way, D is completable and M is not. It remains the case that the infinitistic thesis plus our assumptions about the divisibility of cheese imply the completabilty of M as much as they do the completability of D. It is tempting to regard this as a knock-down refutation of the infinitistic thesis. I shall not say that it is one. But it will be agreed that the completability of M involves difficulties over and above, and of a different kind from, those involved by the completability of D, and that is a fair example of what I said could happen.

One difficulty, then, about the question of whether ω-tasks can be completed is that there are different kinds of them, and there is no reason to think that in regard to completability they stand or fall together. Benacerraf, who hints at this, thinks that there is a special difficulty as well. He suggests that one component of the idea of a completed infinity

[9] Strictly, the remarks should be about the order-types determined by the sets and the natural order on the rationals.

of tasks, namely that of an infinite sequence, "draws the conditions connected with its applicability from an area so disparate from that associated with the other [component] that the criteria normally employed fail to apply." So, "We have what appears to be a conceptual mismatch. Sequences of *tasks* do not exhibit the characteristics of sequences that lend themselves to proofs of infinity" (p. 128). This seems only partly right. We know well enough when a sequence of ordinals or of points or of sets—in general, a sequence of mathematical constructions or objects—is called infinite. On the other hand it is in one way unclear in what circumstances, if any, a sequence of acts or events which happen in space and time could be called infinite. But, after all, only in one way. Those who support the infinitistic thesis will be quick to offer sufficient conditions for a sequence of acts or events to be infinite. Anything we say about the infinitude of a sequence of mathematical objects they will say about the infinitude of a sequence of acts or events, thus in effect claiming for the consistency of their conception whatever we claim for the consistency of ours. They will at least say that *no reason has been given* why a sequence of tasks should not be thought to have *just* those characteristics that "lend themselves to proofs of infinity." This is just what Benacerraf himself seemed at one stage in his article to think, and thus his later remarks do not seem to square fully with his earlier ones.[10] Perhaps it comes closer to an appreciation of the kind of difficulty we face to remark on the apparent necessity of making some idealising assumptions or other before we can even begin to discuss a particular kind of ω-task. Thus it seems that D and M can be discussed only on some rather unrealistic assumptions about the infinite divisibility of some

---

[10] Similarly, when Benacerraf says (p. 126 above) that "there is no circumstance that we could imagine and describe in which we would be justified in saying that an infinite sequence of tasks had been completed," he must mean to rule out such a reply as "We would be justified in saying so if someone had completed the first task and, on finishing some task, always went on and completed the next."

homogeneous material substance. There is something similar to be said about the apparent need for passing from a discussion in terms of the lamp to a discussion in terms of the system S. It is not so clear, of course, what these assumptions involve, or to what extent it is helpful to make them. But it does appear that if we are willing to make them, there is more to be said now about the completability of ω-tasks than Benacerraf seems to allow, and his retreat, in his concluding section, into meta-philosophy and diachronic linguistics will seem unnecessary and premature.

G. E. L. OWEN

Zeno and the Mathematicians

At some time in the first half of the fifth century B.C., Zeno invented the set of paradoxes on which his successors have sharpened their wits. The puzzles have come down to us in various versions, more or less incomplete and more or less reflecting the special interests of later writers. What we have left of Zeno's best-known work comes, on the most hopeful view, to less than two hundred words. Still, this has not stopped Zeno's admirers from trying, with all due caution, to reconstruct the programme of all or some of his arguments. I want to make one such programme plausible and to show how, if I am right, this makes some solutions to the puzzles beside the point.

My second interest in the paper is this. Zeno, it is commonly said, was and wished to be the benefactor of Greek mathematics. By his day the Pythagoreans had brought mathematics to a high level of sophistication. But the foundations of their system were a nest of confusions, and Zeno was out to expose these confusions. One beneficial result of his arguments (on this familiar account) was to compel mathematicians to distinguish arithmetic from geometry.

This picture seems to me mistaken. Zeno neither had nor tried to have this effect on mathematics (though in other ways, no doubt, he did influence contemporary work in the

G. E. L. Owen, "Zeno and the Mathematicians," *Proceedings of the Aristotelian Society*, N.S. LVIII (1957–58), 199–222. Reprinted by permission of the author, and through courtesy of the Editor of the Aristotelian Society.

science). But his arguments had a great effect on a later stage
of mathematics, and the effect was not beneficial.

ZENO'S PROGRAMME

Zeno certainly held, as a philosophical theory inherited
from Parmenides, that there is only one thing in existence.
This is an embarrassment to those who want to portray him
as trying to set up a consistent logic for analysing the structure of space and time. For it means that he thought there
was no such structure: any way of dividing things in time or
space must carry absurdities. If this was his theory we should
expect him to work out an exhaustive list of possible ways
of dividing things and to set about refuting all the possibilities
separately; and this, as I shall try to show, is what he does.

(Let me say at once that this talk of dividing is deliberately
ambiguous. It is not always clear, for instance, whether
Zeno is discussing the possibility of producing a plurality
by actually carving a thing up or by enumerating the fractions it must logically contain; but for most of the way we
shall find the distinction irrelevant.[1] What matters is that
whichever operation Zeno has in mind he is canvassing its
logical and not its physical possibility.)

Some hold that Zeno was not committed to any philosophical tenet whatever. For he is credited with saying "Show
me what the *one* is and then I can tell you what things (in
the plural) are";[2] and this is sometimes taken to show that
he did not profess to understand even the one thing that
Parmenides had left in existence. But the point of his words
is just that, if you want to say that there are a number of
things in existence, you have to specify what sort of thing
counts as a unit in the plurality.[3] If there can be no such in-

---

[1] It is not clear even that Zeno used the word διαιρεῖν and its cognates; but
Parmenides had, and Zeno certainly used equivalent language in discussing
Parmenides' topic (see A1 below).

[2] Eudemus *apud* Simpl. *in Phys.*, 97.12–13, 138.32–33.

[3] Cf. Alexander *apud* Simpl. *in Phys.*, 99.12–16.

dividuals as you claim there can be no such plurality either. And in particular if your individuals have to be marked off by spatial and temporal distinctions you have to be sure that your way of making such distinctions is not logically absurd.

Plato makes it clear that Zeno's major work was divided into separate arguments, each depending on some hypothesis and reducing the hypothesis to absurdity. We do not know the content of these hypotheses, but Plato is emphatic that every argument was designed to refute the proposition that there are a number of things in existence.[4] We certainly have reports of some of the arguments which began "Suppose many things exist." But we also have a report of one which starts "Suppose place exists." And Aristotle treats the familiar puzzles of "Achilles," the "Arrow," the "Stadium," and the "Dichotomy" as though these were designed in the first instance to refute the possibility of movement, not of plurality. It might be, of course, that these latter arguments came from another work of Zeno's.[5] But I shall try to show that they play an essential part in the attack on plurality.

Zeno's major question then is: if you say there are many things in existence how do you distinguish your individuals? The answer in which he is chiefly interested is that the world and any part of it can be broken down into its individual parts by spatial and temporal divisions. And the paradoxes that I am anxious to discuss are those designed to meet this answer, namely those which are jointly planned to show that no method of dividing anything into spatial or temporal parts can be described without absurdity.

For suppose we ask whether such a division could be (theoretically, at least) continued indefinitely: whether any

---

[4] *Parmenides*, 127e–128a, a version which became standard with later commentators (e.g. Simplicius *in Phys.*, 139.5–7).

[5] Not that the evidence that he wrote other works is strong: Plato seems not to know of them, yet he certainly knew of the arguments on motion (cf. *Phaedrus*, 261d and the application of the "Arrow" in *Parmenides*, 15b-e).

division can be followed by a sub-division, and so on,
through an infinite number of steps. Let us say, to begin
with, (A) that it does have an infinite number of steps. Then
could such a division nevertheless ever be (or ever have
been) completed? (A1) One of Zeno's arguments is designed
to show that it could not.

The paradox had two arms. The first began by arguing
that the units in a collection can have no size at all: else
they would have parts and be not units but collections of
units.[6] The second began by arguing that, on the contrary,
there cannot be anything that has no size at all; for there
cannot be a thing which if it were added to or subtracted
from something else would not affect the size of that thing.[7]
So the first arm of the argument assumes that the units it
describes are theoretically indivisible; and the point of this
requirement comes out in the sequel, when Zeno shows
that he is discussing the class of individuals produced by an
exhaustive division of something, a division whose end-
products cannot themselves be further divided. The second
arm of the argument assumes, on the other hand, that its
units must be capable of being added and subtracted in a
sense in which these operations cannot apply to things without magnitude; and the point of this requirement comes
out in the same sequel, for if a thing can be divided into
parts (exhaustively or not) those parts must be capable of
being added to make the thing, and in that case they must
have some size, however small.

Next, to bring these requirements into one focus, Zeno
went on to specify the collection of parts in which he was
interested, namely the collection produced by completing a
division in which every step has a successor. "Each thing,"
he said, "must have some size and thickness, and one part
of it must be separate [or perhaps just 'distinct'] from an-

---

[6] Simplicius *in Phys.*, 139.18–19: this argument at the start of the paradox is
still overlooked by English editors, although its text and sense were settled by
Hermann Fraenkel in "Zeno of Elea's Attacks on Plurality" [24], pp. 14–17.

[7] Simplicius, *op. cit.*, 139.9–15 [see above, p. 13].

other. And the same holds good of the part which is in the
lead—that too will have some size, and of it too some part
will be in the lead. In fact to say this once is as good as saying
it for ever, for no such part of the thing will be the last or
unrelated to a further part."[8] These words define a division
so that there can be no last move in the sequence: for any
fraction that is taken, a similar fraction can be taken of the
remainder (the "part in the lead"). In this, certainly, there is
no clear implication that such a division can have been completed. But Zeno does make that assumption in drawing his
conclusions. For he points out that, on one line of argument
(that of the first arm), the parts produced by this division can
have no size at all: they are end-products whose further
division is logically impossible. And he also points out that,
on the other line of argument (that of the second arm), since
all the parts of such a collection must have some size the
whole collection (and by the same token any part of it) must
be infinite in size. And both conclusions are absurd. They
were presented as an antinomy; but as a dilemma they are
equally lethal. Either the parts have no size, and then there
can be no such parts; or they have some size, and then the
thing you set out to divide becomes infinitely big.

Notice that Zeno is not first setting up a division which
cannot have a last move and then asking, improperly, what
the last move would be.[9] He is asking, legitimately, what the
total outcome of the division would be; and for there to be
such an outcome there must be a smallest part or parts.

The effect of the argument is to show an absurdity in the

---

[8] Simplicius, op. cit., 141.1–6. A commoner but linguistically less easy version
of the words runs "Each thing must have some size and thickness and there
must be another thing separate from it. And the same holds good of the thing
in front: it too will have some size and there will be something in front of
it. . . ." Taken in this way the words do not define the steps in the division but
merely characterize its products by saying that the series has no last member.
And there is no mention of parts (more exactly, none of the Greek genitives
is understood as partitive) before the last line. Otherwise, for our purposes both
versions come to the same.

[9] Cf. James Thomson, "Tasks and Super-Tasks" [reprinted above, pp. 96–97].

alternative for which we opted first, namely that if anything is infinitely divisible such a division can be carried right through. So now (A2) we shall say that anything is infinitely divisible but that such divisions can never be completed. Then, supposing that the puzzle about Achilles and the tortoise[10] is a puzzle about infinite divisibility, it is designed to block this escape route. In order to overtake the tortoise Achilles must first reach the tortoise's starting point; but by then the tortoise will have reached some further point. So then Achilles must reach this point, by which time the tortoise will have got on to another, and so forth: the series comes to no end. The moves which Achilles is required to make correspond to divisions of the intervening country, and the divisions are infinite, determined by the same general formula as in A1. But on our present assumption Achilles cannot complete any such sequence of moves; so he cannot overtake the tortoise, whatever their relative speeds and however short the lead.

Now if I am right about the coupling of Zeno's arguments[11] it is beside the point to maintain, as a general solution of this puzzle, that an infinite division can be completed. For if we say this Zeno will take us back to A1 and ask us about the character of the ultimate parts produced by the division. To make this clear, consider Aristotle's first solution to the puzzle—a solution which he later admits to be unsatisfactory but which he nevertheless thinks to be adequate *ad hominem*.[12] He replies that, provided we recognize that the time of the run can be divided in just the same way as the ground, Achilles can overtake the tortoise in a finite time; for the smaller his moves become the less time he needs to accomplish them, and these component times

---

[10] Aristotle, *Physics* Z, 239b14–29.

[11] Notice the προὔχειν which may have been common to both puzzles: Simplicius, *op. cit.*, 141.4; Aristotle, *op. cit.*, 239b17.

[12] *Op. cit.*, 233a21–31, 263a15–18: the solution is applied first to the "Dichotomy," discussed below, but Aristotle took this to be the same puzzle as the "Achilles."

can diminish without limit. Then suppose we tell Achilles to mark in some way the end of each stage of the course in which he arrives at a point reached by the tortoise in the previous stage. Suppose also we satisfy Aristotle's requirement and allow these successive markings to follow each other at a speed which increases indefinitely, in inverse ratio to the ground covered at each stage; and suppose the marks become proportionately thinner and thinner. Then Zeno, as I understand him, argues that if Achilles claims to have finished his task we can ask about the positions of these marks, and in particular of the last two. If they are in the same place there is no stage determined by them, and if there is any distance between them, however small, this distance is the smallest stage in an infinite set of diminishing stages and therefore the course is infinitely long and not just infinitely divisible.

Two things, I take it, we must give Zeno: first, that of the series of movements that Achilles is supposed to make there can be no last member, just as of the stages of the division described in A1 there can be no last stage; and second, that if either series can be completed it must be possible to describe the resulting state of affairs without absurdity. From these admissions Zeno infers that Achilles can never finish the run that brings him level with the tortoise. Any hope of salvation lies in looking at this inference.

Consider that other series of moves to which Professor Black once likened Achilles' run.[13] Hercules is required to cut off the Hydra's heads, but every time he cuts off a head another grows in its place. When can he finish the assignment? Never, if the task was correctly specified. For if some heads are left on, Hercules has more work to do, and if all are off, it was not the case that for every head cut off another head grows. But these are exhaustive alternatives, so there is *no* subsequent state of affairs of which it is logically possible to say truly: Hercules has finished his task. Now (as Mr.

---

[13] [Above, p. 76.]

Watling has already argued)[14] this is not the case with Achilles. There are plenty of states of affairs compatible with Achilles' having achieved his task of overtaking the tortoise: plenty of positions beside or beyond the tortoise that Achilles can have reached. It is just the case here that Achilles' movements have been so described that they have no last term, but not so that no subsequent state of affairs is compatible with his having completed the series. But to require anyone to finish an infinite division, as in A1, is to start them on a Hydra-operation: there can be no state of affairs, no collection of bits, of which it is possible to say: now the job is done. For either the bits do or they do not have some size, and that exhausts the subsequent possibilities. On this Zeno was right. His error was to construe his A2 example on the model of A1.

In a later paper[15] Black admits this difference in the sense in which Hercules and Achilles can be said to have taken on an infinite set of tasks. But he still holds that in either case "talk of an infinite series of acts performed in a finite time is illegitimate." For he now says that the description of Achilles' movements belongs to "common-sense language" which, in contrast to the mathematical representation of space and time, "does not permit talk of the indefinitely small"—that is, does not have a use for describing Achilles' movements as becoming as short as you like. But a guillotine is not an argument. If someone says, "In making any movement you make an infinite series of decreasing movements," we have no reason yet to reject this as an offence to common usage. It already looks like a recognizable application of mathematical language to the description of familiar events (we recall the graphic problems in school arithmetic): what it needs at once is clarification. We can ask "What do you mean here by 'infinite series'? Do you say that in walking from *a* to *d* I make a set of smaller walks of

[14] "The Sum of an Infinite Series" [117], pp. 41–42.
[15] "Is Achilles Still Running?" [53], pp. 109–126.

which the first takes me beyond *a* and the last brings me level with *d*? For then I cannot see how you define this sequence so as to let me draw on my knowledge of other uses of 'infinite.' " Suppose then he gives us a formula, as in A1 or A2, for defining the class of movements so that there can be no last move in the sequence bringing me level with *d*. Then we know how he is using the redescription of our movements that he has introduced. He has not uncovered an unsuspected set of events in our daily histories and he has not burdened us or Achilles with a new and crippling set of duties: the connexion between our usual descriptions of Achilles' run and this sort of restatement is not in either of these ways a factual connexion. What we have been given is a translation of those usual descriptions; where the second can be known, directly, to apply, the first can be known, derivatively, to apply. So no consequential question can arise about the applicability of the second. If we are told that the equation shows why Achilles never can catch the tortoise, we can only complain that the proffered rules of translation have broken down and go back to our request for clarification. Any attempt at this stage to reconstrue the expression "series of moves with no last member" as specifying a Hydra-operation, an infinite parcelling of the ground such that no state of affairs is compatible with its completion, cancels the equation with our description of Achilles' run. And in this way "common-sense language" is safeguarded; for it is the oscillation between bringing in the infinite series as a logically innocuous translation of ordinary statements and trying to reconstrue it on the model of the task in A1 that breeds the puzzle.

A closely associated paradox is the "Dichotomy."[16] Before reaching your destination you must reach half-way, but before reaching that you must reach half-way to it; and so back. So in this series there is no first move, and you cannot get started. (It can of course also be made to show that there

---

[16] Aristotle, *Physics* Z, 239b11–14 (cf. 233a21–23).

is no last move; Aristotle's report here is ambiguous. But this was taken care of by the "Achilles.") Here again if you insist that there is a first move you are taken back to A1: either this move is no move, or it covers some distance, however small. The solution here is the same as for the Achilles. But Aristotle says that in face of this puzzle some theorists (certainly Xenocrates and apparently at one time Plato) postulated atomic distances, "indivisible lines." [17] That is, they challenged Zeno's disjunction "Either no size at all; or some size, and then divisible" by adding "or some size, but *not* divisible." Then the first or last move towards one's destination would be to cover such an atomic distance; for one could not logically be required to cover any fraction of it first. It is not certain whether the proponents of this theory thought that any measurable distance contained a finite or an infinite number of such distances. An argument for thinking that they meant the former is that this is assumed in the fourth-century polemic *On Indivisible Lines*. An argument for thinking the contrary is that the theory was held at a time when the difficulties of incommensurable lines were fully realized. It was a commonplace that the side and diagonal of a square cannot both be *finite* multiples of any unit of length whatever. If the latter account is true, those who introduced this theory were suggesting that an infinite division can have a last term: the products of such a division are not completely without magnitude, yet they have no finite magnitude such that fractions of it can be specified. They would be, in fact, to all present intents and purposes, infinitesimals, vanishingly small quantities; and movement over such a distance is what writers on mechanics such as Heinrich Hertz have called *infinitely small or minimum displacements*. But whichever interpretation of the theory we give, it was an attempt to evade Zeno's dilemma in A1.

Now it looks as though this attempt is met in advance by another of Zeno's arguments, that known as the "Stadium." [18]

[17] *Physics* A, 187a1–3.
[18] Aristotle, *Physics* Z, 239b33–240a18.

On the prevalent interpretation of the argument this is certainly so; and I wish I could be sure of the truth of the interpretation. But it is fair to warn you that, if the moral of the argument is anything like that now found in it, the Greeks seem to have missed the point by a wide margin. Plato, who converted many of Zeno's arguments to his own use, made no use of this one and apparently saw no objection to postulating infinitesimals. Aristotle rejected infinitesimals, but he missed the sense of an argument that Plato had missed before him.

The puzzle sets up three parallel rows of bodies. All the bodies are equal in size; each row contains an equal number of them; and (a stipulation omitted in Aristotle's report) the bodies in each row are directly adjacent. One row (the As) is stationary. The other two (Bs and Cs) meet at the mid-point of the As and move on past each other at equal speeds, so that when the first B clears the last A in one direction the first C, moving in the opposite direction, clears the last A at the other end. Thus in the time that the first B passes half the As, from mid-point to end, it passes all the Cs. Let this time be t. But then if the first B takes t to pass n bodies (to wit, half the As) it must take not t but 2t to pass 2n bodies (viz. all the Cs). So the move which takes t also takes 2t; this is the alleged puzzle, and plainly it depends on disregarding the relative motions of the bodies. The Cs are moving, the As are not. That is Aristotle's sole comment on the argument, and it is generally felt that if it is refuted by such a comment it was not worth the considerable space he gave it.

Suppose now that Zeno asks how we can specify the relative motions of the bodies. If we say that the first B can pass twice as many Cs as As in a given time, what we say entails that if in a given time it passes one C it also passes half an A. But suppose now that any A (and therefore any B or C) is an *infinitesimal* quantity. Then the B cannot pass half an A: it must pass all or nothing. And since *ex hypothesi* it *is* moving past the As it must pass a whole A in the time that it passes one C. Yet, as we set up the problem, it would pass twice as many Cs as As in a given time. So when it passes one C it also passes two Cs, and this gives Zeno his contradiction. It seems the simplest hypothesis that gives the problem any weight whatever.[19]

There is a familiar argument to show that, if lengths are made up of infinitesimal lengths, everything that moves must move at the same speed.[20] Zeno goes one better than this. He argues (on the present interpretation at least) that, if bodies are made up of infinitesimal lengths, then even if bodies do move at the same speed they cannot move in opposite directions.

This argument, then, seems designed to destroy the last hope that the sort of division described in A1 could theoretically be terminated, in the sense of producing any specifiable end-products. And the "Achilles" and the "Dichotomy" were devised to eliminate the alternative, that the world or any part of it was open to an infinite division that did not terminate in any end-product. The next question is whether Zeno faced the alternative (B) that any division terminates in some finite number of steps beyond which no further step is even logically possible.

Against one arm of this option he did not, so far as we know, think it worth arguing, namely the joint assertion that (a) anything is divisible for only a finite number of steps and (b) the products of such a division will have some finite size. For this could only be a thesis about physical possibilities: Zeno assumes without argument in A1 that the conjunction of size with theoretical indivisibility would be a contradiction. Suppose, on the other hand, that the products of such a division are said to have no size: then the argument of A1 that all parts must have some magnitude goes home against this thesis too. And suppose it is said that the products are

---

[19] But it is possible that Zeno was out to explode the distinction between *moving* and *static*. Given that the distinction is relative, any one of the rows of bodies could be taken as providing the units of distance for assessing the speeds of the others. Trading on the fact that no row had prime right to this status, Zeno gave it to two of the rows in the same argument.

[20] Cf. Russell, *Principles of Mathematics* [102], §322.

vanishingly small, then the "Stadium" argument is equally effective here. For neither of these arguments requires that the end-products with which it deals should be produced by an infinite rather than a finite number of divisions.

However, I think that another of Zeno's arguments may be levelled directly against option B.[21] This is the argument that a collection containing a finite number of parts must also contain an infinite number of them. It must contain just the number that it does, whatever that number is; but between any two members there must be another member, so that the collection is infinitely numerous. The writer who reports this argument takes it to be concerned once again with the results of an infinite division.[22] But it can be understood more generally, as a foretaste of Bradley's paradox. Any two members of a collection must be separated by something if they are to be two things and not one; but by the same argument what separates them must itself be separated from each by something else; and so forth. I suspect that this is the correct interpretation because the argument then becomes complementary to one of Parmenides'. Parmenides had urged that if two things are separated it must be by a gap, nothing; but this is to mistreat nothing as a substantial part of the world.[23] Zeno reinforces this by extracting a different embarrassment from the plea that things are separated not by nothing but by other intervening things, substantial parts of the world. And his argument begins from the consideration of a finite collection; so it may well be aimed at any who thought that there must be some finite number *n* such that the world could be divided into *n* things but not—logically not—into any number higher than *n*.

Certainly, this argument seems patently fallacious. For surely things may be separated by their common boundaries —by their edges, and nothing else. And it is absurd to ask what separates them from their edges, absurd for the reason

---

[21] Simplicius, *op. cit.*, 140.28–33.
[22] *Ibid.*, 140.34–35: Simplicius on his own authority?
[23] Diels-Kranz, *Vorsokratiker*[6] 28 B 8: 22, 46.

that Plato and Aristotle drove home, that the edge of a thing is not another thing of the same type as what it borders, not a part that can be cut off its possessor. The moment that begins a stretch of time or the point that bounds a line is not any stretch, however small, of time or space. Otherwise it in turn has a beginning, and then Zeno's regress is afoot. And Zeno is accused of ignoring this distinction.

If that is so we can turn to the argument through which, if through any, Zeno exercised a major influence on the mathematics of science. For it is in this argument above all that he is accused of confusing edges with the things they border, or more precisely of confusing instants, which are the limits of time-stretches, with time-stretches. But it seems equally likely that he is now characteristically trying to seal off an escape route from the last argument by showing how absurdities come from the attempt to *distinguish* moments from periods of time. This remaining puzzle is that known as the "Flying Arrow." But before discussing it let me bring the mathematicians into the picture.

THE MATHEMATICIANS

Most handbooks written since the time of Paul Tannery will tell you the purpose of the arguments we have examined so far. By Zeno's day Greek mathematics, in the hands of the Pythagoreans, had come to exhibit the familiar picture of a sophisticated superstructure built on badly confused foundations. In his arguments on divisibility Zeno was out to expose these radical confusions, and he succeeded.

Following some other writers I am inclined to think this explanation a myth, and an obstructive myth. For first, the picture of Pythagorean mathematics, to the extent that it is intelligible, rests on quite inadequate evidence. And secondly (and for the present paper more relevantly), if there were such a stage in the history of mathematics, Zeno's arguments would not be directed primarily at it.

Briefly, the theory ascribed to Zeno's contemporaries is this. It is mainly the work of Paul Tannery, but later writers have added to it. Cornford, one of the most important of these, credits the Pythagoreans with failing to distinguish physical bodies from geometrical solids, and with holding about these solids *both* that they are infinitely divisible *and* that they are divisible into atomic bits, which bits *both* have magnitude *and* have the properties of points without magnitude.[24] Indeed they seem to have held every possible opinion about the divisibility of bodies save the opinion that bodies are not divisible. Certainly, Zeno was anxious to find confusions in the claim that bodies are divisible at all. But to ensure that he was writing with a special target in view the target has been enlarged to the point where a shot in any direction will hit it.

   This is not the place to hold an autopsy on the evidence for this theory. Much of the work has been done in print,[25] and what needs to be added can be deferred. What is to our purpose is that Zeno's arguments cannot have been directed against such a theory unless his whole programme was misconceived. For in order to provide his arguments with a target a theory had to be produced which housed every or nearly every incompatible view on the divisibility of bodies. But the direct refutation of such a theory would be to show the absurdity of holding any two or more of these views concurrently. What Zeno does is to distinguish each view and refute it in isolation. Thus he deals separately with absurdities arising from the addition of numbers (in the argument just discussed) and from the addition of magnitudes (in A1), although for Tannery the basic confusion in Pythagoreanism was the confusion between numbers and magnitudes. And he wrings separate embarrassments from the option that the ultimate parts of things have no magnitude and the alternative option that they have some magnitude, and again from the possibilities that a continuous dichotomy can and cannot be

---

[24] Tannery, *Pour l'Histoire de la Science Hellène*, chap. 10; Cornford, *Plato and Parmenides* [11], 58–59, and papers in the *Classical Quarterly*, 1922–23.

[25] In particular by Calogero and Heidel, van der Waerden, Fraenkel, and Vlastos.

completed. In brief, his arguments seem designed to close not some but all avenues of escape to anyone holding the unremarkable belief that there is more than one thing in existence. To suppose that he is merely attacking the possibility of taking more than one of these avenues at once is to wreck the structure of his arguments and to neglect such evidence, internal and external, as we have of their motivation.

Now let me reset the scene by reminding you of some real teething troubles that had overtaken mathematics by the time of Plato and Aristotle. The early Pythagoreans had certainly worked on the assumption that any two lengths can be represented as related to each other by a ratio of whole numbers. Any geometrical theorem could be applied in terms of the theory of numerical proportion that they had developed on this basis. But before Plato's day this assumption had run up against the discovery that lines could be constructed which bore no such proportion to each other. No matter what positive integer is assigned to the side of a square, no corresponding integer can be found to represent its diagonal.[26]

Some textbooks would let you suppose that this discovery compelled mathematicians to jettison the old theory of proportion. But several reactions to it were possible. One was to retain the theory but restrict its scope: and this is just what Euclid does with it in the seventh Book of his *Elements*. One was to retain it *and* apply it to the sides and diagonals of squares by an accommodation that could be made as small as you please.[27] And one was the reaction of Eudoxus: to remodel the theory radically by allowing the concepts of

[26] Cf. Euclid, *Elements* X, app. xxvii (Heiberg).

[27] An ingenious but infertile device. A rule was devised for constructing a series of fractions approaching as close as you please to the ratio between side and diagonal: the lines were described by a series of paired numbers such that always the square on the diagonal equalled twice the square on the side plus or minus one, and the approximate sides and diagonals defined by this construction were called the "rational" sides and diagonals (Theon of Smyrna, 42.10–44.17 (Hiller), cf. Plato, *Rep.*, 546c and Proclus' Commentary, ii.27 (Kroll)).

addition and *greater* and *less* to range over rationals and irrationals alike.

This is enough to certify that the discovery of incommensurables was a real crisis in mathematics, and to introduce another type of reaction to it. Some mathematicians gave up the model of a line as a multiple of unit parts, a model which made sense only on the old theory of proportion. They said instead, as Newton said later,[28] that a line should be considered as generated not by the summation of parts but by the fluxion or motion of a point: the extended line is the path of a moving thing without extension. This is said to be a relatively late reaction,[29] but it is already under attack in Plato's *Parmenides* and Aristotle's *Physics;* and this attack ushered in the period of Zeno's most powerful influence on mathematics. So far, it is plain, Zeno has made no appearance in the crisis. Some writers, hoping to find for him a directly influential rôle in the mathematics of his day, have suggested that the new picture of a line as the path of a moving point was a response not to the discovery of incommensurable lines but to the arguments of Zeno; but this seems incredible. No one who had been vexed by those paradoxes can have hoped to evade them by introducing the idea of motion. In fact it is by an adaptation of some of Zeno's arguments that Plato rejects the new picture of a line; but Zeno himself had probably not talked of points and lines, and the later and precise concept of a point as something with location but without magnitude seems to have been produced to meet a difficulty that had little or nothing to do with his work.

When Plato turns to attack this account of a point in the *Parmenides,* he argues that a thing without parts cannot have a location.[30] For to have a location is to have surroundings,

[28] *Quadr. Curv.* (1704), Intro., §27.

[29] Sextus Empiricus, *adv. math.* X.281–82. The concept of a line that was superseded by the fluxion model is probably not the innocuous one compared with it by Sextus (279–280) and Proclus (*in Eucl.,* i.97–98).

[30] *Parm.,* 138a: part of the attack described by Aristotle in *Metaphysics* A,992a20–22.

and this is to be in contact with something on various sides at various points: but a thing without parts cannot have different sides or points. This equation of location with surroundings is standard with the Greeks: Zeno had built one paradox on it,[31] and Aristotle was to give his own sophisticated version of it in the fourth Book of the *Physics*. Until it was replaced by the method of fixing location by co-ordinates, the formal objection to allowing a point location went unanswered. Aristotle inherited it,[32] as he inherited the corollary argument that a point cannot be said to move.[33] Moreover when Plato goes on to define the conditions under which anything *can* be in contact with different things and, in particular, can be a member of a linear series of such things, he provides both the pattern and the terminology for Aristotle's own treatment of points and lines in the *Physics*.[34] Aristotle's insistence that a line can be composed only of smaller, indefinitely divisible lines and not of points without magnitude rests on Plato's treatment of the point as a thing that cannot have sides or neighbours; and it is more than likely that Plato's argument derives from Zeno's warning that the parts of anything must have some magnitude, however small.

Now it is this same distinction between lines and points that Aristotle turns against Zeno's remaining puzzle, the "Flying Arrow"; and his mishandling of both the distinction and the puzzle is the last topic I want to discuss.

THE ARROW

Zeno's last paradox concerning motion is given by Aristotle in a form which, despite the depravity of the text, can be articulated as follows: Anything which occupies a space just its own size is stationary. But in each moment of its flight

---

[31] Diels-Kranz, *op. cit.*, 29 B 5.

[32] *Physics*, 212b24–25.

[33] *Parm.*, 138c-d; *Phys.*, 240b8–241a6.

[34] Terminology: *contact* (ἅπτεσθαι), *in succession* (ἐφεξῆς), *neighbouring* (ἔχεσθαι), *Parm.*, 148e and *Phys.*, 226b18ff. Plato defines the first by means of the other two, Aristotle defines the last by the first two.

an arrow can only occupy a space just its own size. Hence at each moment of its flight the arrow is not moving but stationary. But what is true of the arrow at each moment of a period is true of it throughout the period. Hence during the whole time of its flight the arrow is not moving but stationary.[35]

Aristotle says that the fallacy lies in assuming that any stretch of time is a collection of moments, a mistake parallel to thinking that any line is a collection of points. Now in a sense his diagnosis is right; but not in the sense that he gave to it. Before we come to this, however, one small point needs to be made. Aristotle is often represented as accusing Zeno of thinking that any time-stretch consists of a *finite* collection of moments. But we shall see that Zeno does not need this premiss (nor its denial, either). And as for Aristotle, he was equally anxious to deny that a period could be composed either of a finite or of an infinite number of moments. Define moments as having no magnitude, and Aristotle has learnt from Zeno to argue that no magnitude can be in either of these ways a sum of such parts.

Let us clear some issues by an imaginary conversation.

Aristotle: You claim that (a) in each moment of its flight the arrow must be stationary, since evidently it has no time to move; but (b) what is true of it at each *moment* is true of it throughout the whole *period*. Hence your conclusion. But you agree that moments have no magnitude (that, of course, is why the arrow cannot move in one). Consequently they cannot be added together to make a period of time, which does have a magnitude.

Zeno: You seem to be attacking my premiss (b). I grant what you say: indeed my argument depends on stressing this characteristic of points and moments. (You remember that I was accused of overlooking it last time.) But the argument does not require that the moments should be added to-

---

[35] Aristotle, *Physics* Z, 239b5–9, 30–33: on the text cf. Lee, *Zeno of Elea* [2], pp. 78–81.

gether. I merely assumed that if something was true at any and every moment of a period it was true throughout a period. It is ordinary sense and not bad logic to say that if at any moment this afternoon I was asleep—at 4:30 as well as 2, and at any such precise time you care to take—then I was asleep throughout the afternoon.

Aristotle: But you cannot describe periods *exhaustively* in this way, in terms of moments. However many moments you can mention you are still only specifying the limits of the periods that separate them, and at any stage of the division you like it is these periods that make up the overall period. You can never have two neighbouring moments. So if it is correct to infer from the fact that at any time this afternoon I was asleep, to the fact that I was asleep all afternoon this can only be because "at any time" means "at all periods, however small." And "at 4:30" can only mean, in this context, "at some period however small round 4:30." Don't misunderstand me: I am not suggesting that such time-references as "4:30" are really specifications of periods of time: if they were, we should have to invent a new set of time-references to say when such periods began and ended; and it is absurd to ask how long 4:30 lasts. I am only suggesting that *here* what parades as a time-reference must be a shorthand specification for some small period of time.

Zeno: In as far as this argument differs from your first, it is trifling. To specify moments is surely enough to specify the limits of periods. But to say that therefore any formula phrased in terms of moments is indirectly about periods of time merely invites the converse reply: for to identify a period is to describe the moments that define it.

Aristotle: Nevertheless you do talk about moments in a way that is only appropriate to periods. You say, for instance, that the arrow is stationary at every moment of its flight. But in the section of my περὶ κινήσεως which introduces an attack on your paradoxes[36] I show that if there is no time in a

---

[36] *Physics* Z, 239a23–239b4.

moment for the arrow to move there is no time for it to be stationary either. Movement involves having different positions at different moments, and accordingly rest involves having the same position at different moments. But we are considering only one moment, so neither of these ideas applies. In making either of them apply you treat the single moment as a period of time itself containing different moments.

Zeno: Now, in effect, you are turning your attack to my premiss (a). But if it is true that at any moment of its flight the arrow is neither moving nor at rest, then, by my second premiss, the arrow is throughout its flight neither moving nor at rest. And as a paradox that will do—unless you can find some independent argument against my second premiss. Of course, if that premiss also depended on treating moments as small periods, the argument would collapse. But you have not shown this so far.

Aristotle: It might be shown like this. Consider a spatial analogy to your argument about time. If a surface is uniformly red all over it is red in every part of it, however small the part. But it is not red or any other colour at every point, if by "point" you mean something without extension. In the ordinary sense of "red" we have no use for calling something without extension red. If we had such a use it must be because "red" was used here in an unfamiliar sense. Likewise, even if it were legitimate to infer from "The arrow was moving (or at rest, or neither) at each moment" to "The arrow was moving (or at rest, or neither) throughout the period," this could only show that the expression "moving" (or the expression "at rest," or both) was being used ambiguously between the two cases. Your second premiss, if it is true, rests on a pun; but if it rests on a pun the conclusion you want will not follow.

Zeno (by now a prey to sharp anachronism): This is surely wrong. For suppose a body is constantly increasing its speed: this state of affairs is naturally explained by saying that *at any moment* it moves at a speed greater than at any previous moment since its motion began. And here notice that the verb "to move" is associated with the common expressions for velocity and that it can be paraphrased by the common equivalents, "to change position" and so forth. So it is false that, if "motion at an instant" had any use, "motion" would have a different sense here from that which it usually carries.

Arbiter: You are both right and both wrong. Consider again the expressions "X was moving at some moment *t*," "X was moving throughout the period *p*." Aristotle denied that the expression "X was moving" had the same sense in both contexts. And in face of Zeno's reply we can add that any expansion of the expression, such as "X was moving at velocity V," could not have the same sense in both. For consider how the methods of confirmation differ. Velocity is distance measured against time. The simple question, With what velocity did X traverse *d* in the period *p?* gets the simple answer, $\frac{d}{p}$. But the question, With what velocity was X moving at a time *t* inside that period ? is complex. It calls for the concept of a limit—the possibility of measuring an indefinitely long series of distances against a corresponding series of times. It can be answered, for instance, by constructing a graph whose curve is indefinitely corrigible by further pairs of measurements. To be sure, once we have this graph we can replace our simple question about speed over a period with a more sophisticated one. For whereas our first question merely demanded the overall speed (not the *average* speed: this is again complex), we can ask now whether X's speed over the period was constant. And this involves a different use of the graph. To say that X moved with a constant speed during the period is to say something doubly general, when to ascribe it that speed at one moment is to say something singly general: for now we ascribe it a speed at each moment in the period. But the possibility of operating on either of these levels of generality depends on being able to answer questions of our first, simple form, and the converse is not true. And thus Zeno's rejoinder fails. For since in this way the possibility of talking about motion at a moment rests on the possibility of talking of motion over a period, the two uses of "motion" are not the same. Likewise we could if we wished give a use to the expression "colour at a point" by building on our ways of describing a colour over a space, but we could not begin the other way round without a radical change in the use of colour-words. But in another way Zeno was right. For to say that these are not the same use is not at all to say that Zeno's second premiss depends on a pun. The premiss is valid, and it is valid precisely because it is the sort of rule whereby we do give a use to such an expression as "moving at a moment." We rule that, when and only when it is correct to say "X was moving throughout the period p," it is also correct to say "X was moving at any moment t in p." Aristotle's fallacy lay in supposing that to infer from the second formula to the first, one must regard the second as specifying a conjunction of moments exactly as long as the period specified in the first. He was in fact applying a simple model of induction, that model which set a premium on the exhaustive enumeration of cases and which Aristotle took to require strict synonymy between different occurrences of the predicate ("X-moving," for instance, in the inference from "Each moment in p is a case of X-moving" to "p is a case of X-moving"). And thus he failed to grasp that the two senses of "moving" are not identical but yet systematically connected; and his failure to see this connexion between two common uses of a common word led him to rule out one use entirely in favour of the other. His reply to Zeno rejects all uses of "movement" other than that which can be described in terms of periods of time, just as the colour-model we considered exhibited all uses of "red" as applicable to colour-stretches. And this is an unjustified departure from usage: it deprives us of a convenient method of characterizing motion which is common idiom for us and for the Greeks.

Now (and here we can drop the pretence of dialogue)

if this is so Zeno's fallacy cannot lie in his second premiss. Therefore it lies in premiss (a), and in particular in the proposition "There is no time to move in a moment" (with or without Aristotle's rider: "and no time to rest either"). The picture we are given is of the arrow bottled up in a piece of time that fits it too closely to allow any movement. The moment is too short to fly in. But such talk of movement is appropriate only when we have in mind periods of time within which movements could be achieved. It is not false that movements can be achieved *within* moments: it is absurd either to say or to deny this, for moments are not pieces of time such that within them any process can either take place or lack the time to take place. But this certainly does not show that the arrow is not moving *at* any moment. It is, of course: we have seen the sense in which it is. Whether it is, is a question of fact and not of logic.

So, despite his contrast between moments and periods of time, Zeno was treating moments as stiflingly small periods. To that extent Aristotle was right in his diagnosis. But he did not apply the diagnosis where it was needed. His denial that there can be any talk of motion except in direct connexion with periods of time is a surrender to Zeno; and his failure to come to grips with premiss (a) compels him to struggle against the wholly respectable premiss (b).

This surrender to Zeno had notable results in the history of dynamics. Notoriously, Aristotelian dynamics failed to deal adequately with acceleration; and it might be thought from what has been said that the failure lay in insisting that acceleration (a phenomenon which Aristotle certainly took seriously) must be analysed in terms of motion and speeds over periods of time, and not in the more manageable shorthand of velocity at an instant. But this is not the root issue. Unable to talk of speed at an instant, Aristotle has no room in his system for any such concept as that of initial velocity or, what is equally important, of the force required to start a body moving. Since he cannot recognize a moment in which the body first moves, his idea of force is restricted to the causing of motions that are completed in a given period of time. And, since he cannot consider any motion as caused by an initial application of force, he does not entertain the Newtonian corollary of this, that if some force F is sufficient to start a motion the continued application of F must produce not just the continuance of the motion but a constant change in it, namely acceleration.[37] It is the clumsy tools of Aristotelian dynamics, if I am right, that mark Zeno's major influence on the mathematics of science.

[37] He would have had another reason for rejecting Newton's account of acceleration, for that account holds good only in a vacuum, and Aristotle thought a vacuum impossible. But some of his followers re-imported the vacuum without abandoning the rest of the system.

Modern Science and Refutation of the Paradoxes of Zeno

ADOLF GRÜNBAUM

About 2500 years ago, a Greek named Zeno of Elea confounded his contemporaries by a series of startling arguments. These were designed to show that the science of geometry is beset by a paradox and that any attempt to provide a mathematical description of motion becomes ensnared in contradictions. So seminal was the scientific challenge bequeathed to posterity by Zeno's polemic that the contemporary philosopher Bertrand Russell paid tribute to him, saying: "Zeno's arguments, in some form, have afforded grounds for almost all the theories of space and

Adolf Grünbaum, "Modern Science and Refutation of the Paradoxes of Zeno," *The Scientific Monthly*, LXXXI (1955), 234–239. Reprinted, with revisions by the author, by permission. This article is a brief, relatively nontechnical introduction to the topics treated at greater length and in more detail in the two selections that follow this one. In all matters of substance and content the following two articles supersede the present one, which predates each of the others by approximately a decade.

time and infinity which have been constructed from his day to our own."[1]

Authorities disagree on the identity of the adversaries at which our searching Greek aimed his intellectual broadside. Disregarding entirely the question of historical authenticity, we shall consider a version of Zeno's paradoxes directly relevant to modern science. To my knowledge, the arguments that I shall offer in refutation of Zeno have not been given by previous writers. It will be best to examine (1) the geometric paradox, which impugns the consistency of the contemporary mathematician's conception of the relationship between a line and its points, and (2) the paradoxes of motion by which Zeno attempted to demonstrate the impossibility of motion.

GEOMETRIC PARADOX[2]

In the geometric paradox, our philosopher asserts that it is self-contradictory to claim that a line segment consists of points, each having zero length.[3] For he reasons that if a line segment of, say, two centimeters actually does consist of points, then the total length of that segment should be computable by adding the individual lengths of its constituent points. But instead of yielding the required value of two centimeters, this computation, says Zeno, unavoidably yields the paradoxical result of zero centimeters, since a summation of zeros can issue in nothing other than zero. By the same token, Zeno argues that it is self-contradictory to maintain that a positive time interval can consist of instants of zero duration. Among those who have taken up their cudgels on this issue, we find such diverse thinkers as

[1] Bertrand Russell, "The Problem of Infinity Considered Historically," reprinted above, p. 54.

[2] See Adolf Grünbaum, "Zeno's Metrical Paradox of Extension," reprinted below, for a full discussion of the issues treated in this section.

[3] See H. Hasse and H. Scholz, Die Grundlagenkrisis der griechischen Mathematik (Charlottenburg: Pan, 1928), p. 11.

Kant,[4] P. du Bois-Reymond,[5] William James,[6] and P. W. Bridgman.[7] Yet the very conception of an interval as a mathematically continuous aggregate of points that Zeno and these writers would proscribe has become commonplace in contemporary science through the work of the German mathematician Georg Cantor.[8] It therefore behooves us to come to grips with this charge of absurdity.

Consider the computation by means of which Zeno deduced his paradoxical result. In order to add the lengths of all the points in an interval of two centimeters, we must first form a precise idea of how many points compose such an interval. And we must be cognizant of the rules governing the additivity of lengths, i.e., the rules available for inferring the length of a total interval from the lengths of disjoint subintervals (or subsets) which jointly constitute it. We note immediately that the number of points in our interval of two centimeters is not finite. But of what avail is the trite observation that it is infinite? Given the additivity rules for length of the standard mathematics, it is to no avail, unless we succeed in giving a mathematically articulate characterization of the particular *kind* of infinite collection with which we are confronted. It was Cantor's achievement to provide precisely this characterization. And since it will give us the means by which to disprove the Zenonian allegation against geometry, we briefly pause to give a statement of its meaning.

Suppose that a very intelligent child who does not, however, know the names of numbers exceeding ten is confronted with two bags of pennies, each containing more

---

[4] I. Kant, *Critique of Pure Reason*, trans. N. K. Smith (London: The Macmillan Company, 1929), pp. 203–204.

[5] P. du Bois–Reymond, *Die allgemeine Funktionentheorie* (Tübingen: Laupp, 1882), Part I, p. 66.

[6] William James, *Some Problems of Philosophy* [44], pp. 185–186.

[7] P. W. Bridgman, "Some implications of recent points of view in physics," *Rev. Intern. Phil.*, III, No. 10 (1949), 490.

[8] G. Cantor, *Gesammelte Abhandlungen*, ed. E. Zermelo (Berlin: Springer, 1932), p. 275. For an English translation of Cantor's fundamental papers, see [123].

than ten pennies, and is then asked to determine which of the two bags contains more pennies. By virtue of his limited knowledge of numbers, the child would find it awkward to make a separate count of the contents of either bag. But his intelligence will enable him to make the required determination expeditiously: he will try to pair off each coin in bag *A* with a specific coin in the other bag *B*. If he exhausts the coins in bag *B* and still has coins left over in bag *A*, then he will conclude that there are more pennies in bag *A* than in bag *B*. On the other hand, if the supply in *B* outlasts the supply in *A*, he will know that the *B* collection is richer than the one in *A*. And if he comes out even, he will know, *without* having had to make *separate* counts, that bag *A* contains the same number of pennies as bag *B*. By the same kind of reasoning, we know that, in a monogamous society, there are just as many husbands as wives at any one time, although we have not taken a census.

Cantor saw that this method of one-to-one pairing lends itself to the solution of the problem of comparing two *infinite* collections as to cardinality: two such collections are equinumerous, if there is at least one way of pairing off their members so as to secure for each member in either collection exactly one partner in the other. In the event that no such pairing is possible, the collection that is left with some unpaired objects in every case is the *larger* of the two. Now, Cantor was able to show[9] that the infinity of points in a unit line segment is larger in precisely this sense than the infinity of positive integers. Having called the latter infinity "denumerable," he then called the former "super-denumerable."

In the context of modern mathematics, Zeno is thus defying us to obtain a result differing from zero upon adding all the lengths of the super-denumerable infinity of points that compose a unit segment. This means that we are being asked to add as many zeros. To Zeno's mind, it was axiomatic (1) that such an addition is necessarily feasible and permis-

[9] *Gesammelte Abhandlungen,* pp. 278–280.

sible and (2) that the result of any addition of zeros would be zero, regardless of the cardinality of the set of zeros to be added. But he could not anticipate that the addition of a super-denumerable infinity of numbers, be they zero or positive, presents a problem altogether different from adding *either* a finite sequence of numbers such as 3, 4, 7 *or* a *denumerable* infinity of numbers such as $1, \frac{1}{2}, \frac{1}{4}, \frac{1}{8}, \frac{1}{16}, \frac{1}{32}, \frac{1}{64}, \ldots$ Although arithmetic has evolved a definition of the "sum" of a *denumerable* infinity of numbers by a consistent generalization of the concept of finitary sum on the basis of the limit concept, this definition is utterly useless and irrelevant when the addition of a *super*-denumerable infinity of numbers is called for. Thus, while length is denumerably additive in standard mathematics, the addition of the lengths of all the points composing a unit segment is a meaningless (undefined) operation in analytic geometry and hence cannot be used to compute a value for the total length of the segment. In particular, the deduction of Zeno's paradoxical result zero for the length of a unit segment is precluded by this arithmetical fact. And what holds for the unit segment also holds for a segment of two centimeters and for any other. For *mirabile dictu,* Cantor demonstrated that no matter what their length, all line segments contain the same super-denumerable infinity of points. Therefore, if the concept of super-denumerable infinity is itself free from contradictions, then Zeno's charge of inconsistency is false, both in regard to the postulate that the line is an aggregate of mathematical points and that a time interval is a set of instants each of which has no duration.

Proponents of Zeno's view might still argue that this *arithmetical* rebuttal is unconvincing on purely geometric grounds, maintaining that if extension (space) is to be composed of elements, these must themselves be extended. Specifically, geometers like Veronese objected[10] to Cantor

---

[10] See E. W. Hobson, *The Theory of Functions of a Real Variable,* 2nd edn. (Cambridge: Cambridge University Press, 1921), Vol. I, pp. 56–57.

that in the array of points on the line, their extensions are all, as it were, "summed geometrically" before us. And from this geometric perspective, it is not cogent, in their view, to suppose that even a super-denumerable infinity of un-extended points would be able to sustain a positive interval, especially since the Cantorean theory claims arithmetical consistency here on the strength of the obscurities that oblig-ingly surround the meaning of the arithmetic "sum" of a super-denumerable infinity of numbers.

Is this objection to Cantor conclusive? I think not. Whence does it derive its plausibility? It would seem that it achieves persuasiveness via a tacit appeal to a *pictorial* representa-tion of the points of mathematical physics in which they are arrayed in the consecutive manner of beads on a string to form a line. But the properties that any such representation imaginatively attributes to points are not even allowed, let alone prescribed, by the formal postulates of geometric theory. The spuriousness of the difficulties adduced against the Cantorean conception of the line becomes apparent upon noting that not only the cardinality of its constituent points altogether eludes pictorialization but also their dense ordering: between any two points, there is an infinitude of others. Thus, in complete contrast to the discrete order of the beads on a string, *no* point is immediately adjacent to any other.

These considerations show that from a genuinely geo-metric point of view, a physical interpretation of the formal postulates of geometry cannot be obtained by the inevitably misleading pictorialization of *individual* points of the theory. Instead, we can provide a physical interpretation quite un-encumbered by the intrusion of the irrelevancies of *visual* space, if we associate *not* the term *"point"* but the term *"linear Cantorean continuum of points"* of our theory with an appropriate body in nature. By a point of this body we then mean nothing more or less than an element of it pos-sessing the formal properties prescribed for points by the postulates of geometry. And, on this interpretation, the

ground is then cut from under the geometric *parti pris*
against Cantor by the modern legatees of Zeno.

Apart from the *metrical* consistency of the modern conception of an interval as an aggregate of unextended points,
mathematicians have succeeded during the current century
in proving, by means of the *topological* theory of dimension,
that there is also no contradiction in regarding the one-
dimensional line as consisting of zero-dimensional points.[11]
This proof is not redundant with the foregoing analysis, since
it turns out that the concepts of positive length and one-
dimensionality are not at all the same.

In addition to refuting Zeno's geometric paradox, our
analysis yields the following result: unless substantial modifications are made simultaneously throughout the body of
analytic geometry, the proposal of some writers that we replace the Cantorean conception of the line as continuous by
the postulate that it consists of only a *denumerable*, discontinuous infinity of points must be rejected on logical
grounds of inconsistency alone. For the length or measure of
a denumerable point set is zero within standard mathematics, as can be seen upon denumerating any such set and
then applying the familiar arithmetic definition of the sum of
a denumerable sequence to the sequence of zeros representing the lengths of its members in accord with the standard
additivity rules for length.

PARADOXES OF MOTION[12]

Among the four paradoxes with which Zeno sought to dis-
credit the possibility of physical motion, two are of primary
relevance to contemporary mathematical physics, because
of that discipline's affirmation that the time variable ranges

[11] See W. Hurewicz and H. Wallman, *Dimension Theory* (Princeton, N.J.:
Princeton University Press, 1941), p. 18, and Adolf Grünbaum, "A Consistent
Conception of the Extended Linear Continuum as an Aggregate of Unextended
Elements" [69], pp. 290–295. See also P. S. Aleksandrov, "The present status of
the theory of dimension," *Am. Math. Soc. Translations*, 2, 1, 1 (1955).

[12] See "Modern Science and Zeno's Paradoxes of Motion," in this anthology,
for a full discussion of the issues raised in the remainder of this essay.

over the real numbers just as the space variable does. More particularly, it is the denseness of the ordering of the points of space and of the instants of time that provides the point of application for Zeno's polemic. The claim that for any point on the path of a moving object, there is *no* next point, anymore than there is an immediately following or preceding instant for any instant during the motion, enables Zeno to ask incisively: In what sense can the events composing the motion be significantly said to succeed one another temporally, if they succeed one another densely rather than in the consecutive manner of a discrete sequence? This question takes the form of asking (1) how can a temporal process even begin, if, in order to survive the lapse of a positive time interval *T,* a body must first have endured through the passage of an infinite regression of overlapping subsidiary time intervals $\frac{T}{2^n}$ ($n = \ldots, 3, 2, 1$), which has *no first term* because the denseness postulate entails infinite divisibility, and (2) how can a temporal process be completed in a finite time, if its completion requires the elapsing of an endless progression of temporal subintervals $\frac{T}{2^n}$ ($n = 1, 2, 3, \ldots$) in which there is *no last term* as a consequence of the denseness postulate?

The more familiar versions of these two queries are the "Dichotomy" paradox and the paradox of "Achilles and the Tortoise." In the former, whose argument was endorsed by A. N. Whitehead,[13] Zeno contends that the mathematical theory of motion entails the impossibility of the very process that it purports to describe. For if there is indeed no point *next* to the starting point on the path of a runner that he can occupy immediately after leaving the starting point, then an infinity of points and, hence, intervals are inevitably

---

[13] A. N. Whitehead, *Process and Reality* [48], pp. 53, 96, 105–107, and *Science and the Modern World* [49], p. 186. See also Galileo Galilei, *Dialogues Concerning Two New Sciences*, trans. H. Crew and A. de Salvio (New York: Macmillan, 1914), pp. 162–164.

interposed between the starting point and *any* other point
to which the runner would move. And thus the motion is
nipped in the bud, as it were. On the other hand, even if
per impossibile the motion had begun, the paradox of Achilles shows that its completion in a finite time is quite
unachievable. Having granted a head start d to the slow tortoise, which moves with velocity v, Achilles can never catch
up with the turtle, despite his greater speed V: the fleet-
footed warrior will *not* overtake the reptile after a time
$\frac{d}{V-v}$, because there is no last term in the series of time
intervals

$$\frac{d}{V} + v\frac{d}{V^2} + v^2\frac{d}{V^3} + \dots,$$

a series whose terms represent the successive times required
by Achilles to traverse the successive distances separating
him from the tortoise, beginning with the head start d of the
tortoise.

According to a view that is as widespread as it is erroneous, Zeno's argument is no more than a mathematical
anachronism. We are told that if he had only known,
as we do today, that the arithmetic sum of a suitably convergent infinite series of numbers is finite rather than infinite, then he would have recognized that he had merely
posed a pseudoproblem. More particularly, the sum formula
for a geometric series would have convinced him at once
that the sum of the series considered in the "Dichotomy"
is actually T and the series of times needed by Achilles
to come abreast of the tortoise does add up to the finite
value $\frac{d}{V-v}$. This retort is based on the fact that in modern
mathematics, Cauchy has *defined* the arithmetic "sum" of
an infinite convergent series as the limit of the sequence of
its partial sums. But it overlooks that the *arithmetic* theory
of limits *as such* cannot be invoked to dismiss the allegation
that kinematical theory entails temporal paradoxes. For the
issue posed by Zeno is the following: Is the ordinal and
metrical structure of time such as to *justify* the *application* of

the arithmetic theory of limits to the phenomena of motion as well as the postulate of kinematics that the instants of time are *densely* ordered?

What is required in order to refute Zeno's objections to the mathematical theory of motion is a proof that neither the denseness of its ordering of the constituent events of the motion nor such features of this process as are entailed by this denseness property constitute obstacles to its inception and consummation either ordinally or metrically.

To lay the groundwork for this proof, we ask: What is the basis for the view that the very meaning of temporal succession involves that events follow upon one another *seriatim*, like the consecutive beats of the heart, and not densely? The answer can be none other than that this feeling derives from a tacit appeal to the properties of the time-order experienced intuitively in human consciousness. Since each act of thought takes a minimum positive amount of time rather than a mere instant of zero duration, it is inevitable that when we analyze the stream of consciousness into a succession of constituent moments or "nows," these elements are experienced as occurring in a discrete sequence. No wonder therefore that on such an intuitively grounded meaning of temporal succession, there is an ever present feeling that if physical events are to succeed one another in time, their order of occurrence must also be discrete, if it is to be a temporal order at all. It follows that a refutation of Zeno will be at hand if the psychological criterion of temporal sequence can be supplanted by a strictly physical criterion of "event B is later than event A" that does not entail a discrete temporal order, but allows a dense order instead.[14]

Fortunately, a criterion of time-order based on the statis-

[14] While the present essay provides an explication in terms of the asymmetric relation of *later than*, "Modern Science and Zeno's Paradoxes of Motion" utilizes a symmetric relation of *causal connectedness*. For a full discussion of the physical relation of *later than*, as well as an explanation of the relations between the two kinds of treatment, see Adolf Grünbaum, *Philosophical Problems of Space and Time* [139], chaps. 7–8, and "The Anisotropy of Time," in T. Gold and D. L. Schumacher, eds., *The Nature of Time* (Ithaca, N.Y.: Cornell University Press, 1967), pp. 149–186.

tics of the thermodynamic behavior of classes of physical systems each of whose members is quasi-isolated for a limited time provides a criterion with precisely these required properties. For the numerous relevant details, I must refer the reader to other publications.[15]

Our analysis has shown that we are absolved from the necessity of answering "how" a succession of events can occur by exhibiting a discrete sequence of occurrence. Upon freeing ourselves from the limitations of the psychological criterion of time-order by means of the constructive elaboration of an alternative, autonomous physical criterion, it becomes clear that the dense temporal ordering of the constituent point-events of a motion is no obstacle whatever to either its inception or its completion in a finite time. And thus to ask "how" the motion can occur despite the dense temporal order, or what the runner does immediately after leaving his point of departure or immediately prior to arriving at his destination, is seen to be entirely unwarranted.

Once the physical intelligibility of temporal denseness is established, the following can be shown: There is no more reason to infer that a temporally dense set of physical events must be of infinite duration by virtue of thus being dense, than for concluding untutoredly that a spatially dense set of physical points must be of infinite spatial extent on the strength of its denseness.

QUANTUM THEORY

Standard quantum theory has discretized or quantized some physical properties whose counterparts in classical physics were mathematically continuous. When coupled with reports of *speculations* about incorporating minimal distances ("hodons") and times ("chronons") in some elaborated future form of the theory, this kind of quantization has insinuated the belief to some that standard quantum mechanics affirms the atomicity of space and time. But space

---

[15] *Ibid.*

and time are *not* quantized or granular in standard quantum theory: every point of continuous physical space is a *potential* sharply defined position of, say, an electron, and separately, every instant of a continuous time is *potentially* the time of a physical event, speculations about hodons and chronons notwithstanding. And since the space and time of standard quantum mechanics are each *dense*, the ordinal and time-metrical features of the refutation of Zeno's "Dichotomy" and "Achilles" which I have outlined are not rendered superfluous or invalid by that theory, even though these paradoxes involve quantum-mechanically proscribed, well-defined classical particle trajectories.

In regard to speculations envisioning a genuine quantization of space and time which repudiates their mathematical continuity altogether, it is well to be mindful of the following perceptive comment by H. Weyl:

> So far, the atomistic theory of space has always remained mere speculation and has never achieved sufficient contact with reality. How should one understand the metric relations in space on the basis of this idea? If a square is built up of miniature tiles, then there are as many tiles along the diagonal as there are along the side; thus the diagonal should be equal in length to the side.[16]

[16] H. Weyl, *Philosophy of Mathematics and Natural Science* [130], p. 43. For a discussion of the Democritean conception of *mathematical* atomism and its reception in antiquity, see S. Luria, "Die Infinitesimaltheorie der antiken Atomisten," in *Quellen u. Studien zur Gesch. d. Math. Astr. u. Phys.*, Abt. B, Studien II (Berlin: Springer, 1933), pp. 106–185.

Zeno's Metrical Paradox of Extension

ADOLF GRÜNBAUM

§1. THE PROBLEM

It is a commonplace in the analytic geometry of physical space and time that an *extended* straight-line segment, having positive length, is treated as "consisting of" *unextended* points, each of which has zero length. Analogously, time intervals of positive duration are postulated to be aggregates of instants, each of which has zero duration.

Ever since some of the Greeks defined a point as "that which has no part,"[1] philosophers and mathematicians have questioned the consistency of conceiving of an extended continuum as an aggregate of unextended elements. On the long list of investigators who have examined this question in the context of the specific mathematical and philosophical theories of their time, we find not only Zeno[2] but also such

From *Modern Science and Zeno's Paradoxes* (Middletown, Conn.: Wesleyan University Press, 1967), pp. 115–135. Reprinted by permission. British edition, revised (London: George Allen & Unwin Ltd., 1968).

---

[1] This definition is given in Euclid, *The Thirteen Books of Euclid's Elements*, translated by T. L. Heath (New York: Cambridge University Press, 1926), p. 153.

[2] S. Luria, "Die Infinitesimaltheorie der antiken Atomisten," *Quellen und Studien zur Geschichte der Mathematik, Astronomie, und Physik*, Abteilung B, Studien II (Berlin, 1933), p. 106.

thinkers as Aristotle,[3] Cavalieri,[4] Tacquet,[5] Pascal,[6] Bolzano,[7] Leibniz,[8] Paul du Bois-Reymond,[9] and Georg Cantor,[10] to mention but a few. Thus, William James wrote:

> If, however, we take time and space as concepts, not as perceptual data, we don't well see how they can have this atomistic constitution. For if the drops or atoms are themselves without duration or extension it is inconceivable that by adding any number of them together times or spaces should accrue.[11]
>
> . . . that being should be identified with the consummation of an endless chain of units (such as "points"), no one of which contains any amount whatever of the being (such as "space") expected to result, this is something which our intellect not only fails to understand, but which it finds absurd.[12]

Writing on this issue more recently, P. W. Bridgman declared:

> With regard to the paradoxes of Zeno . . . if I literally thought of a line as consisting of an assemblage of points of zero length and of an interval of time as the sum of moments without duration, paradox would then present itself.[13]

[3] Aristotle, On Generation and Corruption, Book I, Chapter ii, 316a15–317a17; A. Edel, Aristotle's Theory of the Infinite (New York: Columbia University Press, 1934), pp. 48–49, 76–78; T. L. Heath, Mathematics in Aristotle [14], pp. 90, 117.

[4] C. B. Boyer, The Concepts of the Calculus (New York: Hafner Publishing Co., Inc. 1949), p. 140. [Dover edn. [31]].

[5] Ibid.

[6] Ibid., p. 152.

[7] Ibid., p. 270; and B. Bolzano, Paradoxes of the Infinite, edited by D. A. Steele (New Haven: Yale University Press, 1951).

[8] B. Russell, The Philosophy of Leibniz (London: George Allen & Unwin Ltd., 1937), p. 114.

[9] P. du Bois-Reymond, Die Allgemeine Funktionentheorie, Vol. I (Tübingen: Lauppische Buchhandlung, 1882), p. 66.

[10] G. Cantor, Gesammelte Abhandlungen, edited by E. Zermelo (Berlin: Springer-Verlag, 1932), pp. 275, 374.

[11] W. James, Some Problems of Philosophy [44], p. 155.

[12] Ibid., p. 186.

[13] P. W. Bridgman, "Some Implications of Recent Points of View in Physics," Revue Internationale de Philosophie, III, No. 10 (1949), p. 490.

This Zenonian criticism of the mathematical theory of physical space and time by James and Bridgman is a challenge to the basic Cantorean conceptions underlying analytic geometry and the mathematical theory of motion.[14] Their view also calls into question such philosophies of science as rely on these conceptions for the interpretation of our mathematical knowledge of nature. Accordingly, it is essential that we inquire whether contemporary point-set theory succeeds in avoiding an inconsistency upon postulating positive linear intervals to be aggregates of extensionless point-elements.

In the present chapter I shall endeavor to exhibit those features of present mathematical theory which do indeed preclude the existence of such an inconsistency. It will then be clear what kind of mathematical and philosophical theory does succeed in avoiding Zeno's mathematical (metrical) paradoxes of plurality, paradoxes that I have distinguished from his paradoxes of motion in the Introduction.* As before, my concern with the views which various writers have attributed to Zeno is exclusively systematic, and I make no claims whatever regarding the historicity of Zeno's arguments or concerning the authenticity of views which I shall associate with his name. According to S. Luria,[15] Zeno invokes two basic axioms in his mathematical paradoxes of plurality. Having divided all magnitudes into positive and "dimensionless," i.e., unextended magnitudes, Zeno assumed that (1) the sum of an infinite number of equal positive magnitudes of arbitrary smallness must necessarily be infinite, and (2) the sum of *any* finite or *infinite* number of "dimensionless" magnitudes must necessarily be *zero*.

The second of these axioms seems to command the assent of P. W. Bridgman and was also enunciated by the mathematician Paul du Bois-Reymond,[16] who then inferred that we

---

[14] G. Cantor, *Gesammelte Abhandlungen*, p. 275.
*[In *Modern Science and Zeno's Paradoxes*, p. 3.]
[15] S. Luria, "Die Infinitesimaltheorie der antiken Atomisten," p. 66.
[16] P. du Bois-Reymond, *Die Allgemeine Funktionentheorie*, Vol. I, p. 66.

cannot regard a line as an aggregate of "dimensionless" points, however dense an order we postulate for this aggregate. Zeno himself is presumed to have used these axioms as a basis for the following dilemma:[17] If a line segment is postulated to be an aggregate of infinitely many *like* elements, then two and only two cases are possible. Either these elements are of equal positive length and the aggregate of them is of infinite length (by Axiom 1) or the elements are of zero length and then their aggregate is necessarily of zero length (by Axiom 2). The first horn of this dilemma is valid but does not have relevance to the modern analytic geometry of space and time. It is the second horn that we must refute in the context of present mathematical theory if we are to solve the problem which we have posed.

To carry out this refutation, we must first ascertain the logical relationships between the modern concepts of metric, length, measure, and cardinality, when applied to (infinite) point-sets. For in the second horn of his dilemma, Zeno avers that a line cannot be regarded as an aggregate of points no matter what cardinality we postulate for the aggregate. And du Bois-Reymond endorsed this contention by reminding us that points are "dimensionless," i.e., unextended, and by maintaining that if we conceive the line to be "merely an aggregate of points" then we are *eo ipso* abandoning the view that "A line and a point are entirely different things."[18]

We see that du Bois-Reymond is conforming to the long intuitive tradition of using the concepts of length and dimensionality interchangeably to characterize (sensed) extension. It will therefore be best to begin our analysis by noting that we must distinguish the traditional *metrical* usage of the term "dimensionless" from the contemporary *topological* meaning of "zero dimension." This distinction has become necessary by virtue of the autonomous development of the topological theory of dimension apart from metrical geome-

[17] H. Hasse and H. Scholz, *Die Grundlagenkrisis der griechischen Mathematik* (Charlottenburg: Pan-Verlag, 1928), p. 11.
[18] P. du Bois-Reymond, *Die Allgemeine Funktionentheorie*, Vol. I, p. 65.

try. Prior to this development, any positive interval of Cartesian n-space was simply called "n-dimensional" by definition. Thus, line segments having length were called "one-dimensional" and surfaces having area "two-dimensional." By contrast, in the topological theory of dimension developed in the present century, it is a non-trivial *theorem* that lines are topologically one-dimensional, surfaces two-dimensional, and, generally, that Cartesian n-space is n-dimensional. In fact, it is this theorem which warrants the use of the name "dimension theory" for the branch of topology dealing with such non-metrical properties of point-sets as make for the validity of this theorem.[19]

By contrast, the traditional *metrical* sense of dimensionality identifies dimensionality with length or measure of extendedness. It is only the latter sense of "dimension" and "dimensionless" which is relevant to the metrical problem of this chapter. Hence I refer the reader to another publication[20] for an account of how the twentieth-century theory of dimension can *consistently* affirm the following *additivity* properties for dimension in the *topological* sense of "zero-dimensional" and "one-dimensional": The point-set constituting the number axis or any finite interval in it (e.g., an infinite straight line or a finite line segment, respectively) is *one*-dimensional even though it is the set-theoretic sum of *zero*-dimensional subsets. The zero-dimensional subsets are: (1) any unit point-set (such a set has a single point as its only member and hence can be loosely referred to as a "point," whenever such usage does not permit ambiguities), (2) any *finite* collection of one or more points, (3) any denumerable set (in particular the set of rational real points), and (4) the set of irrational real points, which is non-denumerably infinite.

Accordingly, we must now deal with the following *metrical* question: Within the framework of the standard mathematics used in physics, how can the definition of length

---

[19] K. Menger, *Dimensionstheorie* (Leipzig: B. G. Teubner, 1928), p. 244.

[20] A. Grünbaum, "A Consistent Conception of the Extended Linear Continuum as an Aggregate of Unextended Elements" [69], pp. 290–295.

consistently assign zero length to *unit* point-sets or individual points while assigning positive finite lengths to such unions (sums) of these unit point-sets as constitute a finite interval? To furnish an answer to the latter question will be to refute the second horn of Zeno's dilemma. We shall furnish an analysis satisfying these requirements after devoting some attention to the consideration of prior related problems.

§2. THE ADDITIVITY OF LENGTH AND MEASURE

Length, measure, or extension is defined as a property of point-sets rather than of individual points, and zero length is assigned to the *unit set,* i.e., to a set containing only a single point. While it is both logically correct and even of central importance to our problem that we treat a line interval of geometry as a set of point-elements, strictly speaking the definition of "length" renders it incorrect to refer to such an interval as an "aggregate of unextended points." For the properties of being extended or being unextended each characterize unit point-*sets* but are not possessed by their respective individual point-elements, much as temperature is a property only of aggregates of molecules and not of individual molecules. The entities which can therefore be properly said to be unextended are *included in* but are not *members of* the aggregate of points constituting a line interval. Accordingly, the line interval is a union of unextended unit point-sets and, strictly, not an "aggregate of unextended points." Though strictly incorrect, I wish to use the latter designation in order to avoid the more cumbersome expression "union of unextended unit point-sets."

I shall now present such portions of the theory of metric spaces as bear immediately on our problem.

The structure characterizing the class of all real numbers (positive, negative, and zero) arranged in order of magnitude is that of a linear Cantorean continuum.[21]

---

[21] E. V. Huntington, *The Continuum and Other Types of Serial Order,* 2nd edition (Cambridge: Harvard University Press, 1942), pp. 10, 44. [Dover edn. [126].]

The Euclidean point-sets or "spaces" which we shall have occasion to consider are "metric" in the following complex sense:[22]

1) There is a one-to-one correspondence between the points of an n-dimensional Euclidean space E^n and a certain real coordinate system $(x_1, \ldots, x_n)$.

2) If the points x, y have the coordinates x_i, y_i, then there is a real function $d(x, y)$, called their (Euclidean) *distance*, given by

$$d(x, y) = \left[\sum_1^n (x_i - y_i)^2 \right]^{\frac{1}{2}}$$

The basic properties of this function are given by certain distance *axioms*.[23]

A finite interval on a straight line is the (ordered) set of all real points between (and sometimes including one or both of) two fixed points called the "end-points" of the interval. Since the points constituting an interval satisfy condition (1) above in the definition of "metric," it is possible to define the "distance" between the fixed end-points of a given interval. The *number* representing this distance is the *length* of the point-set constituting the interval. Let "a" and "b" denote, respectively, the points a and b *or* their respective real-number coordinates, depending upon the context. We then define the length of a finite interval (a, b) as the non-negative quantity $b - a$, regardless of whether the interval $\{x\}$ is closed ($a \leqq x \leqq b$), open ($a < x < b$), or half-open ($a \leqq x < b$ or $a < x \leqq b$). (It is understood that the symbols "$<$" and "$=$" have a purely ordinal meaning here.) Therefore, the set-theoretic addition of a single point to an open interval (or to a half-open interval at the open end) has no effect at all on the *length* of the resulting interval as compared with the length of the original interval. In the limiting case of $a = b$,

[22] S. Lefschetz, *Introduction to Topology* (Princeton, N.J.: Princeton University Press, 1949), p. 28.

[23] *Ibid.*

the interval is called "degenerate," and here the closed interval reduces to a set containing the single point $x = a$, while each of the other three intervals is empty. *It follows that the length of a degenerate interval is zero.* Loosely speaking, a single point has zero length.[24]

Zeno is challenging us to obtain a result differing from zero when using the additivity of lengths to determine the length of a finite interval on the basis of the known zero lengths of its degenerate subintervals, each of which has a single point as its only member. But since each positive interval has a *non-denumerable* infinity of degenerate subintervals, we see already that the result of determining the length of that interval by "compounding," in some unspecified way, the zero lengths of its degenerate subintervals is far less obvious than it must have seemed to Zeno, who did not distinguish between countably and non-countably infinite sets!

Although length is similar to cardinality in being a property of *sets* and not of the elements of these, it is essential to realize that the cardinality of an interval is not a function of the length of that interval. The independence of cardinality and length becomes demonstrable by combining our definition of length with Cantor's proof of the equivalence of the set of all real points between 0 and 1 with the set of all real points between *any* two fixed points on the number axis. It is therefore not the case that the longer of two positive intervals has "more" points. In the case of two unequal intervals, one of which is a proper part of the other, the longer interval contains points which are *not* also contained in the shorter one. In this latter sense of the specified *difference in the identity and comprehensiveness of membership,* the longer of two such intervals may be said to contain "more" points, i.e., points other than the points belonging to the shorter interval. But this "more" of differing identity and comprehensiveness must *not* be confused with the

[24] H. Cramér, *Mathematical Methods of Statistics* [134], pp. 11, 19.

"more" of greater numerosity (cardinality). And it is the specified kind of greater comprehensiveness that makes for greater spatial (or temporal) extension.

Once the independence of cardinality and length of intervals is established, it is possible to eliminate several of the confusions which have vitiated certain treatments of the infinite divisibility of intervals, as we shall see below. Thus, it will become impossible to infer in finitist manner that the division of an interval into two or more subintervals imparts to each of the resulting subintervals a cardinality lower than the cardinality of the original interval.

An interesting illustration of the independence of cardinality and length is provided by the so-called "ternary set" (Cantor discontinuum). This set has measure zero (and zero dimension) while having the cardinality of the continuum.[25] And the existence of this set shows that the cardinality as such is *not* sufficient to confer positive extension on *an interval* but that its positive extension depends on the *structural arrangement* of its elements.

We shall be concerned with ascertaining why Zeno's *paradoxical* result that the length of a given *positive* interval (a, b) is zero is *not* deducible from the following two propositions in our geometry in the context of its rules governing the additivity of lengths: (1) Any positive or non-degenerate interval is the union of a continuum of degenerate subintervals, and (2) the length of a degenerate (sub) interval is zero. It is obvious that *if the theory is consistent,* Zeno's result cannot be deducible. Such a result would contradict the proposition that the length of the interval (a, b) is b − a (a ≠ b). Furthermore, this result would be incompatible with Cantor's theorem that all positive intervals have the same cardinality regardless of length, for this theorem shows that no inference regarding the length of a non-degenerate interval can be drawn from propositions (1) and (2) via the ad-

[25] R. Courant and H. Robbins, *What Is Mathematics?* [133], p. 249. Also, A. D. Aleksandrov, A. N. Kolmogorov, and M. A. Lavrent'ev, *Mathematics*, Vol. III, translated by K. Hirsch (Cambridge: The M.I.T. Press, 1963), pp. 24 and 28.

ditivity of lengths permitted by the theory. In order to show later that the standard mathematical theory used in physics does have the required consistency, i.e., that it does not lend itself to the deduction of Zeno's paradoxical result, we must now consider the determination of (1) the length of the union of a *finite* number of non-overlapping intervals of known lengths, and (2) the length of the union of a *denumerable* infinity of such intervals.

If an interval i is the union of a *finite* number of intervals, no two of which have a common point, i.e., if

$$i = i_1 + i_2 + i_3 + \ldots + i_n \qquad (i_p i_q = 0 \text{ for } p \neq q),$$

it follows readily from the theory previously developed that the length $b - a$ of the total interval is equal to the *arithmetic sum* of the individual lengths of the subintervals. We therefore write

$$L(i) = L(i_1) + L(i_2) + L(i_3) + \ldots + L(i_n).$$

If we now *define* the arithmetic sum of a progression of finite cardinal numbers as the limit of a sequence of partial arithmetic sums of members of the sequence, then a nontrivial proof can be given[26] that the following theorem holds: The length of an interval which is subdivided into an *enumerable* number of subintervals without common points is equal to the arithmetic sum of the lengths of these subintervals.[27] It follows at once that if the standard mathematical theory containing this result *were* to assert as well—which it does *not!*—that an interval consists of an enumerable number of points, then Zeno's paradox would be deducible.

Thus, both for a finite number and for a countably infinite number of non-overlapping subintervals, the length $L(i)$ of the total interval is an additive function of the interval i. The length of an interval is a numerical measure of the comprehensiveness (extension) of that interval's *membership* relative to the standard of length but not of its cardinality. The latter

---

[26] Cf. H. Cramér, *Mathematical Methods of Statistics* [134], pp. 19–21.

[27] See also the discussion in [*Modern Science and Zeno's Paradoxes*] Chapter II, §2A.

does not depend upon the comprehensiveness of the membership of an interval.

It will be recalled that "length" was defined only for intervals. So far, we have not assigned any property akin to length to other kinds of point-sets. There are many occasions, however, when it is desirable to have some kind of *measure* of the extensiveness, as it were, of point-sets quite different from intervals. Problems of this kind as well as problems encountered in the theory of (Lebesgue) integration have prompted the introduction of the generalized metrical concept of "measure" $L(S)$ of a set S to deal as well with sets other than intervals. This metrical concept extends the definition of the interval function $L(i)$ so as to obtain a non-negative and additive set function $L(S)$ which coincides with $L(i)$ in the special case when S is an interval i. And the principles of the resulting measure theory relevant to our concern with Zeno's metrical paradox are the following:

1) The measure of a set of points is to be a number dependent on the set, such that the measure of the sum of two sets, which have no point in common, is the sum of the measures of the two sets. . . . The measure of a set being regarded as a function of the set, is thus required to be an *additive* function, i.e., a function such that its value for the set $E_1 + E_2$ is the sum of its values for E_1 and E_2.[28]

2) . . . any sum . . . of a finite or enumerable number of measurable sets [all contained in a non-infinite interval] is itself measurable.[29]

3) The measure of the sum of an enumerably infinite sequence of sets, no two of which have a point in common, is to be the limiting sum of the measures of the sets, whenever that limiting sum exists.[30]

4) Every enumerable set of points is measurable, and its measure is zero.[31]

[28] E. W. Hobson, *The Theory of Functions of a Real Variable*, Vol. I [New York: Dover Publications, Inc., 1953], p. 166.
[29] H. Cramér, *Mathematical Methods of Statistics* [134], p. 32.
[30] E. W. Hobson, *The Theory of Functions of a Real Variable*, Vol. I, p. 166.
[31] *Ibid.*, p. 176.

It will be noted that in virtue of (2) and (3), the standard mathematical theory asserts that the measure is *countably additive* (or enumerably additive), just as it had asserted for length, as is evident from our earlier discussion of the additivity of length.[32]

Since the theory of infinite divisibility has been used fallaciously in an attempt to deduce Zeno's metrical paradox, we shall now point out the relevant fallacies before dealing with the crux of our problem to refute the second horn of Zeno's metrical dilemma.

§3. INFINITE DIVISIBILITY

In an exchange of views with Leibniz, Johann Bernoulli committed an important fallacy: He treated the actually infinite set of natural numbers as having a *last* or "∞th" term which can be "reached" in the manner in which an inductive cardinal can be reached by starting from zero.[33] Bernoulli's view is clearly self-contradictory, since no such discrete denumerable infinity of terms could possibly have a last term.

When giving arguments in behalf of his theory of infinitesimals, C. S. Peirce[34] committed the same Bernoullian fallacy by reasoning as follows: (1) The decimal expansion of an irrational number has an infinite number of terms; (2) the infinite decimal expansion has a *last* element at the "infinitieth place," and since the latter is "infinitely far out" in the decimal expansion, this element is infinitely small or infinitesimal in comparison to finite magnitudes; and (3) since continuity requires irrationals, continuity presupposes infinitesimals. Furthermore, the method of defining irrational points by nested intervals[35] was *misconstrued* by du Bois-

---

[32] For details on the definition of "measure" for various kinds of point-sets, the reader is referred to H. Cramér, *Mathematical Methods of Statistics* [134], pp. 22ff., and P. R. Halmos, *Measure Theory* [135].

[33] H. Weyl, *Philosophy of Mathematics and Natural Science* [130], p. 44.

[34] C. Hartshorne and P. Weiss (eds.), *The Collected Papers of Charles Sanders Peirce*, Vol. VI (Cambridge: Harvard University Press, 1935), paragraph 125.

[35] R. Courant and H. Robbins, *What is Mathematics?* [133], pp. 68–69.

Reymond[36] such that he was then able to charge it with committing the Bernoullian fallacy.[37]

We are now concerned with this fallacy, because it is always committed when the attempt is made to use the *infinite divisibility* of positive intervals as a basis for deducing Zeno's metrical paradox and for then denying that a positive interval can be an infinitely divisible extension. Precisely this kind of deduction of the paradox is attributed to Zeno by H. D. P. Lee[38] and P. Tannery,[39] both of whom seem to be unaware of the fallacy involved.

The following basic assumptions are involved in their version of Zeno's arguments:

1) Infinite *divisibility* guarantees the possibility of a *completable* process of "infinite division," i.e., of a completable infinite sequence of sets of division operations.

2) The completion of this process of "infinite division" is achieved by the last set of division operations in the sequence and terminates in "reaching" a last product of division in each of the parts—a mathematical point of zero extension.[40]

---

[36] P. du Bois-Reymond, *Die Allgemeine Funktionentheorie*, Vol. I, pp. 58–67.

[37] Du Bois-Reymond's fundamental error lies in supposing that the method of nested intervals allows and requires the "coalescing" of the end-points of a supposedly "next-to-the-last" interval into a single point such that this "coalescing" is the *last step* in an infinite progression of nested interval formations. If the method in question did require such a coalescing, then it would indeed be as objectionable logically as is the Bernoullian conception of the ∞th or last natural number. This is not the case, however, for while the method does indeed make reference to a progression of intervals, it neither allows nor requires that the irrational point is the "last" or "∞th" such "contracted" interval. Instead of appealing to "coalescence," the method specifies the irrational point *by the mode of variation* of the intervals in the *entire sequence*. It is therefore a property of the entire sequence which enables us to define the kind of point which is being asserted to exist. It would seem that du Bois-Reymond permitted himself to be misled by such pictorial language as "The interval contracts into a point."

[38] H. D. P. Lee, *Zeno of Elea* [2], p. 23.

[39] P. Tannery, "Le Concept Scientifique du Continu: Zénon d'Élée et Georg Cantor," *Revue Philosophique*, XX, No. 2 (1885), pp. 391–392.

[40] This assumption is to be likened to the supposition that the printing of all the $\aleph_0$ digits in the infinite decimal representation of π would be completed by printing a *last* digit; cf. the discussion in Chapter II, §4 [pp. 222–226 below].

3) The *actual infinity* of distinct point-elements constituting the interval is generated by such an alleged process of "infinite division."

4) Since the sets of divisions begin with a first operation on the total interval, each has an immediate successor, and each set, except the first, has a specific predecessor, they jointly constitute a progression of sets of one or more operations.

By assumptions (3) and (4), the "final elements" or points of the interval to which Zeno's metrical argument is to be applied are each presumed to have been generated by the last step in a *progression of division operations*. This consequence, however, is absurd. For it is the very essence of a progression not to have a last term and not to be completable in that ordinal sense! To maintain the self-contradictory proposition that in such an actually infinite aggregate of order type ω, there is a "last" set of divisions which ensures the completability of the process of "infinite division" by "reaching" a "final" product of division is indeed to commit the Bernoullian fallacy.

Several consequences follow at once:

1) We do not ever "arrive" by this kind of "infinite division" of an interval at its actual, super-denumerable infinity of mathematical points in the sense of first *generating* this actual infinity of unextended elements by "infinite division."

2) *The facts of infinite* (i.e., indefinite) *divisibility do not by themselves legitimately give rise to the metrical paradoxes of Zeno,* which may arise if we postulate an actual infinity of point-elements *ab initio*. It is because Cantor's theory rests on this latter postulate and not because every interval on his number axis is infinitely (i.e., indefinitely) divisible that we must inquire whether the line as conceived by Cantor is beset by the metrical difficulties pointed out by Zeno.

To show that this latter assertion is justified within the context of point-set theory, we shall now construct on the foundations of that theory a treatment of infinite divisibility consistent with it.

No clear meaning can be assigned to the "division" of a line unless we specify whether we understand by "line" an entity like a sensed "continuous" chalk mark on the black-board or the very differently continuous line of Cantor's theory. The "continuity" of the *sensed* linear expanse consists essentially in its failure to exhibit visually noticeable gaps as the eye scans it from one of its extremities to the other. There are no distinct *elements* in the sensed "continuum" of which the seen line presents itself as a structured aggregate. By contrast, the continuity of the Cantorean line consists precisely in the complicated structural relatedness of (point) *elements* which is specified by the postulates for real numbers.[41]

We cannot always perceive a distinct third gap between any two visually discernible gaps (sections) in the sensed line. Thus the visually discernible gaps (sections) in that line do not constitute a discernibly dense set. This means that any significant assertion concerning possible divisibility of a *sensed* line must be compatible with the existence of thresholds of perception. Division of the *sensed* line will mean the creation of one or more perceptible gaps in it. Con-trariwise, any attribution of (infinite) "divisibility" to a Can-torean line must be based on the fact that *ab initio* that line and its intervals are already "divided" into an actual dense infinity of point-elements of which the line (interval) is the structured aggregate. Accordingly, the Cantorean line can be said to be already actually *infinitely divided*. "Division" of the line can therefore mean neither the creation of visual gaps in it nor the "separation" of the point-elements from one another to make them distinct. *What we will mean in speaking of the "division" of the Cantorean line is the sin-gling out of positive non-overlapping subintervals from (proper or improper) intervals of the line,* and in the case of finite point-sets in general and of the degenerate interval in particular, "division" will mean the formation of proper non-

---

[41] See the earlier discussion in [*Modern Science and Zeno's Paradoxes*] Chapter II, end of §2A.

empty *subsets.* A positive interval is *infinitely* divisible in the sense of permitting the SINGLING OUT of at least one *denumerable* infinity of positive, non-overlapping subintervals.

It follows from our definition of division and from the properties of finite sets that the division of a *finite* point-set of two or more members necessarily effects a reduction in its cardinality. This reduction is in marked contrast to the behavior of *intervals,* whose division yields subintervals of the same cardinality as the original interval. It is of fundamental importance to be aware in this context that the division of an interval effects *no* reduction in the cardinality of the resulting subintervals as compared to that of the original interval. For the unwitting *denial* of this fact seems to be implicit (along with the Bernoullian fallacy) in the false supposition that the infinite divisibility of an interval assures the obtainability of all of its constituent individual points as "products of infinite division." Since the degenerate interval has no proper non-empty subset, that unique kind of interval is *indivisible.* We see that on our theory, (infinite) divisibility and indivisibility are respectively *set-theoretic* rather than metrical properties. This theory has enabled us to assign a precise meaning to the indivisibility of a unit point-set by (1) defining division as an operation on sets only and not on their elements, (2) defining divisibility of finite sets as the formation of proper non-empty subsets of these, and (3) showing that the degenerate interval is indivisible by virtue of its lack of a subset of the required kind.

Note that division is a kind of *operation* on specified point-sets while divisibility and being super-denumerably infinite are respective *properties* of certain point-sets in the case of the Cantorean line. And the infinite divisibility of an interval does not make for a kind of "infinite division" which would first generate its super-denumerably many constituent points.[42]

It is of importance to realize that our analysis has shown

---

[42] Nevertheless, it is often convenient by way of *elliptic parlance* to designate the membership of a set through mention of an actual infinity of operations which, as it were, "identify" the elements of the set in question.

how we can assert the following *two* propositions *perfectly consistently:*

1) The line and positive intervals in it are *infinitely divisible.*

2) The line and positive intervals in it are each a union of *indivisible* degenerate intervals.

We are now prepared to deal with the crux of our problem by using point-set theory to refute the second horn of Zeno's metrical dilemma.

§4. THE STATUS OF ZENO'S PARADOX OF EXTENSION

Since a positive interval is the union of a continuum of degenerate intervals,[43] we must now determine what meaning, *if any,* we can assign to "summing" the lengths of all these degenerate intervals with a view to obtaining the paradoxical value zero for the length of the total interval. The answer we shall give to this problem will not be *ad hoc,* since the reasoning on which it is based will not depend upon the particular lengths which Zenonians wish us to "compound" but rather on the fact that the number of lengths to be "added" is *not denumerable.*

Earlier, we determined the length of the union of a *finite* number of non-overlapping intervals of known lengths on the basis of these latter lengths. In addition, we made a corresponding determination of the length of the union of a *denumerable* infinity of non-overlapping intervals. If we now attempt to subdivide an interval into a *non-denumerable* infinity of non-overlapping intervals, we find that they *cannot be non-degenerate.* For Cantor has shown that any collection of positive non-overlapping intervals on a line is at most denumerably infinite.[44] It follows that the degenerate subintervals which are at the focus of our interest are the only kind

---

[43] The word "continuum" can designate either the ordering structure of the real numbers or their cardinality. The context will indicate which of these meanings is intended or whether both are jointly involved.

[44] G. Cantor, *Gesammelte Abhandlungen,* p. 153.

of non-overlapping subintervals of which there are non-denumerably many in a given interval. Quite naturally, therefore, they create a special situation. The latter is due to the fact that our theory does *not* assign any meaning to "forming the arithmetic sum," when we are attempting to "sum" a *super-denumerable* infinity of individual numbers (lengths)! This fact is independent of whether the individual numbers in such a non-denumerable set of numbers are zeros or finite cardinal numbers differing from zero.

Consequently, the theory under discussion cannot be deemed to be *ad hoc* for precluding the possibility of "adding," in Zenonian fashion, the zero lengths of the continuum of points which "compose" the interval (a, b) to obtain zero as the length of this interval. Though the finite interval (a, b) is the union of a continuum of degenerate subintervals, *we cannot meaningfully determine its length in our theory by "adding" the individual zero lengths of the degenerate subintervals.* We are here confronted with an instance in which set-theoretic addition (i.e., forming the union of degenerate subintervals) is meaningful while arithmetic addition (of their lengths) is not.

We have shown that the standard set-theoretical geometry here presented does not have the paradoxical feature of both assigning the non-zero length $b - a$ to the interval (a, b) *and* permitting the inference via the additivity of lengths that (a, b) must have zero length on the grounds that its points each have zero length. More precisely, we have shown that geometrical theory can consistently affirm the following four propositions simultaneously in the context of its rules of additivity for lengths:

1) The finite interval (a, b) is the union of a continuum of degenerate subintervals.

2) The length of each degenerate (sub)interval is 0.

3) The length of the interval (a, b) is given by the number $b - a$.

4) The length of an interval is not a function of its cardinality.

Our analysis has manifestly refuted the Zenonian allegation of inconsistency if made against the standard set-theoretical geometry.

The set-theoretical analysis of the various issues raised or suggested by Zeno's paradoxes of plurality has enabled me to give a *consistent* metrical account of an extended line segment as an aggregate of unextended points. Thus Zeno's mathematical paradoxes are avoided in the formal part of a geometry or chronometry built on Cantorean foundations. Given the aforementioned additivity rules for length of the standard mathematical theory, the consistency of the metrical analysis which I have given requires the *non-denumerability* of the infinite point-sets constituting the intervals on the line. Thus, if any infinite set of *rational* points were regarded as constituting an extended line segment, then the customary mathematical theory under consideration could assert the length of that merely denumerable point-set to be greater than zero only at the cost of permitting itself to become self-contradictory! For we saw that in the standard theory the length of an interval and the measure of a point-set are each countably additive. And hence if an interval (a, b) between the *rational* points a and b were claimed to consist *only* of the denumerable *rational* points between a and b, the following logical situation would result: The denumeration of this set of points coupled with the countable additivity of their zero lengths would permit the deduction that the length of (a, b) is (paradoxically) zero. This zero result is deducible without any reference at all to the congruences and unit of length furnished by a transported standard of length, which is extrinsic to (a, b). To emphasize the independence of this result from a length-standard extrinsic to (a, b), we can say that the *"intrinsic"* length of a denumerable "interval" of rational points is zero—similarly for the measure of such an "interval."[45]

It might seem that this conclusion concerning the fun-

---

[45] Cf. also H. Cramér, *Mathematical Methods of Statistics* [134], p. 25.

damental logical importance of non-denumerability could be criticized in the following way: The need for non-denumerably infinite point-sets to avoid metrical contradictions derives from the countable additivity of length and measure. Without these additivity rules, it would not have been possible to infer that the length and the measure of an enumerable point-set turn out to be *zero*. Consequently, by omitting these additivity rules, it would presumably have been possible to assign a finite length to certain enumerable sets without contradiction and to base physical theory on a denumerable geometry. Thus it might be argued that a non-denumerably infinite point-set is only unimportantly indispensable for consistency, since this indispensablity obtains only relatively to a formulation of the theory in which length and measure are countably additive.

To assess the merits of this objection, two points must first be noted:

1) The rejection of *countable* additivity for length and measure would entail incurring the loss of those portions of standard applied mathematics which depend on the presence of countable additivity in the foundations. Thus, for example, one would need to sacrifice some of the mathematics of Fourier series and of the eigenfunctions of quantum mechanics as well as of probability theory and statistics. For countably additive set functions enter into these branches of applied mathematics in one or another form via the Lebesgue integral, the Lebesgue measure, or the Lebesgue-Stieltjes integral.

2) Apart from being required for metrical consistency in the context of countable additivity, the super-denumerability of intervals is inherent in the assumption of the mathematical continuity of space and time and thus in everything that depends on this assumption in the theories of empirical science. Those who maintain that super-denumerably infinite point-sets are only quite unimportantly essential to physical theory are making a gratuitous claim and have so far given us nothing more than the *recommendation* to attempt to

erect the physics of space and time on *denumerable* foundations. For to substantiate their claim, they must demonstrate that the implementation of their recommendation is feasible by showing the following: At least one kind of mathematics which avoids Zeno's paradox by dispensing with countable additivity in the interest of postulating the denumerability of space and of time is fully as viable for empirical science as the standard mathematics used in actual physical theory.[46] But in the light of the physical considerations put forward in favor of countable additivity in [72] Chapter II, §2A, it is quite doubtful that physicists would acquiesce in its sacrifice. In this significant sense, Zeno's metrical paradox of extension does pose a challenge to theorists whose philosophical commitments do not allow them to avail themselves of super-denumerably infinite sets.

Proponents of Zeno's view might still argue that this *arithmetical* rebuttal, which appeals to the fact that arithmetic addition is not defined for a super-denumerable infinity of numbers, is unconvincing on purely geometric grounds, maintaining that if extension (space) is to be composed of elements, these must themselves be extended. Specifically, geometers such as Veronese objected[47] to Cantor that in the array of points on the line, their extensions are all, as it were, "summed geometrically" before us. And from this geometric perspective, it is not cogent, in their view, to suppose that even a super-denumerable infinity of unextended points would be able to sustain a positive interval, especially since the Cantorean theory can claim arithmetical consistency here only because of the obscurities that obligingly surround the meaning of the arithmetic "sum" of a super-denumerable infinity of numbers.

Is this objection to Cantor conclusive? I think not. Whence

---

[46] For doubts about the thesis that the warrant for the mathematical continuity of space and time is conventional rather than empirical, cf. my *Philosophical Problems of Space and Time* [139], pp. 334–336.

[47] See E. W. Hobson, *The Theory of Functions of a Real Variable*, 2nd edition, Vol. I (New York: Cambridge University Press, 1921), pp. 56–57.

does it derive its plausibility? It would seem that it achieves persuasiveness via a tacit appeal to a *pictorial* representation of the points of mathematical physics in which they are arrayed in the consecutive manner of beads on a string to form a line. But the properties that any such representation imaginatively attributes to points are not even allowed, let alone prescribed, by the formal postulates of geometric theory. The spuriousness of the difficulties adduced against the Cantorean conception of the line becomes apparent upon noting that not only the cardinality of its constituent points altogether eludes pictorialization but also their dense ordering: between any two points, there is an infinitude of others. Thus, in complete contrast to the discrete order of the beads on a string, *no* point is immediately adjacent to any other. The futility, irrelevance, and misleading effect of attempts to visualize the Cantorean interval structurally become apparent from the following: If we were to exclude one end-point of an initially closed interval from that interval, the now open "end" of that interval would *defy* pictorialization because of the non-existence of a point *next to* the excluded point.

These considerations show that from a genuinely geometric point of view, a physical interpretation of the formal postulates of geometry cannot be obtained by the inevitably misleading pictorialization of *individual* points of the theory. Instead, we can provide a physical interpretation quite unencumbered by the intrusion of the irrelevancies of visual space, if we associate *not* the term *"point"* but the term *"linear continuum of points"* of our theory with an appropriate body in nature. By a point of this body we then mean nothing more or less than an element of it possessing the formal properties prescribed for points by the postulates of geometry. And, on this interpretation, the ground is then cut from under the geometric *parti pris* against Cantor by the modern legatees of Zeno.

It has been overlooked in some quarters that the issues posed by Zeno's paradox of extension are no less important philosophically than are those raised by his paradoxes of motion. Two examples will illustrate that there has been insufficient appreciation of the philosophical lesson to be learned from the avoidance of Zeno's paradox of extension within the framework of the standard mathematical theory.

1) In his discussion of the mathematical theory of motion, Russell neglected the essential contribution made by the cardinality and ordinal structure of the linear Cantorean continuum toward the avoidance of Zeno's paradox of extension. This philosophical neglect of his is clear in the following passages:

> Mathematicians have distinguished different degrees of continuity, and have confined the word "continuous," for technical purposes, to series having a certain high degree of continuity. But for *philosophical* purposes, all that is important in continuity is introduced by the lowest degree of continuity, which is called "compactness" [i.e., denseness]. . . . What do we mean by saying that the motion is continuous? It is not necessary for our purposes to consider the whole of what the mathematician means by this statement: *Only part of what he means is philosophically important.* One part of what he means is that, if we consider any two positions of the speck occupied at any two instants, there will be other intermediate positions occupied at intermediate instants. . . .[48]

We know that the mere existence of the denseness property guarantees only a denumerably infinite point-set. But in the context of the standard mathematical additivity rules for length, a super-denumerably infinite point-set is required by the demands of metrical consistency. And it could be reasonably maintained that the *physical relevance* of the metrical concept of length requires its countable additivity. Hence in this sense there are *philosophical* reasons for requiring a higher degree of continuity than is ensured by the denseness property alone.

2) The Greeks certainly were *not* led to the discovery of

---

[48] B. Russell, *Our Knowledge of the External World* [100], pp. 144, 146, my italics.

incommensurable magnitudes by merely *operationally* carrying out the iterative transport of measuring sticks.[49] And it is impossible to show by direct physical operations alone that there are hypotenuses whose length cannot be represented by any rational number. For the limits of experimental accuracy and the denseness of the rational points guarantee that we can never claim anything but a rational result on the strength of operational accuracy alone. A radical operationist approach to geometry might therefore suggest that this science be constructed so as to use only the system of rational points.[50] The analysis given in this chapter has aimed to show that in the absence of a denumerable alternative to the standard mathematical theory which is demonstrably viable for the purposes of physics, such an operationist approach to geometry and to the theoretical measurables of physics must be rejected on logical grounds.[51]

[49] For the historical details, see K. von Fritz, "The Discovery of Incommensurability by Hippasus of Metapontum," *Annals of Mathematics*, XLVI (1945).

[50] Cf. the approximative geometry of J. Hjelmslev ("Die natürliche Geometrie," *Abhandlungen aus dem mathematischen Seminar der Hamburger Universität*, Vol. II [1923], pp. 1ff.) and Weyl's comments on it (H. Weyl, *Philosophy of Mathematics and Natural Science* [130], pp. 143–144).

[51] In §3 (pp. 336–338), G. J. Massey, "Toward a Clarification of Grünbaum's Conception of an Intrinsic Metric," *Philosophy of Science*, XXXVI (1969), pp. 331–345, offers some criticisms of the formulation of the thesis of this chapter. For a discussion of these criticisms, see A. Grünbaum, "Reply to Critiques, and Critical Exposition," *Philosophy of Science*, XXXVII (1970), forthcoming.

Modern Science and Zeno's Paradoxes of Motion

ADOLF GRÜNBAUM

In his book *Philosophy of Mathematics and Natural Science*, the renowned mathematical physicist Hermann Weyl raised the following question: Is it *kinematically* feasible that a machine carry out an *infinite* sequence of distinct operations in a finite time? And he gave a conditional answer to it as follows: If a machine obeying the principles of classical kinematics cannot carry out a denumerable infinity of operations in a finite time, then the received interpretation of

The Introduction and Part I, "The Zenonian Runners," are taken from "Can an Infinitude of Operations Be Performed in a Finite Time?" to be included as a chapter in a forthcoming collection of Monday Lectures delivered at the University of Chicago, to be published by the University of Chicago Press; also published in the *British Journal for the Philosophy of Science*, XX, No. 2 (October, 1969). Reprinted by permission of the University of Chicago and the author. Part II, "The Infinity Machines," and Part III, "Zeno's Paradoxes of Motion and Standard Quantum Mechanics," are taken from *Modern Science and Zeno's Paradoxes*, British edition (London: George Allen & Unwin Ltd., 1968), chap. 2. Reprinted by permission. The original footnote numbering of these three selections has been retained.

the classical mathematical theory of motion is beset by one of Zeno's kinematical paradoxes. Thus, Weyl refers to Achilles' task of traversing a unit space interval by successively traversing the infinite series of decreasing subintervals of lengths

$$\tfrac{1}{2}, \tfrac{1}{4}, \tfrac{1}{8}, \tfrac{1}{16}, \ldots \frac{1}{2^n} \ldots (n = 1, 2, 3, \ldots).$$

And Weyl writes:

> The remark that the successive partial sums . . . of the series . . . do not increase beyond all bounds but converge to 1, by which one nowadays thinks to dispose of the paradox, is certainly relevant and elucidating. Yet, if the segment of length 1 really consists of infinitely many subsegments of lengths $\tfrac{1}{2}, \tfrac{1}{4}, \tfrac{1}{8}, \ldots$, as of "chopped-off" wholes, then it is incompatible with the character of the infinite as the "incompletable" that Achilles should have been able to traverse them all. If one admits this possibility, then there is no reason why a machine should not be capable of completing an infinite sequence of distinct acts of decision within a finite amount of time; say, by supplying the first result after $\tfrac{1}{2}$ minute, the second after another $\tfrac{1}{4}$ minute, the third $\tfrac{1}{8}$ minute later than the second, etc. In this way it would be possible, provided the receptive power of the brain would function similarly, to achieve a traversal of all natural numbers and thereby a sure yes-or-no decision regarding any existential question about natural numbers!

Weyl's contention has generated a literature alleging the kinematic absurdity of hypothetical machines which are presumed to be capable of carrying out an infinite sequence of operations *in a finite time*. Hereafter I shall often speak of $\aleph_0$ operations instead of saying "an infinite sequence of operations." These so-called "infinity machines" have included a device that would print *all* of the digits of an infinite decimal on a finite strip of paper, a machine that would recite the names of all the natural numbers in a suitable code, a lamp that would be switched on and off $\aleph_0$ times, and a device that would transfer a marble back and forth $\aleph_0$ times.

Charges of paradox have been leveled against infinity machines by such various authors as G. J. Whitrow, M. Black, C. S. Chihara, and J. F. Thomson.[1] Their allegations of absurdity pertain to the distinctively kinematical aspects of the $\aleph_0$ operations which are to be executed. Hence the physiological, chemical, electrical or other feasibility of the $\aleph_0$ operations will not be at issue, unless it has a bearing on the assessment of their kinematic possibility. But if there are physiological, electrical or other *non*-kinematic grounds for deeming the infinity machines to be physically or technically impossible, is it then not an idle exercise to inquire whether they are *kinematically* paradoxical? I think not. Of course, I grant instantly that such an inquiry may not be productive for engineering. But I hope to show that it is indeed illuminating with respect to the kinematical component of the class of physical theories which assert the mathematical continuity of space and time, as relativity theory does, for example. Even standard quantum theory employs continuous space and time variables, although it has, of course, repudiated the well-defined particle trajectories of Newtonian and relativistic mechanics.

In this paper, I shall offer an *affirmative* though *multiply-qualified* answer to Weyl's question concerning the performability of $\aleph_0$ operations in a finite time. But I shall endeavor to show that Weyl's own mildly conditional affirmative answer is too strong, viz., his claim that if the unit interval traversed by Achilles in unit time "really consists" of $\aleph_0$ geometrically decreasing subintervals, then a machine must be able to complete an infinite sequence of "distinct acts of decision" (e.g., calculations).

It will turn out that the fundamental kinematic issues posed by Weyl's contention can be confronted by comparing

[1] For details, see my book *Modern Science and Zeno's Paradoxes*, Chapter II, §4, and my article "Are 'Infinity Machines' Paradoxical?" [67].

the motion of Achilles, who runs *continuously* at an average unit velocity, with the motion of another runner who is presumed to traverse the same unit space interval in the same unit time but runs *intermittently* as follows: he interrupts his motion by $\aleph_0$ pauses of rest whose successive durations have the following geometrically decreasing magnitudes:

$$\tfrac{1}{4}, \tfrac{1}{8}, \tfrac{1}{16}, \tfrac{1}{32}, \ldots,$$

and so on ad infinitum. Thus, the latter intermittent motion, which I shall call the *"staccato"* run, will serve as our prototype of the $\aleph_0$ operations which are to be executed by the infinity machines in a finite time.

Preparatory to inquiring whether the *staccato* run is beset by kinematic absurdities, I must explain in detail my reasons for denying Zeno's charge of paradox against the mathematical description of Achilles' *uninterrupted* motion through a unit space interval. I shall refer to Achilles' smooth run as the *"legato"* motion in order to distinguish it from the intermittent motion of his *staccato* running mate. And for our entirely nonhistorical purposes, I take Zeno's challenge to be the following: Kinematic theory tells us convincingly enough that a *legato* runner moving with average unit velocity can traverse a unit space interval in unit time. But, this theory *also* asserts that Achilles' *legato* run involves, among other things, an *infinite* sequence of submotions through a progression of non-overlapping spatial subintervals of respective lengths $\tfrac{1}{2}, \tfrac{1}{4}, \tfrac{1}{8}, \ldots$, and so on. It is true that the successive *durations* of these submotions can be such as to form a sequence which suitably converges to zero. Nonetheless, Zeno continues, the *legato* motion cannot be completed in a finite time, since the theory tells us that the elapsing of a unit time interval involves the successive elapsing of an *endless* progression of subintervals. And he contends that kinematics thereby contradicts itself, because its *unending* sequences of submotions render the *completion* of any motion *temporally unintelligible*.

I. The
Zenonian Runners

THE LEGATO RUN

In honor of Zeno, let us apply the name "Z-sequence" to an infinite progression of intervals of space or time whose successive magnitude are $\frac{1}{2}, \frac{1}{4}, \frac{1}{8}, \ldots$, and so on. For the sake of arithmetic simplicity, I shall follow Zeno's procedure and assume that the successive *durations* of the *legato* runner's submotions form a Z-sequence just as the subintervals of space which are covered by these submotions. Thus, it is being assumed that the *legato* runner's *average* velocity is unity in each of the $\aleph_0$ subintervals traversed by him up to the terminal instant of his motion. But we shall see later in our discussion of the *staccato* run that this *constancy* of the average velocity makes for a kinematically dubious discontinuity in the velocity function at the terminal instant. Fortunately, the *legato* runner can alternatively be assumed to run such that his velocity function yields average velocities in the subintervals that converge to zero at the terminal instant. But let us disregard this arithmetically more complicated *legato* motion until we discuss the *staccato* run. And let us furthermore adopt the terminology used by Vlastos[2] and refer to the traversal of any of the spatial *sub*intervals of our Z-sequence as "making a Z-run." Vlastos notes that as commonly used, the term "run" individuates uniquely the physical action to which it applies, much as "heart-beat" does. And he points out that in *this* sense of "run," the runner's *legato* traversal of the Z-sequence could only be described as a *single* run and not as having involved a denumerable infinity of "Z-runs." But clearly, in order to traverse the unit interval in one smooth and uninterrupted "run" in the ordinary sense, the runner must—among other things—traverse all the members of the Z-sequence and, in the latter sense, make $\aleph_0$ Z-"runs." To distinguish between these two quite

[2] See G. Vlastos, "Zeno's Race Course" [29].

different uses of the noun "run," Vlastos writes "run$_a$" for the single motion which we can perceive with our unaided senses in daily life contexts, and "run$_b$" for the kind relevant to the Z-sequence of kinematics.

Human awareness of time exhibits a positive threshold or minimum. This fact can now be seen to have a consequence of fundamental relevance to the appraisal of Zeno's argument. For it entails that *none* of the infinitely many temporal subintervals in the progression whose magnitude is less than the human *minimum perceptibilium* can be *individually experienced as elapsing* in a way that does *metrical* justice to its actual lesser duration. To succeed, the attempted individual *contemplation* of all the subintervals would require a denumerable infinity of mental acts, each of which requires or exceeds a positive minimum duration. *Thus, we do not experience these subintervals individually as elapsing in a metrically faithful way. Instead, we gain our metrical impression of duration in this context from the time needed by our mental acts of contemplation and not from the respective duration numbers which we associate intellectually with the contemplated subintervals when performing these mental acts.* And the resulting compelling feeling that an infinite time is actually needed to accomplish the traversal in turn insinuates the deducibility of this paradoxical result from the theory of motion. Specifically, the existence of a duration-threshold of time awareness guarantees that there is a *positive lower bound* on the duration of any run$_a$. And this fact enters into several of the following fallacies here committed by Zeno in his so-called Dichotomy paradox:

1) Zeno's claim that the progression of Z-runs$_b$ requires an infinite future time is made plausible by a tacit appeal to our awareness that $\aleph_0$ runs$_a$ would indeed last forever, because there is a positive lower bound on the duration of any run$_a$. The threshold governing our acts of awareness likewise induces the feeling that after the first instant of the motion, a unique next event must happen in the motion *and* that there must be a unique next-to-the-last event that happens before

the final instant of the motion, if there is to be a final instant at all. But since the successive subintervals converge to zero by decreasing geometrically, the threshold-governed one-by-one contemplation which Zeno invites cannot be metrically faithful to the actual physical durations of the contemplated subintervals. And our intuitive time awareness rightly boggles at *experiencing* each of $\aleph_0$ subintervals of time as elapsing individually. But, justified though it is, Zeno *illicitly* trades on this boggling. For it cannot detract from the following crucial fact: *any and every* one of the $\aleph_0$ temporal subintervals of the motion is over by the end of one unit of time. To see this, note that for *every n*, the sum of the first *n* terms of the geometric series of duration numbers

$$\tfrac{1}{2}, \tfrac{1}{4}, \tfrac{1}{8}, \ldots, \frac{1}{2^n}$$

is given by a total duration less than 1, namely by the sum

$$S_n = 1 - (\tfrac{1}{2})^n \ (n = 1, 2, 3, \ldots).$$

And note further that here I have invoked the undisputed fact that the clock-measures of time intervals are *finitely additive* to claim that one unit of time is the least upper bound on the total duration of all the $\aleph_0$ subintervals of the motion. It follows that both distributively and *collectively* all $\aleph_0$ temporal subintervals of the motion elapse within one unit of time. The justification for this conclusion becomes further apparent upon becoming cognizant of the next error, by which Zeno buttresses his conclusion that the runner would *never* reach his destination.

2) With respect to the relation of temporal precedence, the set comprising the temporal subintervals of the progression *and* the instant of the runner's arrival at his destination has the form of an *infinite* progression *followed* by a last element. And this ordered set is said to be of ordinal type $\omega + 1$. Furthermore, the instant of the runner's arrival at his destination point 1 does *not* belong to *any* of the temporal subintervals of the progression. Thus, the closed time interval required by the runner's completed motion consists of all

the instants belonging to any of the subintervals of the progression *and* of the instant of arrival at the point 1: by failing to include the instant of arrival, the membership of the subintervals of the progression fails to exhaust the entire membership of the closed time interval required by the completed motion. Indeed, the union of the subintervals of the progression constitutes a half-open time interval precisely because it fails to include the terminal instant of the motion.

Zeno illicitly exploits the fact that it is *logically* impossible for the *terminal* instant of the motion to belong to any of the subintervals of the unending progression, since it is *later* than all of them. Zeno appeals to this fact to infer wrongly that *there cannot be* any terminal instant at which the runner reaches his destination. Once we have become victimized by our threshold of time awareness, we are set up to commit this otherwise transparent fallacy. In this way, Zeno seeks to lend further credence to his claim that the union of the subintervals of the progression is of infinite duration. But what can be deduced from the logical impossibility of finding the terminal instant in any of the subintervals forming the unending progression? The failure of the terminal instant to belong to the union of the $\aleph_0$ subintervals amounts to no more than that this instant is not to be found in the half-open time interval which has been left half open by *excluding the terminal instant;* the half-openness of the resulting time interval does *not* show that the union of the temporal subintervals must be of infinite *duration* just because that union has no terminal instant, and just because the infinite progression of subintervals has no last member. For the terminal instant is the *earliest* instant *following every* instant belonging to *any* subinterval of the unending progression, while the durations of these subintervals suitably converge to zero. The nonexistence in the progression of a last subinterval during which the motion would be completed does not preclude the existence of an instant later than all the subintervals which is the last instant of the motion.

In the case of Zeno's arithmetically simple example, this state of affairs expresses itself *arithmetically* in the following compound way:

1) If the runner departs at $t = 0$, then corresponding to the nonexistence of a last temporal subinterval of the motion in the progression, the respective times by which he has traversed the successive subintervals of the Z-sequence are given by the *infinite* sequence

$$\frac{1}{2}, \frac{3}{4}, \frac{7}{8}, \frac{15}{16}, \frac{31}{32}, \ldots, \frac{2^n - 1}{2^n}, \ldots \qquad (n = 1, 2, 3, \ldots).$$

2) Although the number 1 is not a member of this infinite sequence of time numbers, the arithmetic limit of this infinite sequence on the number axis is constituted by the number 1, which is the time coordinate of the last instant of the motion and represents the total duration of the union of the subintervals belonging to the progression.

3) The runner traverses ever shorter subintervals of the unit racecourse in proportionately ever shorter subintervals of time, thereby traveling at constant average speed.

What then are we to think of the charge that the arithmetic theory of limits has been lifted uncritically out of the context of its legitimate application to physical *space* and adduced irrelevantly in an effort to refute Zeno's allegations of *temporal* paradox? We saw that the mathematical apparatus of the theory of limits is ordinally and metrically no less appropriate to physical time than it is to physical space. Note that I have *not* invoked the *arithmetical* theory of limits *as such* to dismiss the allegation that kinematical theory entails *temporal* paradoxes. Instead, my contention has been that we are *justified* by the ordinal and metrical structure of physical time in applying that arithmetical theory *and* that Zeno's specific deductions of metrical contradictions in the Dichotomy paradox are each vitiated by fallacies which I am engaged in pointing out.[3]

---

[3] In the wake of Zeno, A. N. Whitehead, W. James and others have claimed that the elements of time must succeed one another *discretely* and hence cannot intelligibly possess the denseness property of the linear mathematical

The highly misleading role played by Zeno's one-by-one contemplation of the members of his progression becomes conspicuous upon noting the following fact: *It would even take us forever to contemplate one by one the progression of DURATIONLESS instants which divide one temporal sub-interval from the next, and yet the durational measure of this progression of instants is ZERO within standard physical theory!* By the same token, the fact that our contemplation of the $\aleph_0$ subintervals would last forever is not a basis for concluding that the union of the progression of them would be of infinite duration. In summary, Zeno would have us infer that the runner can *never* reach his destination, just because (1) in a finite time, we could not possibly contemplate one by one *all* the subintervals of the progression, and (2) for purely *logical* reasons, we could not possibly find the terminal instant of the motion in *any* of the $\aleph_0$ subintervals of the progression, since the terminal instant is not a member of any of them. But it is altogether fallacious to infer Zeno's conclusion of infinite duration from these two premises.

The recent literature on Zeno continues to provide illustrations of the intellectual havoc resulting from an irrelevant *though tacit* appeal to the fact that there is a positive lower bound on the duration of any single mental act of ours such as *conscious counting*. Thus, G. J. Whitrow seems to have engaged in precisely such an unwitting appeal in his endeavor to show that the mathematical continuity which we attribute to finite intervals of space cannot similarly be attributed to physical time without thereby generating logical antinomies. After stating that "We must not assume that . . . in *time*, any infinite sequence of operations can be performed,"[4] Whitrow considers the consequences of assuming that our *legato* runner passes through the entire progression

---

continuum, which requires that between *any* two instants, there exists at least one other. I must refer to my *Modern Science and Zeno's Paradoxes*, Chapter II, §2, B and C for a statement of my reasons for rejecting this contention.

[4] G. J. Whitrow, *The Natural Philosophy of Time* [119], p. 148.

of positions envisaged by Zeno as the respective termini of his subintervals. Whitrow invites us to assume that in so doing, the runner would *number* all these positions consecutively and concludes that then the runner's task would involve exhausting "the infinite set of positive integers by counting."[5] Thus Whitrow conjures up the image of conscious counting in a manner akin to Zeno's illicit appeal to the eternity of one-by-one contemplation in the Dichotomy. But it is wrong to identify the metrical features of the process of conscious counting (say, in English) with those of traversing Zeno's progression of points in a finite interval. For we must not allow our human psycho-neurophysiology of time awareness to intrude itself and to victimize us in this mathematically most misleading way.

We recall that Zeno's *legato* runner requires $\frac{1}{2}$ unit of time to traverse the first $\frac{1}{2}$ of the unit space interval, $\frac{1}{4}$ unit of time to traverse the next $\frac{1}{4}$ of the distance, $\frac{1}{8}$ unit of time for the next $\frac{1}{8}$ of the distance, and so on. Let us now examine the different motion of the *staccato* runner, who departs simultaneously and runs on an equal and parallel racetrack.

Our description of the *staccato* run so far did not specify the magnitudes of the successive distances traversed by the *staccato* runner during the times allotted to his intermittent runs. For the sake of arithmetic simplicity, I shall first treat the *staccato* run by taking the successive distances to be proportional to the times of the intermittent runs by a factor of 2. Thus all $\aleph_0$ intermittent motions of the *staccato* runner are first assumed to proceed at the *same* average velocity. But our assessment of the kinematic feasibility of the *staccato* run will *not* be made to rest on the arithmetically simple

[5] In here using everyday words such as *doing* and *things* in technical contexts, we are fully alerted against such confusions as misidentifying a run$_b$ as a run$_a$ no less than when we use technical terms such as *work* and *energy* in physics. We need to use language to describe the physical process constituting the *legato* runner's traversal of the total interval. And in determining whether this process can occur in a finite time, as described, we need to heed the commitments of ordinary language only to the extent of guarding against being victimized or stultified by them.

case of constant average velocity, any more than in the case of the *legato* run. For we shall see that this simple case involves the following kinematically problematic feature: at the terminal instant of the runner's arrival at his final destination, his velocity exhibits a *finite* discontinuity. Hence after having treated this arithmetically simple case, I shall be concerned to note that alternatively, the *intermittent* runs of the *staccato* runner no less than the uninterrupted sequence of *legato* runs could demonstrably proceed at *suitably decreasing* average velocities so as *not* to exhibit any kind of discontinuity. In this way, the *staccato* run will turn out to be just as unproblematic kinematically as the *legato* run.

Having entered this caution, I shall first confine my attention entirely to the arithmetically simple case.

THE STACCATO RUN

By contrast to the *legato* runner, his *staccato* mate is required to traverse each subinterval of the Z-sequence in half the time needed by the *legato* runner and then to wait for the latter to catch up with him before traversing the next Z-interval. Specifically, the *staccato* runner takes $\frac{1}{4}$ of a unit of time to traverse the first Z-interval of length $\frac{1}{2}$ and rests for an equal amount of time; then he takes $\frac{1}{8}$ of a unit of time to traverse the second Z-interval of length $\frac{1}{4}$ and rests for an equal amount of time, and so on ad infinitum. Thus, the *staccato* runner interrupts his motion by $\aleph_0$ pauses of rest whose successive durations are

$$\frac{1}{4}, \frac{1}{8}, \frac{1}{16}, \frac{1}{32}, \dots.$$

And he suspends his motion at each of his Z-stops just long enough to enable his *legato* colleague Achilles to catch up with him. It might *appear* quite legitimate to require the *staccato* runner to plant a flag at each of his Z-stops while he pauses at them and awaits his friend Achilles. Indeed, even the *legato* runner Achilles has been called upon in the literature to engage in flag-planting at each of the progression of points terminating the subintervals of the Z-sequence on his track. This demand has been addressed to the *legato* runner on Zeno's behalf in the recent literature, notwithstanding the fact that Achilles spends only a mathematical instant of zero duration at each of the specified space points while running uninterruptedly.

But if the *staccato* runner is to carry out the $\aleph_0$ operations of starting and stopping during a finite time, kinematic theory will not allow him to carry out the $\aleph_0$ operations of planting a flag at each of the designated Z-stops. To see this, note first that the erection of a flag at each of the $\aleph_0$ Z-stops would presumably require the *staccato* runner to translate his own limbs and rotate the flag *each* time into the vertical direction through a minimum positive distance, however small. And in that case, the *staccato* runner would have to perform $\aleph_0$ upward (or downward) *equal* minimal spatial displacements during ever shorter times at boundlessly increasing average velocities. Thus, he would have to effect a *spatially infinite* total displacement of his own limbs and of the flags during a finite time in the following manner: the successive *maximum* vertical velocities of his limbs required to erect the flags consecutively in ever shorter times would *increase boundlessly* with time up to the instant $t = 1$ at which *he comes to rest* at his destination, since the successive average velocities would have to increase boundlessly. But such a motion has two kinematically objectionable features: (a) at the instant $t = 1$ of arrival at the destination point P, the motion of his hands violates the requirement that the *position* of a body be a continuous function of the time, since the vertical position of a point on either hand does not approach any limit as $t \rightarrow 1$, and (b) at the terminal instant $t = 1$, the fluctuating *velocity* function of his hands has an instant of *infinite discontinuity*, since that velocity function is unbounded in every earlier neighborhood of the terminal instant.

By contrast, if he is *not* required to plant any flags, then at $t = 1$, the (vertical and horizontal) *position* of a point on the *staccato* runner's hands or feet is a continuous function of time, and his horizontal velocity will fluctuate only between zero and some fixed finite maximum value so as to yield an *average* two units for his intermittent horizontal motions. But since this *average* horizontal velocity maintains the *same* positive value up to the terminal instant of rest, the successive *peak* velocities cannot fall below this positive value and *cannot* converge to zero. Hence in this arithmetically simple example, the continuity of the horizontal position at the terminal instant $t = 1$ obtains alongside the following discontinuity: the horizontal velocity function exhibits an instant of *finite* discontinuity at $t = 1$, just as the graph of a step function has points of finite discontinuity. Moreover, since there is a minimum velocity change (from zero to the average) during each of the $\aleph_0$ *ever shorter* time intervals, the horizontal *accelerations* increase (and decrease) boundlessly as $t \to 1$, and the acceleration function has an instant of infinite discontinuity at the terminal instant of rest-and-zero-acceleration.

Thus, we see that the requirement to plant a flag $\aleph_0$ times at the Z-stops calls for a kinematically forbidden discontinuity in the vertical position along with an infinite discontinuity in the vertical velocity. On the other hand, the execution of the $\aleph_0$ start-and-stop operations of the *staccato* run without flag-planting requires no discontinuity in the position. But if we demand that all the *staccato* motions proceed at the same average velocity, then this run involves a finite discontinuity in the horizontal velocity along with an infinite discontinuity in the horizontal acceleration.

It is clear, therefore, that the flag-planting is ruled out kinematically. But in view of the remaining discontinuities in the horizontal velocity and acceleration, our arithmetically simple kind of *staccato* and *legato* runs may well be kinematically problematic. As far as I know, books on classical or prequantum mechanics do not spell out whether motions involving these particular discontinuities are kinematically possible or not.

If the specified discontinuities in the horizontal velocity

and acceleration are *not* impermissible, then it can now be shown to follow that the arithmetically simple *staccato* run is no less feasible kinematically than the corresponding *legato* motion. And in that case, the arithmetically simple *staccato* run can be consummated simultaneously with the *legato* run.

To see this, note that in the arithmetically simple case, the *staccato* runner at no time lags behind his *legato* colleague during the closed unit interval but is either ahead of him or abreast of him. While running within each of the Z-intervals, the *staccato* runner's average velocity is twice that of his *legato* colleague, but his overall average velocity for the total interval is equal to his colleague's velocity and is less than the velocity of light *in vacuo*. And if the aforementioned *finite* discontinuity in the horizontal velocity of the runners at $t = 1$ is not kinematically impermissible, then we can conclude the following: if the *legato* runner reaches his destination in 1 unit of time after traversing the Z-sequence, then so also does the *staccato* runner.

There *may*, of course, be specifically *dynamical*—as distinct from kinematical—difficulties in effecting the infinitude of horizontal accelerations and decelerations required by the *staccato* runner's alternate starting and stopping. Indeed, calculation shows[6] that the total energy (work) expended by that runner in imparting the same average velocity to his body $\aleph_0$ times is *infinite*. Thus, the runner would have required an infinite store of energy when he set out on his run. For he sustains $\aleph_0$ *uncompensated* losses of kinetic energy in the decelerations, and the total magnitude of these losses is infinite. The availability of an infinite amount of energy is a matter of the *de facto* dynamical boundary conditions of the world, or at least, not a matter of kinematical law.

Fortunately, as Richard Friedberg has pointed out,[7] the intermittent runs no less than the uninterrupted sequence of *legato* runs can each proceed at suitably decreasing average

[6] Cf. A. Grünbaum, "Are 'Infinity Machines' Paradoxical?" [67], p. 401.

[7] Private communication from Professor Richard Friedberg of the Department of Physics at Columbia University.

velocities such that each runner's velocity, acceleration (and *all* of the higher time-derivatives as well) vary continuously throughout the closed unit time interval during which he traverses a unit distance. Thus, Friedberg's version of the *legato* and *staccato* runs obviates all of the kinematically and dynamically problematic features of the arithmetically simple example. In particular, the successive *peak* velocities and accelerations attained by Friedberg's *staccato* runner during the decreasing subintervals converge to zero as we approach the terminal instant.[8] In the case of Friedberg's *legato* and *staccato* runs we can therefore conclude without qualification that the *staccato* run is no less feasible

[8] More specifically, let $K = \sum\limits_{n=0}^{n=\infty} e^{-n^2}$, which equals about 1.38. Then

Richard Friedberg's $\aleph_0$ intermittent runs cover the successive distances

$\dfrac{e^{-n^2}}{K}$ ($n = 1, 2, 3, \ldots$). He lets

$$g\,(x) = e^{-csc^2 \pi x} \text{ for } 0 < x < 1$$

and

$$g\,(x) = 0 \text{ for } x \geq 1 \text{ or } x \leq 0.$$

And he notes that the function g and all of its derivatives are continuous for all real values of x.

Upon putting $\quad I \equiv \displaystyle\int_0^1 g(t)dt = \int_0^1 e^{-csc^2 \pi t}dt,$

he lets the *legato* runner have a velocity

$$v_l = \frac{g(t)}{I}\ .$$

It is then obvious that the distance $\displaystyle\int_0^1 v_l dt$ covered by the *legato* runner during the unit time interval is *one* unit.

Friedberg requires the *staccato* runner to run at the velocity

$$v_s = \frac{1}{IK} \sum_{n=0}^{n=\infty} 2^{n+2} \cdot g(2^{n+2}\,[t - 1 + 2^{-n}])\, e^{-n^2}$$

which has the following properties: (a) *all* of the infinitely many terms of this sum vanish during all those time intervals when the *staccato* runner is required to rest, and (b) during the time of the nth intermittent run (beginning with $n = 0$), the positive velocity function v_s is given entirely by the nth term, kinematically than the *legato* motion and that both are indeed kinematically possible.

This conclusion has the following important consequence: Given that the pauses separating the individual traversals carried out by the *staccato* runner form a geometric progression whose terms converge to zero, it is *immaterial* to the traversability of the total unit interval in a finite time that the process of traversal consists of $\aleph_0$ motions separated by pauses of rest (as in the *staccato* run) instead of being one uninterrupted motion which *can be analyzed* into an infinite number of submotions (as in the *legato* run). And if we wish to call the *staccato* runner's execution of the $\aleph_0$ *separate* motions "doing infinitely many things," then his performance shows that infinitely many things can be done in a finite time. Of course, if the pauses between the individual traversals of the *staccato* run were all *equal*, then this run could not be carried out in a finite time, no matter how small each of the equal pauses might be.

In view of the thresholds which govern the physiological reaction times of the *staccato* runner and his times of *conscious* execution of a set of instructions, it is clear that this runner cannot be "programmed" to perform the *staccato*

---

since all the other terms of the sum from $n = 0$ to $n = \infty$ vanish for that time interval.

The minimum value 1 of $\csc^2 \pi x$ is yielded by $x = \frac{1}{2}$, so that the maximum value of $g(x)$ is given by $g(\frac{1}{2})$, which is $\frac{1}{e}$. Since the maximum value $g(\frac{1}{2})$ corresponds to the *temporal* midpoint of the nth intermittent run, the peak value P_n of v_s during the nth intermittent run occurs at its temporal midpoint. Hence Friedberg concludes that in the case of the velocity function v_s, the successive peaks in the intermittent runs (beginning with $n = 0$) are

$$P_n = \frac{2^{n+2}}{Kele^{n^2}}$$

and converge to zero. And he shows that the distance $\int_0^1 v_s dt$ traversed by the *staccato* runner during the unit time interval is likewise 1. The *staccato* runner moves and rests intermittently for the required geometrically decreasing times. But he gets ahead of the *legato* runner, who first catches up with him at $t = 1$, though Friedberg notes that the use of a more complicated formula would allow the *legato* runner to catch up as well at the earlier times $\frac{1}{2}, \frac{3}{4}, \ldots$, as in the simplest example.

run in accord with the required metrical specifications, when the times during which he is to run or rest become small enough to fall below his thresholds. But this fact does not vitiate my contention that, in principle, kinematically the *staccato* run as described is physically possible. For kinematic theory allows us to assume that a body's separate motions have the prescribed metrical properties.

In claiming to have shown that the *staccato* run is kinematically feasible, I have, of course, *not* offered a formal consistency proof of kinematic theory as supplemented by the description of the *staccato* run. It seems to me that instead, we can reasonably be content with the following kind of "proof" that the *staccato* run is kinematically possible: a demonstration that the alleged deducibility of the paradoxical *infinite* duration is unfounded and that, given the kinematical principles of the theory along with the boundary conditions, the theory entails the *finitude* of the total duration of the *staccato* run.

We have been mindful of *ruling out* any flag-planting or other marking processes that would require *any* discontinuous change in any of the three position coordinates of the *staccato* runner's limbs. But the *staccato* runner can be held to have "marked" each one of a progression of space points by the act of stopping at each one for the prescribed length of time. If I may presume that this waiting at the stops qualifies as "marking" them, then the *staccato* runner's total motion constitutes an important counterexample to one of the theses recently put forward by C. S. Chihara as part of his critical response to Weyl's comparison of the Z-run with the performance of an infinity machine. Chihara believes that for *logical* reasons the difference between Achilles' mere *legato* traversal of the interval and a runner's marking all the end points of the subintervals in the course of his journey makes for the difference between completability in a finite time and requiring an infinite time. He says:

> ... to give a more intuitive characterization of the difference between Achilles' journey and Achilles' task of marking the end points, in the former case we start with the task and

analyze it into an infinite sequence of stages, whereas in the latter case we start with the stages and define the task as that of completing the infinite sequence of stages. To complete the journey, one must simply perform a task which can be analyzed ad infinitum, but to complete the task of marking all the end points, one must really do an infinite number of things.[9]

But as we saw, the *staccato* runner does "really do an infinite number of things" in what is kinematically a demonstrably *finite* time. It would appear that here Chihara has misdiagnosed the source of the difference between completability in a finite time and requiring an infinite time. The *staccato* run is *not* one uninterrupted motion which can be merely *analyzed* into a particular infinite set of submotions, as in the case of the *legato* run. Instead it consists of $\aleph_0$ motions separated by pauses of rest. And yet kinematically it is physically possible to complete it in a finite time in the context of classical physics.

We had to rule out the successive planting of $\aleph_0$ flags by the *staccato* runner as kinematically impossible, because it would involve a discontinuity in the position function. It turns out that in the case of all the other infinity machines mentioned at the outset, we must likewise predicate the assertion of their kinematic possibility on their at least *not* involving an illicit discontinuity in the position function.

II. The
Infinity Machines

1. THE π-MACHINE

The putative process of this machine is to print *all* the digits 3.1415926535 . . . constituting the infinite decimal representation of π such that the first digit is printed in $\frac{1}{2}$ of a minute, the second in $\frac{1}{4}$ of a minute, the third in $\frac{1}{8}$ of a

[9] C. S. Chihara, "On the Possibility of Completing an Infinite Process" [60], p. 86.

minute, and so on. We disregard here whether an infinite time might not be required for the more complicated process by which this progression of digits might first have been *computed seriatim* via, say, Archimedes' method of exhaustion for determining the area of a unit circle. For it suffices for our purposes that a progression of digits is to be printed as described, and, if necessary, these digits may be any digits whatever. Furthermore these $\aleph_0$ numerals might all have been inserted *simultaneously* into the printing press in a spatial arrangement to be discussed below. I shall refer to any such process as "the π-printing" and to the hypothetical printing press executing it as the "π-machine." And our problem will be to determine the conditions, IF ANY, under which the π-printing could be completed in 1 minute.

2. THE PEANO MACHINE

Let a mechanical device capable of reciting the sequence of natural numbers $n = 1, 2, 3, \ldots$ depart from the leftmost point 1 and move continuously to the right through a unit interval in 1 minute to the point 0. Now focus on the progression of points $\frac{1}{n}$ $(n = 1, 2, 3, \ldots)$ within that interval, a progression which contains the point 1 but *not* the point 0. And suppose that the device might perform recitations as follows: For every one of these points $\frac{1}{n}$ $(n = 1, 2, 3, \ldots)$, when reaching that point it begins to recite the number n and completes the recitation of n by the time it arrives at the next point in the progression. Thus, for every natural number n, the device takes $\frac{1}{n} - \frac{1}{n+1}$ of a minute to recite it. But in so doing, it does *not* employ the English noises which name the natural numbers; instead it employs a sequence of names whose successive lengths are governed by a restriction to be discussed below. I shall refer to this traveling number-reciting device as "the Peano machine." Our problem will be whether the prescribed names of all the natural numbers will have been recited when the Peano machine reaches the point 0 after 1 minute. By answering this question, we shall also have appraised Whitrow's afore-mentioned contention that his runner cannot exhaust all the positive integers by counting "however fast he counts."

3. THE THOMSON LAMP

There are reading lamps equipped with buttons which, if pressed, switch the lamp on when it is off and switch it off when it is on. If the lamp is off and its button is then pressed an odd number of times, the lamp will be on, but if it is pressed an even number of times, the lamp will be off. Let the lamp be off, and now suppose that the button might be pressed such that the first jab requires $\frac{1}{2}$ of a minute, the second $\frac{1}{4}$ of a minute, and so on. Our problem is under what conditions, if any, the lamp button can thus be pressed to switch the lamp on and off $\aleph_0$ times within the finite time of 1 minute. Since J. F. Thomson introduced the putative process of these $\aleph_0$ on-off lamp switchings into the literature,[47] I shall refer to it as "the Thomson process." But it is to be noted that Thomson argued that the process thus named is logically impossible.

4. BLACK'S TRANSFERRING MACHINE

Max Black has invited consideration of several processes involving $\aleph_0$ transfers of marbles:

(1) The first process is carried out by an infinity machine called "Alpha," whose function Black describes as follows:

> Let us suppose that upon our left a narrow tray stretches into the distance as far as the most powerful telescope can fol-low; and that this tray or slot is full of marbles. Here, at the middle, where the line of marbles begins, there stands a kind of mechanical scoop; and to the right, a second, but empty tray, stretching away into the distance beyond the farthest reach of vision. Now the machine is started. During the first

---

[47] James Thomson, "Tasks and Super-Tasks" [113], reprinted above.

minute of its operation, it seizes a marble from the left and transfers it to the empty tray on the right; then it rests a minute. In the next half-minute the machine seizes a second marble on the left, transfers it, and rests half-a-minute. The third marble is moved in a quarter of a minute, with a corresponding pause; the next in one-eighth of a minute; and so until the movements are so fast that all we can see is a gray blur. But at the end of exactly four minutes the machine comes to a halt, and now the left-hand tray that was full seems to be empty, while the right-hand tray that was empty seems full of marbles.[48]

(2) Infinity machine Beta is characterized by comparison with Alpha:

Imagine the arrangements modified as follows. Let there be only *one* marble in the left-hand tray to begin with, and let some device always return *that same marble* during the time at which the machine is resting. Let us give the name "Beta" to a machine that works in this way. From the standpoint of the machine, as it were, the task has not changed. The difficulty of performance remains exactly the same whether the task, as in Alpha's case, is to transfer an infinite series of qualitatively similar but different marbles; or whether the task, as in Beta's case, is constantly to transfer the *same* marble—a marble that is immediately returned to its original position. Imagine Alpha and Beta set to work side by side on their respective tasks: every time the one moves, so does the other; if one succeeds in its task, so must the other; and if it is impossible for either to succeed, it is impossible for each.[49]

And Gamma functions as an accessory to Beta:

I said, before, that "some device" always restored the marble to its original position in the left-hand tray. Now the most natural device to use for this purpose is another machine—Gamma, say—working like Beta but *from right to left*. Let it be arranged that no sooner does Beta move the marble from left to right than Gamma moves it back again. The successive working periods and pauses of Gamma are then equal in

[48] M. Black, *Problems of Analysis* [53], p. 102. [See p. 74 above.]
[49] *Ibid.*, p. 103. [See p. 75 above.]

length to those of Beta, except that Gamma is working while
Beta is resting, and vice versa. The task of Gamma, moreover,
is exactly parallel to that of Beta, that is, to transfer the marble
an infinite number of times from one side to the other.[50]
I shall now discuss the various infinite processes involved
in the "infinity machines."

THE π-MACHINE

In considering kinematically whether it is physically possible that the π-machine achieve the π-printing in a finite
time, I must immediately stipulate that the heights from
which the press descends to the paper to print the successive
digits may *not* be equal but must form a geometrically decreasing series converging to zero. In this way, I can assure
that the spatial magnitude of the successive tasks does *not*
remain the same while the time available for performing
them decreases toward zero: Just as in the case of the runners, the π-machine is thereby called upon to move at only
a constant average speed by traversing ever smaller distances
in proportionately ever smaller times. My reason for requiring the heights of descent to converge to zero in a suitable fashion becomes apparent upon recalling the analysis
I gave of the flag-planting in the case of the *staccato* runner. If the heights of descent did not converge to zero, the
successive velocities required for the printing would soon
exceed the velocity of light and would vary with time in a
manner that is kinematically objectionable even in the context of the Newtonian theory. Here, no less than in the case
of the *staccato* runner, I ignore the *dynamical* problems of
programming the π-machine so that the successive spatially
and temporally shorter descents of the press can be *triggered*
as required.
I require furthermore that the widths of the successive
numerals to be printed converge to zero in such a way that
ALL the $\aleph_0$ digits can be printed in a horizontal line on a
FINITE strip of paper. In laying down this second require-

[50] *Ibid.*, p. 104. [See p. 76 above.]

ment, I blithely ignore as logically irrelevant the blurring of the digits on the paper through smudging of the ink when their widths become sufficiently small, not to speak of the need for ink droplets of width dimensions below those of an electron!

Under the fundamental restriction of my first proviso regarding the heights of descent, the π-printing no more requires an infinite time than do either the *legato* or the *staccato* runner. And, given my second requirement concerning the widths of the successive digits, the spatial array of the $\aleph_0$ digits no more requires an infinite space than the *unending* progression of Z-intervals which collectively fit into the space of a finite unit interval: As long as the sequence 3.1415926535 . . . is printed so that the successive widths of the digits converge to zero in the manner of the Z-intervals, the question "What does this array *look like at the right end?*" receives the same kind of answer as the corresponding question about the progression of Z-intervals. We have been cautioned [p. 197] against the misguided attempt to form a *visual* picture of the *open end* of a finite space interval, and we are aware that the metrically finite union of the Z-intervals is open at the right "end" as is the total space interval formed by the progression of horizontally shrinking digits. Although we cannot visually picture the *non*-existence of a rightmost point, our very characterization of the openness of the right end shows that we clearly understand in ordinal terms "what that end looks like." Just as the interval constituted by the union of the Z-intervals can be closed at the right end by the addition of a rightmost (last) point, so also, of course, can the interval formed by the horizontal cross section of the unending π-sequence.

Precisely analogous remarks apply to the time intervals that correspond to (1) the process of traversing all the Z-intervals, and (2) the process of printing all the digits of π as specified. In the case of either Z-runner, we naturally tend to include in the *motion process* the event of his arrival at his destination where the runner *first* comes to rest: In so doing, we seem to be interested not only in those states of the *legato* runner in which his velocity is positive but also in the *earliest* of his states of rest. But in the case of the π-printing process, there may be a tendency to include in the *printing process* only those states of the π-machine belonging to the printing motion and to exclude the *earliest* subsequent event when it is no longer engaged in the printing. Thus, by virtue of our decision as to whether to include a terminal event in a given temporally finite process or not, the time interval corresponding to either Z-motion process turns out to be closed at the later end, whereas the time interval corresponding to the π-printing process does not. But the exercise of our decisional option to omit from the time interval corresponding to the π-printing the *earliest* instant following all the instants at which the press is busy printing must not be allowed to abet the following fallacious inference: drawing the conclusion that there exists no such earliest subsequent instant and that the π-printing cannot be over or completed within a finite time after its start. One might as well infer that the spatial interval constituted by the union of the unending progression of Z-intervals must be spatially infinite!

Let me assume that I am right in claiming that the completion of the kind of π-printing process which I described is physically possible kinematically no less than the completion of the total *staccato* Z-run. Then my π-printing process constitutes a further counterexample to Chihara's cited claim that an infinite number of things cannot be done in a finite time. And furthermore we see that the kind of infinite π-printing process and machine I have described does *not* have the characteristics of the quite different kind of process and machine which Chihara invoked in support of his plea as follows:

> Granted that Thomson's argument [for the logical impossibility of the "Thomson process"] breaks down, however, I am sympathetic with his suggestion that there is something unintelligible about these hypothetical machines. The diffi-

culty, as I see it, is not insufficiency of time, tape, ink, speed, strength or material, power, and the like, but rather the inconceivability of how the machine could actually finish its super-task. The machine would supposedly print the digits on tape, one after another, while the tape flows through the machine, say from right to left. Hence, at each stage in the calculation, the sequence of digits will extend to the left with the last digit printed being "at center." Now when the machine completes its task and shuts itself off, we should be able to look at the tape to see what digit was printed last. But if the machine finishes printing all the digits which constitute the decimal expansion of pi, no digit can be the last digit printed. And how are we to understand this situation?[54]

I am not arguing that the concept of a super-machine is self-contradictory. The above difficulty can be easily avoided: one might argue that the above considerations show no more than that a super-machine would have to be radically different from anything we now have (which, after all, should not be surprising). But even if we allow that no decisive argument has been given to show the inconceivability of such a super-machine, can we really conceive of such a machine actually finishing its computation?[55]

Suppose that I had not explicitly ruled out the equality of all the heights from which the printing press is to descend but had countenanced their equality. In that case, we can conclude the following from our discussion of the *staccato* runner: Quite apart from the incompatibility of the then required super-light speeds with the special theory of relativity, these super-light *speeds* would have been *sufficient* to assure the Newtonian kinematic impossibility of the completion of the printing in a finite time. For the speeds that would be needed would not accord with the requirement that the velocity function of a body may not have an instant of infinite discontinuity, as in the flag case (*staccato* run). In this respect, Chihara's quoted account overlooks the

[54] C. S. Chihara, "On the Possibility of Completing an Infinite Process" [60], p. 80.
[55] Ibid.

relevance of speed as a sufficient condition for the unintelligibility of completability. But unless Weyl could show that the successive spatial displacements (or "tasks") performed by a machine to CALCULATE (not just print!) seriatim the digits of π can, in principle, suitably converge to zero, my account of the π-machine does sustain the following conclusion reached by Chihara[56]: Weyl was mistaken in claiming that only if an infinite sequence of calculations can be completed in a finite time can Achilles traverse all the Z-intervals.

THE PEANO MACHINE

If we were to allow the use of the English-language names of the numbers to be recited, then there would be a number beyond which the lengths of the names—each measured by the name's syllable content—would increase boundlessly. And even if these name lengths remained the same, the "syllable-size" of the successive recitation tasks would remain the same while the time available for their performance would decrease indefinitely. To assure that the average speed of the mechanical "lips" engaged in the recitation can remain constant instead of having to increase boundlessly, we would require non-English names of the successive numbers such that the successive distances traversed by the mechanical lips as they perform their recitations would decrease in proportion to the available time. It is quite unclear how distinctive names capable of being pronounced by the mechanical lips in accord with this stringent requirement could be generated by a rule.

Let us postpone this difficulty for the moment and turn from the modulating mechanical lips to the vibrating membrane of the mechanical voice. We note that each of the required $\aleph_0$ distinct sound-names or noises requires at least one vibration of the voice membrane. But the time available for the utterance of these successive noises converges to

---

[56] Ibid., pp. 83 and 87.

zero. Hence the *frequency* of the noises and also of the membrane must *increase indefinitely*. It has been suggested to me by A. Janis that the ensuing denumerable infinity of frequencies permits each natural number to be named by a sound of distinctive pitch. And it seems to me that such a pattern of noises constitutes an acceptable code language for numbers.

The energy imparted to the air particles by the vibrator is proportional to the square of the frequency and to the square of the amplitude. We can assure though that the frequency pattern required by the total recitation does *not* necessitate the expenditure of an infinite amount of energy in a finite time. For although the frequencies of the membrane must increase indefinitely, we can require that the amplitudes of the successive vibrations of the total recitation decrease in such a way that the total energy expended is finite.

A decrease in the successive amplitudes is required not only on these *dynamical* grounds. For in order that the vibratory motion of the membrane be *kinematically* possible, the amplitudes of the vibrations corresponding to the successive noises must decrease and suitably converge to zero: Even if the membrane executes only one vibration for each noise, the membrane would have to vibrate through an infinite total distance in a finite time, if the amplitudes of all the $\aleph_0$ noises were equal.

The assumed fulfillment of this proviso regarding the decrease in the amplitude does enable us to conclude that it is physically possible kinematically for the traveling Peano machine to complete the recitation in a finite time. Just as in the case of the π-machine, there is a tendency to think of the number *recitation process* as *not* including the earliest of the states of the Peano machine in which it is *no longer* engaged in reciting. This essentially classificatory decision on our part thus prevents the *finite* time interval required for the total recitation from being closed at its later end. But I remind the reader of the *caveat* I issued on this point a propos of the π-machine: It should not be inferred that a time interval *must* be metrically infinite just because it is ordinally open at either the later or the earlier "end."

It is now clear why I objected to Whitrow's linking of Achilles'. traversal of a progression of points in a finite time with expecting Achilles to number them all by counting. I take it that the kind of counting to which Whitrow was appealing would take the form of *reciting* all the natural numbers *in English* or performing the infinitude of threshold-governed mental acts of thinking seriatim of all of them. And we saw that either of these forms of counting would take forever. If we were to grant Whitrow that Achilles can traverse the progression of points in a unit space interval *only* if he can thus count them all, then indeed Whitrow would be warranted in concluding that Achilles cannot accomplish the traversal in a finite time. But the separate temporal analyses which I gave of the processes of traversal and of vocal or mental counting in English show that Whitrow has misidentified the durational features of counting with those of Achilles' traversal of the progression of Z-points.

THE THOMSON LAMP

In a careful and penetrating paper, P. Benacerraf has demonstrated that Thomson's attempt to establish the logical impossibility of performing the $\aleph_0$ on-off switchings by the time 1 minute has elapsed is a *non sequitur*.[57] Let t_1 be the instant 1 minute after the start of the switching process at t_0. In substance, Benacerraf makes the following points.

The information we are given is that for any time t in the interval $t_0 \leqq t < t_1$, if the lamp is off at t, then there exists a later time in the interval at which it is on, *and* if the lamp is on at t, then there is a later instant in the interval at which it is off. Thomson infers fallaciously from the first premise

---

[57] P. Benacerraf, "Tasks, Super-Tasks, and the Modern Eleatics" [reprinted above].

that the lamp must be on at t_1 and from the second premise that it must be off at t_1, whereupon he is able to claim that the process of $\aleph_0$ on-off switchings must be logically impossible. But from these premises no conclusion follows about the state of the lamp *at time t_1* with respect to being on or off. Although it is true that the lamp must be either on or off if it still exists at time t_1, no conclusion as to which of these two mutually exclusive situations obtains at t_1 is *deducible* from the given information: Thomson erroneously assumes it to be a matter of logic that the description of a sequence of acts of order type ω *must* be *determinate* with respect to the character of the outcome of a sequence of acts of order type $\omega + 1$. In so doing, he overlooks that he is insisting on deducing a conclusion about the state of affairs at an instant *following* a progression of time intervals from information pertaining *only* to the states of affairs prevailing at instants *within* the progression.

In this way, Benacerraf showed that Thomson failed to prove the logical impossibility of performing in a finite time $\aleph_0$ on-off lamp switchings whose successive durations geometrically converge to zero. Benacerraf then turns to the question of what would be involved in establishing either the logical impossibility or the logical possibility of such a process. Speaking of an infinite number of tasks as a "super-task,"[58] he writes:

> To show that the concept of super-task is self-contradictory, it must be shown that there is something self-contradictory in the concept of a completed infinite series of tasks. . . . In order to show this, it would suffice, for example, to show that it is part of the meaning of "task" that nothing can be called a task that does not take some time to perform *and* that there is a lower bound on the length of time allowable for the performance of a single task.
>
> Similarly, to show that super-tasks are not logically impossible, it would suffice to show that a correct analysis of each of the concepts involved permits their conjunction without

[58] *Ibid.* [p. 106 above].

explicit contradiction. . . . I strongly suspect that . . . there is probably no set of conditions that we can (nontrivially) state and show to be includable in a correct statement of the meaning of the expressions in question whose satisfaction would lead us to conclude that a super-task had been performed. . . . I mean only that there is no circumstance that we could imagine and describe in which we would be justified in saying that an infinite sequence of tasks had been completed.[59]

. . . We have what appears to be a conceptual mismatch. Sequences of *tasks* do not exhibit the characteristics of sequences that lend themselves to proofs of infinity.[60]

. . . Thomson is . . . successful in showing that arguments *for* the performability of super-tasks are invalid.*

Thus Benacerraf doubts the feasibility of furnishing a proof of the logical possibility of performing a super-task. Note that to his mind the issue of logical possibility raised by the $\aleph_0$ on-off switchings of Thomson's lamp in the prescribed times seems to be the following: Can a physical process thus involving $\aleph_0$ subprocesses of suitably decreasing durations be held to occur in a finite time *without* explicit contradiction, IF we *also* describe that process as constituting the performance of $\aleph_0$ "TASKS" in the *ordinary* sense of that term? But to my mind, the essential and interesting question of logical possibility within the framework of the theory arises from the fact that the specified subprocesses which are collectively presumed to have occurred in a finite time constitute an infinite set of a particular ordinal type whose members must *collectively and severally satisfy certain kinematic requirements*. And I do *not* see why *this* question of logical possibility should be interlaced with the further question whether it can be shown that no contradiction is then introduced by calling the production of each of these subprocesses the performance of a "task" in the everyday sense

[59] *Ibid.* [pp. 125–126 above].
[60] *Ibid* [p. 128 above].
*[*Ibid.*, p. 129 above. In this edition (above), Benacerraf has changed "invalid" to "inadequate."]

of that term. I wish to recall the comment I made when I discussed the *staccato* run à propos of Max Black's invocation of ordinary language: In considering whether it is logically possible kinematically that the $\aleph_0$ separate motions of this process occur in a finite time, we need to heed the commitments of ordinary language only to the extent of guarding against being victimized or stultified by them.

If, with Benacerraf, one disregards in this context whether "the concept of the infinite is itself self-contradictory,"[61] I cannot see that here one should demand more in the way of a "proof" of logical possibility than the provision of a kind of physical model via a kinematic description devoid of the explicit metrical contradictions which have been alleged against it.[62] Hence let us conceive in this way of "proving" kinematically whether or not the Thomson lamp can be consistently held to have carried out its $\aleph_0$ switching operations in a finite time.

Let us simplify our consideration of the problem by disregarding the question of the following electromagnetic possibility: the realizability of the conditions required for the emission of visible photons from the filament of the lamp bulb during each of $\aleph_0$ geometrically decreasing "on"-periods before t_1, and possibly at t_1 and thereafter. Instead, let any state in which the lamp circuit is merely electrically closed qualify as an "on"-state of the lamp, while an "off"-state is one in which the circuit is thus broken or open. We can therefore confine our consideration to the kinematics of the motions of the button or switch whose alternating states correspond to closed or open states of the circuit by virtue of the electrical coupling or de-coupling between them.

Let the button have the form of a *rotating* little knob whose circular base has a periphery consisting of one elec-

---

[61] *Ibid.* [p. 125 above].

[62] Benacerraf himself seems to offer this kind of "proof" of logical possibility when he writes [p. 127]: "We have recognized that the shrinking genie covers all the Z-points but fails to occupy 1. . . . how could we recognize this if . . . Thomson were right and this was a contradictory notion . . . ?"

trically conducting and one non-conducting circular arc. Every triplet of on-off-and-on-again states will then require that any point on the periphery move circularly through a *fixed* positive distance. And since there are to be $\aleph_0$ such triplets during the time $t_1 - t_0$, any such point would have to traverse an infinite spatial distance in a finite time. As is clear from our discussion of our earlier "infinity machines," if the button is to be at rest at time t_1 or to be moving then with a particular finite velocity, even Newtonianly this arrangement would involve a kinematically impossible infinite discontinuity in the time variation of the button's velocity, quite apart from requiring relativistically prohibited superlight velocities.

Alternatively, let a button be equipped with an electrically conducting base which can close a circuit by fitting into the space between the exposed circuit elements E_1 and E_2. And let the button be depressed through a *fixed* distance d to close the circuit *every* time the lamp is to be turned on, while it is restituted upward to the same starting position to break the circuit each of the $\aleph_0$ times when the lamp is to be turned off. Then the same kinematic impossibility results.

Since Thomson imposed no restrictions on the operation of the reading lamp button other than the durations of the successive jabs, he may reasonably be presumed to have envisioned this kind of motion of the switch button and of the circuit elements. Now consider the question "What is the state of the lamp at time t_1?" Benacerraf rightly charged Thomson's deduction of *contradictory answers* to it with being fallacious. But granting our presumption as to the kind of process which Thomson envisioned, we see that this question is unanswerable for the following reason: kinematic theory *rules out* the process which is expected to issue in exactly one of the two states on or off at time t_1. Hence I must dissent from Chihara's view concerning supermachines like Thomson's lamp when he says: "Indeed the question . . . is unanswerable. But one cannot conclude that it is unanswerable because there is a contradiction in the notion of such a super-machine, since it seems quite reasonable to maintain that not enough information about the machines was supplied to answer it."[63] I dissent, because the kinematic impossibility here is, of course, not a matter of insufficient mechanical information.

Moreover, on the basis of the explicit information given by Thomson, there are certain conditions which must be satisfied by both the switch (button) and the circuit elements to make his process kinematically possible. And, as A. Janis has pointed out to me, these conditions are such that the state of the circuit at time t_1 is *predictably closed*. To see this, let us first recall the discussion of our earlier infinity machines. It is then clear that the consecutive downward and upward jabs of the switching button which alternately close and break the circuit must produce displacements of the button whose length Δx are a suitably decreasing sequence converging to zero. And we must assume that there is no electric arcing or sparking across *any* space gap Δx, however small, between the conducting button base, on the one hand, and the exposed circuit ends E_1 and E_2 on the other. For if there were electrical sparking-across for all Δx equal to or less than some minimum ϵ, then the kinematic requirement that Δx suitably converge to zero as $t \rightarrow t_1$ would have the following result: there would be a time t_ϵ *before* t_1 such that the circuit would be electrically *closed* for all instants t belonging to the interval $t_\epsilon \leqq t < t_1$. And this result would obviously violate Thomson's requirement that the lamp is still to be switched *off* $\aleph_0$ times during this time interval.

At time t_0, when the lamp is off, let $\frac{1}{2}$ be the *initial* vertical distance between the button base and the horizontal circuit-opening E_1E_2, as shown in the diagram below, which is *not* drawn to scale. Then after the base of the button has been depressed once to close the circuit, let it be raised after each

[63] C. S. Chihara, "On the Possibility of Completing an Infinite Process" [60], p. 80.

such depression *not* all the way to its initial position A but to intermediate points $A_1, A_2, A_3, \ldots, A_n, \ldots$ whose respective distances Δx from $E_1 E_2$ are

$$\tfrac{1}{8}, \tfrac{1}{32}, \tfrac{1}{128}, \ldots \frac{1}{2^{2n+1}}, \ldots \qquad (n = 1, 2, 3, \ldots).$$

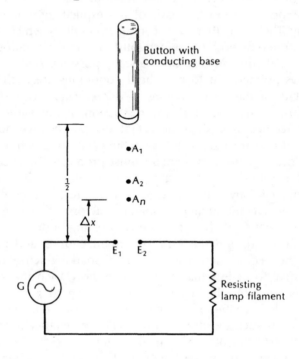

Then the $\aleph_0$ circuit-closing jabs involve a sequence of downward displacements Δx

$$\tfrac{1}{2}, \tfrac{1}{8}, \tfrac{1}{32}, \ldots \frac{1}{2^{2n+1}}, \ldots \qquad (n = 0, 1, 2, 3, \ldots).$$

The corresponding sequence of available time intervals Δt is

$$\tfrac{1}{2}, \tfrac{1}{8}, \tfrac{1}{32}, \ldots \frac{1}{2^{2n+1}}, \ldots \qquad (n = 0, 1, 2, 3, \ldots).$$

If all of the downward jabs were to proceed at unit velocity, then the circuit would be closed for only an instant each time during these particular time intervals. On the other hand, if only some fixed proper fraction $\frac{1}{k}$ of these available times Δt were devoted to the downward motions, then the velocity of the button would have the same value k each time, thereby satisfying the Newtonian kinematic requirement of having an upper bound during the time interval $t_0 \leqq t < t_1$. And, if the downward motion were to start each time at the *beginning* of the time interval available for it, the lamp would be on at least for the sequence of time intervals Δt $(1 - \frac{1}{k})$, i.e., at least during the time intervals

$$\frac{1}{2^{2n+1}}\left(1 - \frac{1}{k}\right) \qquad (n = 0, 1, 2, 3, \ldots).$$

To conform to the requirements of the theory of relativity, the velocity k must be less than that of light in the units we are using. But even Newtonianly the button velocity would impermissibly increase boundlessly, if only *decreasing fractions* $\frac{1}{n}$ $(n = 1, 2, 3, \ldots)$ rather than a fixed proper fraction $\frac{1}{k}$ of the above decreasing time intervals Δt were granted successively for the downward motions in order to secure successive on-states of durations

$$\frac{1}{2^{2n+1}}\left(1 - \frac{1}{n+1}\right) \qquad (n = 0, 1, 2, 3, \ldots).$$

Turning to the $\aleph_0$ circuit-*breaking* jabs, we note that they involve a sequence of decreasing upward displacements

$$\tfrac{1}{8}, \tfrac{1}{32}, \tfrac{1}{128}, \ldots \frac{1}{2^{2n+1}}, \ldots \qquad (n = 1, 2, 3, \ldots).$$

The corresponding sequence of decreasing time intervals Δt available to break the circuit by moving the button upward is

$$\tfrac{1}{4}, \tfrac{1}{16}, \tfrac{1}{64}, \ldots \frac{1}{2^{2n}}, \ldots \qquad (n = 1, 2, 3, \ldots).$$

Let $\frac{1}{k}$ be the particular fixed fraction of the available time interval Δt which is devoted each time to the button's circuit-breaking motion. Clearly $\frac{1}{k} \leqq 1$, and the button's upward velocity v is given by $v = \frac{k}{2}$. Under the relativistic restriction that v have values less than the velocity c of light, we also have $k < 2c$, or $\frac{1}{k} > \frac{1}{2c}$, so that

$$\frac{1}{2c} < \frac{1}{k} \leqq 1.$$

Suppose that $\frac{1}{k}$ has some value in this interval *other than* 1, and let the upward motion terminate each time at the *end* of the time interval available for it. Then the lamp will *also* be *on* during the following initial positive subintervals of the intervals available for the button's upward circuit-breaking motions

$$\left(1 - \frac{1}{k}\right) \frac{1}{2^{2n+1}} \qquad (n = 1, 2, 3, \ldots).$$

The state variable characterizing the lamp as either on or off is clearly a discrete variable by ranging over only two values rather than over a continuum of values. But we took a closed state of the circuit to be tantamount to an on-state of the lamp, while a broken state of the circuit is equivalent to an off-state of the lamp. And the positions of the button needed to close and break the circuit in the prescribed fashion must exhibit the kinematically required continuity. Therefore, $\Delta x \to 0$ as $t \to t_1$ and $\Delta x = 0$ at $t = t_1$, i.e., the required spatially continuous motion of the base of the switching button issues in the coincidence of the base with E_1E_2 at time t_1. Hence the circuit is *predictably closed* at time t_1, i.e., the lamp must be *on* at the termination of the unit time interval $t_1 - t_0$.

Indeed there is an important respect in which the motion of the button can be understood on the model of the runner's traversal of a *progression* of Z-intervals in the Dichotomy (cf. Ch. II, §3, B [72]). The button's $\aleph_0$ downward motions involve the traversal of a total space interval of length

$$L_d = \sum_{n=0}^{n=\infty} \frac{1}{2^{2n+1}} = \frac{4}{6}.$$

And the button's $\aleph_0$ upward motions involve a total spatial displacement of length

$$L_u = \sum_{n=1}^{n=\infty} \frac{1}{2^{2n+1}} = \frac{1}{6}.$$

But, of course, the button actually moves alternately down and up, starting at $t = t_0$ with a downward motion through the initial distance $\frac{1}{2}$. And after traversing this initial distance, it traverses *twice* each of the space intervals

$$\frac{1}{2^{2n+1}} \qquad (n = 1, 2, 3, \ldots)$$

by executing first an upward and then a downward motion through the same interval. Hence the button has the task of traversing a total interval of length

$$L_d + L_u = \frac{5}{6}$$

by traversing first an interval of $\frac{1}{2}$ and then an infinite progression of subintervals

$$\frac{1}{4}, \frac{1}{16}, \frac{1}{64}, \cdots \frac{1}{4^n}, \cdots \qquad (n = 1, 2, 3, \ldots).$$

Our mention of the runner's traversal of a progression of subintervals in the Dichotomy does *not* overlook that all of the *legato* runner's $\aleph_0$ Z-runs to his destination point are spatially in the *same* direction and proceed without velocity fluctuations, while the suitably decreasing motions of the button which terminate in a closed state of the circuit at time t_1 are $\aleph_0$ alternately *down and up* motions. Specifically, the *legato* runner's uniform motion involves only one initial acceleration of particular finite magnitude and one final deceleration of specific finite magnitude, whereas the accelerations (though *not* the velocities!) of the button increase indefinitely. And, as Wesley Salmon has noted illuminatingly, *except* for the *legato* motion, all the processes we are discussing involve indefinitely large *accelerations*. But this difference between the *legato* motion and all of the rest does not militate against a crucial similarity between them, with respect to which the completability of the latter is no less intelligible than that of the former. [The above discussion of Friedberg's *staccato* runner shows, moreover, how this difference can be circumvented. See pp. 214–216.]

For what matters is that the runner reaches his destination at time t_1 after traversing a *progression* of Z-runs, while there does not exist any last Z-run in the progression by means of which the termination of the motion could be effected. And what matters especially is that the terminal instant t_1 of the motion does *not* belong to *any* member of the progression of temporal subintervals corresponding to the $\aleph_0$ Z-runs, although *every other* instant of the motion belongs to at least one such member. In short, what matters is that the runner's arrival at his destination at time t_1 does not belong to any of the Z-runs and is surely *not* effected by the traversal of a non-existent *last* Z-run terminating in that arrival. Similarly, the jabbing motions form a suitably decreasing progression which issues in an on-state at time t_1, even though that on-state is *not* the terminus of any *continuously downward* jabbing motion of positive duration during which the lamp would be off. Nor can the on-state at time t_1 belong to any continuous on-state of positive duration whose first instant terminates a single continuously downward jab. Thus, if t_1 were the start of a continuous on-state of positive duration, the particular instantaneous on-state *at* t_1 would *not* be the terminus of a continuously downward jab. By contrast, within the confines of the half-open time-interval $t_0 \leqq t < t_1$ *before* t_1, the first instant of any continuous on-state of positive duration *is* the terminus of a continuously downward jab of positive duration. And, again within the confines of that half-open interval *before* t_1, any instantaneous on-state which separates two continuous off-states is likewise the terminus of a continuously downward jabbing motion of positive duration.

These considerations will enable us to see that the production of Thomson's $\aleph_0$ on-off states would *not* be feasible under the following alternative switching arrangement even if we were to assure the finitude of the total spatial displacement of the switching button.[64] Let our modified switch button be movable through a linear space interval which is divided by a middle point into up and down, or left and right respectively. And assume that the coupling between the positions of the base of the button and the lamp circuit is such as to satisfy the following conditions: (i) when the button base is at any point in the upper (or left) segment, the circuit is open and the lamp is off, (ii) when the button base is at any point in the lower (or right) segment, the circuit is closed and the lamp is on, (iii) when the button-base point coincides with the center point C in the middle, the lamp is on or off depending on whether it had arrived at C from above (left) or below (right) respectively, and (iv) if the button base is at the mid-point C at a time *t*, the existence of an on-state of the circuit at *t* requires that the button base have reached C from above (left) at or before *t*, and—unless a circuit-component (e.g., the lamp filament) has burnt out— the existence of an off-state at *t* while the base is present at C requires the base to have reached C at or before *t* from below (right). To assure the kinematically required finitude of the total spatial displacement of the button base during the allowed finite time $t_1 - t_0$ (1 minute), let the button base journey back and forth across C $\aleph_0$ times so as to traverse suitably decreasing distances and reach C at time t_1. After t_1, we leave the switch in the position which it attained at t_1.

Our previous considerations now enable us to assert that at time t_1, the button base *cannot* have reached C either by a continuous approach *from above* (left) or by a continuous approach *from below* (right). For this much is required if the execution of Thomson's jabbing instructions is to be kine-

[64] I am indebted to Allen Janis for having concocted this alternative switching arrangement and for having pointed out instructively that it cannot produce Thomson's process.

matically feasible. But, in that case the posited conditions governing the coupling of the switching button to the lamp circuit entail the following conclusion: if the lamp circuit is still intact at t_1 and thereafter, then the lamp is *neither on nor off at time* t_1 and thereafter. Yet if the lamp circuit still exists intact at that time, it must be either on or off. And it can easily be observed which of these two states prevails at t_1 and thereafter by looking at the lamp. Even if the lamp filament should have burned out at time t_1, we can replace the bulb by a new one at that time and observe its state thereafter. Hence if Thomson's required $\aleph_0$ on-off states of the lamp circuit are claimed to permit the endurance of the lamp circuit until and beyond the instant t_1, a contradiction is introduced by the assumption that these $\aleph_0$ states can be produced by the present *modified* switching arrangement.

Thus, in the case of the latter switching arrangement, no less than in the case of the kinematically impossible jabbing motions discussed initially, the inability to predict the state of the lamp circuit at time t_1 is not at all a matter of insufficient information. And we see that the latter impossible switching arrangement (S_2) differs from the one yielding a *predictably closed* circuit at time t_1 (S_1) as follows: in the case of S_1, on and off respectively involve coincidence and non-coincidence of the button base with E_1E_2, while the on-state at t_1 is *not* the terminus of any *continuously unidirectional* (e.g., downward or rightward) jab; but arrangement S_2 requires that the one lamp state associated with the base's center position at time t_1 and thereafter be the outcome of a continuously unidirectional jab terminating at time t_1. And precisely this is ruled out by the kinematics required for Thomson's process.

BLACK'S TRANSFERRING MACHINE

For the reasons given when we discussed the other infinity machines, the marbles of Max Black's marble transferring machines would have to be so positioned and the two trays so moved (e.g., toward the line half-way between their initial separation) that the distances through which the successive marble transfers would have to be effected would decrease in proportion to the available successive times and thus would suitably converge to zero by the time the 4 minutes have elapsed. And, in that case—dynamical difficulties aside —I claim that (1) by the end of 4 minutes of Alpha's intermittent operation, the centers of mass of all the $\aleph_0$ different marbles will be to the right of the line of contact at which the left and right trays are joined at the end of 4 minutes, and (2) by the end of 4 minutes of alternate operation by Beta and Gamma, the center of mass of the single marble would be on the line of contact, and at rest there.

Max Black maintains that it is logically impossible for either machine Alpha or machine Beta (assisted by Gamma) to carry out its assigned task in a finite time. And his reasons are that there is the kinematic difficulty of a discontinuity in the position function which we just obviated by our restrictions, and also that Beta and Gamma exhibit this logical impossibility as follows:

> . . . the single marble is always returned, and each move of the machine accomplishes nothing . . . the very act of transferring the marble from left to right immediately causes it to be returned again; the operation is self-defeating and it is logically impossible for its end to be achieved. Now if this is true for Beta, it must be true also for Alpha.[65]

> Somebody may still be inclined to say that nevertheless when the machine Beta finally comes to rest (at the end of the four minutes of its operation) the single marble might after all be found in the right-hand tray, and this, if it happened, would *prove* that the machine's task had been accomplished.

> . . . Let it be arranged that no sooner does Beta move the marble from left to right then Gamma moves it back again.[66]

> . . . If the result of the whole four minutes' operation by the first machine is to transfer the marble from left to right, the result of the whole four minutes' operation by the second machine must be to transfer the marble from right to left. But

[65] M. Black, *Problems of Analysis* [53], pp. 103–104. [See p. 76 above.]
[66] *Ibid.*, p. 104.

there is only one marble and it must end somewhere. If it ought to be found on the right, then by the same reasoning it ought to be found on the left. But it cannot be both on the right and on the left. Hence neither machine can accomplish its task, and our description of the infinity machine involves a contradiction.[67]

We noted that under Black's conditions of a *fixed* positive separation of the two trays, there is the kinematic impossibility of a discontinuity in the position function to which he rightly calls attention. But the appreciation of *that* difficulty must not be allowed to confer acceptability on his further contention that the description of the functions of Beta and Gamma permit the deduction of contradictory conclusions regarding the spatial location of the one marble after 4 minutes. For his reasoning in support of *this* contention is vitiated by errors, some of which are analogous to those committed by Thomson and pointed out by Benacerraf.

Black says that "Each move of the machine [Beta] accomplishes nothing," and that "The operation is self-defeating and it is logically impossible for its end to be achieved." He mistakenly believes here to be able to deduce that the marble does *not* end up in the right tray after 4 minutes. But the facts about the marble's transfers *to which he calls attention here* merely fail to sustain the conclusion that the marble does end up on the right. And he invokes the following false supposition: The assumption of the occurrence of all of Beta's prescribed one-way transfers in a finite time, if true, *must* enable us to *deduce* that the marble will end up on the right side at the *first* instant t_1 following *all* these transfers. If such deducibility does not obtain, Black feels entitled to conclude that Beta could not have effected the $\aleph_0$ one-way transfers in a finite time.

But Gamma's recurring return of the marble after every transfer by Beta does not provide a basis for concluding that the marble does *not* end up on the right, just as the recurring off-switchings of the Thomson lamp do not enable us to infer

[67] *Ibid.*, pp. 104–105.

that the lamp will not be on at time t_1. We are given that after any *even* number of oppositely directed one-way transfers of the marble by Beta and Gamma, beginning with one from left to right, the marble will be back on the left, and after any *odd* number of such transfers it will be on the right: For any time t in the interval $t_0 \leq t < t_1$, if the marble is on the left at t, then there exists a later time in the interval at which it is on the right, and if it is on the right at t, then there exists a later time in the interval when it is on the left. But this information does not entail where the marble would or would not be after Beta and Gamma have each carried out $\aleph_0$ one-way transfers.

Nor can the non-deducibility of the marble's location *at* time t_1 serve to show that Beta could not have effected the $\aleph_0$ transfers in a finite time *before* t_1. The belief that if $\aleph_0$ transfers are to have taken place before t_1, the position of the marble *at* t_1 ought to be deducible from the information specifying its movements *prior and up to the time t_1* seems to spring from the following tacit assumption: Given a point at any distance d, however small, from the marble's final rest location at time t_1, there is a closed positive time interval containing t_1 as its last instant during which the marble is spatially confined to being at one of the points of the closed space interval on its path corresponding to that distance. But this tacit assumption is *incompatible* with the stated conditions governing the operation of Beta and Gamma, which alternately operate between trays that are a *fixed* distance apart and do so during the entire interval $t_0 \leq t < t_1$. Why then should the marble's location at time t_1 be deducible? It is indeed true that Beta's violation of Black's tacitly made assumption shows that the performance demanded from it calls for a kinematically impermissible discontinuity in the time variation of the position, as I explained when I proscribed the flag-planting by the *staccato* runner. But what are we to make of the fact that *if applicable,* Black's tacitly made assumption would permit the deduction of the location of the marble at t_1? Surely it does not sustain the following inference: Beta could not have effected all the $\aleph_0$ transfers within 4 minutes, *because* the marble's location at time t_1 is *not* deducible from conditions violating Black's tacit assumption. The latter inference is a *non sequitur* even though we know *independently* that its conclusion is true on the strength of the kinematically impermissible position pattern required by $\aleph_0$ transfers across a *fixed* distance in a finite time.

III.
Zeno's
Paradoxes of Motion
and Standard
Quantum Mechanics

Recalling the points concerning quantum mechanics mentioned in §1 (Ch. II),* the first question is whether Zeno's Arrow and Stadium paradoxes—both interpreted as being predicated on and directed against the *discreteness* of space and time—pose a challenge for standard quantum mechanics, just as the Dichotomy and Achilles did for the continuity theory of motion. The belief that the Arrow and the Stadium are thus challenging seems to have been suggested by the following line of thought. Standard quantum theory has discretized or quantized some physical properties whose counterparts in classical physics were mathematically continuous. When

---

*["Newtonian physics, relativity theory, and standard quantum mechanics all assume that spatial and temporal betweenness are each dense as opposed to discrete. We shall note . . . that standard quantum theory has discretized or quantized some physical properties whose counterparts in classical physics were mathematically continuous. But we must emphasize that standard quantum theory has *not* quantized *space* or *time*, lest it be overlooked here that the time of this theory is dense. For in standard quantum theory, every point of continuous physical space is a *potential* sharply defined position of, say, an electron, and separately, every instant of a continuous time is *potentially* the time of a physical event." Adolf Grünbaum, *Modern Science and Zeno's Paradoxes* [72], pp. 37–38.]

coupled with reports of *speculations* about incorporating minimal distances ("hodons") and times ("chronons") in some elaborated future form of the theory, this kind of quantization has led some people to the belief that standard quantum mechanics affirms the atomicity of space and time. Whitrow writes:

> . . . since the rise of the quantum theory, it has become commonplace to regard energy as being ultimately atomic. Whether physical length should also be pictured in the same way is still a moot point, although it would seem to be in general accord with the trend of modern ideas to postulate a lower limit to spatial extension in nature. Closely linked with this concept is the hypothesis of minimal natural processes and changes, according to which no process can occur in less than some atomic unit of time, the *chronon*.[78]

But in the case of energy, the eigenvalues form a discrete set for *some* kinds of systems while forming a *continuous* set for other systems. More generally, a standard treatise on the subject points out that

> In general, whenever there is some boundary condition to satisfy, the eigenvalues will turn out to be discrete. . . . On the other hand, in free space, with no boundaries . . . the spectrum is continuous. This is also a general rule; if there are no boundary conditions limiting the region where the wave function is large, then operators will usually have a continuous spectrum. In some cases, such as the hydrogen atom . . . part of the spectrum is discrete and part is continuous. The discrete part of the spectrum corresponds to various quantum states of the hydrogen atom; the continuous part corresponds to states in which the atom is ionized.[79]

And indeed after making the statement about quantum theory which I quoted from him in this paragraph, Whitrow goes on to admit that

> So far, however, most physicists have felt no need to adopt the concept of temporal atomicity, the quantum concept of *stationary* state being reconciled with a continuous time

[78] G. J. Whitrow, *The Natural Philosophy of Time* [119], p. 153.

[79] D. Bohm, *Quantum Theory* (Englewood Cliffs, N.J.: Prentice-Hall, Inc., 1951), p. 217.

variable through quantum mechanics. . . . Until there is general agreement concerning the chronon, the concept of mathematical time underlying physical science, including microphysics, will continue to be based on the hypothesis of continuity or infinite divisibility.[80]

The fact that there are some physical attributes of single-particle systems in quantum mechanics (spin, intrinsic angular momentum) such that *all* the eigenvalues of the associated operator form a discrete set must not mislead us into supposing that space and time are quantized in the theory. For they are not: Every point of continuous physical space is a *potential* sharply defined position of, say, an electron, and, separately, every instant of a continuous time is *potentially* the time of a physical event, speculations about hodons and chronons notwithstanding.[81] Of course, this sense of affirming the continuity of space and time fully allows the quantum theory to repudiate via the conjugate parameters of the Heisenberg Uncertainty Relations the existence of well-defined particle trajectories in the sense of classical mechanics.

Since space and time are not quantized in standard quantum theory, Zeno's Arrow and Stadium do not challenge that theory. At best, a genuinely atomic space and time is nowadays a gleam in the eyes of hopeful speculative theoreticians, as is a physical theory whose fundamental laws take the form of difference equations. And since the time of standard quantum mechanics is *dense* and shares essential metrical features with the time of non-quantum physics, the time-metrical features of my refutation of Zeno's Dichotomy and Achilles are not rendered superfluous by quantum theory, even though these paradoxes involve quantum mechanically proscribed classical trajectories.

As we just saw, the hypothesis of atomicity of space and

---

[80] G. J. Whitrow, *The Natural Philosophy of Time* [119], pp. 156–157.

[81] See Adolf Grünbaum, *Modern Science and Zeno's Paradoxes* [72], Chapter I, §5, where it is pointed out that energy, no less than other attributes of quantum mechanical systems, *can* be measured in an arbitrarily short time in that theory.

time on which Zeno's Stadium is predicated is not part of any elaborated or seasoned contemporary physical theory. Nonetheless, I shall discuss the Stadium, since I wish to call attention to an important *cautionary lesson* implicit in it for the speculations envisioning a genuinely atomic space and time. In speaking of such an envisionment, it is well to bear in mind that there is both a weak sense and a strong sense in which a discrete space and time might be contemplated: (1) The weak sense is to imagine a world of which it would be appropriate to say that it has a granular space and time,[82] and (2) the strong sense is to specify those further empirical conditions which would justify that we *reinterpret* our present information about the physical space and time of our actual world so as to attribute genuine atomicity to them. It is difficult enough to carry out the weaker kind of envisionment. And it is all the more unclear how future developments in quantum theory might implement the stronger program of quantization of space and time.

Turning now to Zeno's Stadium, we are confronted with a row of points *A* which passes a fixed stadium *S*, likewise composed of points. Zeno assumes space and time to be discrete, and the rate at which *A* passes *S* is one point per instant. In addition, suppose that another row of points *B* moves in the direction opposite to that of *A* but at the same minimum rate as *A*. At consecutive instants, we then have the situations indicated in Figure 5. Now Zeno points out that at *consecutive instants*, *B*1 is vertically aligned with *A*1 and then with *A*3. And he maintains that this is absurd, for the

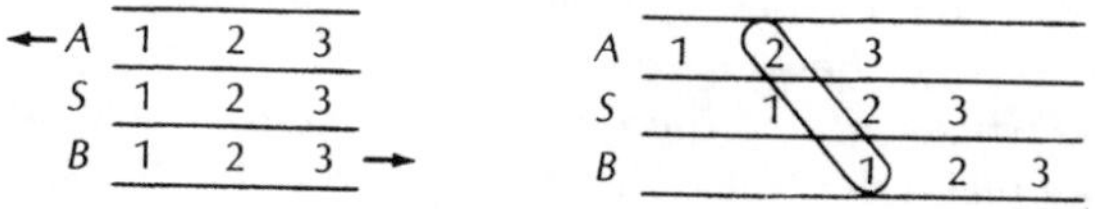

FIGURE 5. The slanted combination *A*2, *B*1 is the *non-event* vertical alignment.

[82] For a brief characterization of such a logically possible world, see my essay 'The Falsifiability of a Component of a Theoretical System" in *Mind, Method, Matter*, Festschrift for Herbert Feigl, edited by P. Feyerabend and G. Maxwell (Minneapolis: University of Minnesota Press, 1966), pp. 298–299.

following reason: As rows A and B were moving in opposite directions, there must have been a temporally *intervening* instant at which B1 was vertically aligned with A2, which is between A1 and A3.

Whitrow's comment on Zeno's Stadium is as follows:

> Despite its ingenuity, this is one of the easiest of Zeno's arguments to answer. For, if space and time are composed of discrete units, then relative motions must be such that the situations typified by the diagrams . . . *can* occur at successive instants [i.e., a point row A can move with respect to a point row B at the rate of two granular points per indivisible moment]. . . . Indeed, Zeno is in fact guilty of a logical error himself when he makes this appeal, for in fact he is tacitly invoking a postulate of continuity which is incompatible with the hypotheses adopted at the beginning of the argument.[83]

Similarly, in 1903 Bertrand Russell cited the opinion of M. Evellin[84] that A2 and B1 did not cross each other at all. For given that instants are indivisible, all we can say is that at one instant A1 is over B1 and at the very next instant, A3 is over B1. Nothing has happened between the instants, since the supposition that A2 and B1 have crossed springs from the tacit but illicit assumption of denseness. And in 1903 Russell's comment on Evellin's opinion was: "This reply is valid, I think, in the case of motion."[85] But without telling us what prompted him to change his mind, Russell retracted the very point endorsed by him here by declaring later à propos of the Arrow:

> At each of the thousand instants, the arrow is where it is, though at the next instant it is somewhere else. It is never moving, but in some miraculous way the change of position has to occur *between* the instants, that is to say, not at any time whatever. . . . The more the difficulty is meditated, the more real it becomes. The solution lies in the theory of continuous series. . . .[86]

---

[83] G. J. Whitrow, *The Natural Philosophy of Time* [119], pp. 136–137.

[84] B. Russell, *The Principles of Mathematics* [102], p. 352.

[85] *Ibid.*

[86] B. Russell, *Our Knowledge of the External World* [100], p. 179.

To state what lesson I believe to be implicit in Zeno's Stadium and to have been overlooked by Whitrow's and Evellin's replies to him, I invite attention to Figure 6. Whereas in Figure 5, rows *A* and *B* moved in opposite directions at

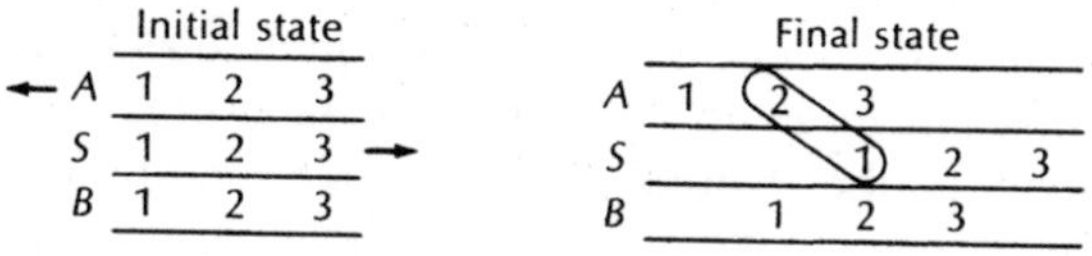

FIGURE 6. The slanted combination *A*2, *S*1 is the *non*-event vertical alignment.

the rate of one point per instant with respect to row *S*, in Figure 6 assume that *A* and *S* move oppositely at the unit rate with respect to *B*. Thus, while a relative "double jump" is exhibited in Figure 5 by *A* and *B*, in Figure 6 rows *A* and *S* engage in relative "double jumps."

Now let us compare the *event-status* of the vertical alignment of *B*1 with *A*2 as between the situations in Figures 5 and 6, and let us make a like comparison for the vertical alignment of *S*1 with *A*2. That both alignments *exist* in both situations is assertible on the strength of the *spatial* relations of betweenness, alignment, and contiguity inherent in the several states of affairs involving rows of discrete sets of points; the affirmations of these vertical alignments do *not* depend on an illicit and covert appeal to temporal continuity. But whether these vertical alignments *also* qualify as having *event-status within the conceptual framework of spatio-temporal atomicity* depends on there *also existing an instant* at which the points in question can be vertically aligned. Thus, having distinguished, as the atomicity theory is driven to do, between vertical point alignments that also qualify as *events* and those which do not, our comparison yields the following important findings: The vertical alignment of *B*1 with *A*2 is *not* an event in the situation of Figure 5 but it is an event in the situation of Figure 6, and the vertical alignment of *A*2 with *S*1 *is* an event in Figure 5 but is *not* an event in Figure 6.

Hence whether a given spatial vertical alignment qualifies as an event or not depends on the magnitude of the *relative* velocity of the two rows: If it is *two* "jumps," then a vertical alignment need not qualify as an event, whereas it does so qualify when the relative velocity is one "jump."

I wish to call attention to this consequence as a *cautionary lesson* implicit in Zeno's Stadium to be borne in mind by proponents of the stronger program of space-time granulation. This consequence has the significance of a *caveat* for the following reason: As far as I am aware, none of our present-day kinematic knowledge even gives a hint of the possibility of the aforementioned dependence of event-status on relative motion. This important fact was overlooked by Whitrow when he wrote:

> . . . *on the hypothesis of temporal atomicity*, Achilles will not traverse anything in an indivisible element of time; at each instant he will be in a definite place, at one instant he will be here, at the next instant there, and that is all there is to it.[87]

I have endeavored to show that there is more to it than that!

[87] G. J. Whitrow, *The Natural Philosophy of Time* [119], p. 154.

Appendix:
Sets and
Infinity

Since a certain rudimentary knowledge of the theory of sets is essential to an understanding and appreciation of the arguments concerning Zeno's paradoxes, this appendix presents, for the benefit of readers who have had little or no exposure to the discipline, a few of the basic facts relating directly to the essays in this volume.[1]

From our everyday use of the English language we all have some general understanding of words like "class," "set," "collection," and "aggregate." In the context of this book all of these terms may be regarded as synonyms, and may be used interchangeably. Roughly, then, a *set* or *class* is simply a collection of entities, concrete or abstract, that can be brought together intellectually and considered as an aggregate. The objects x belonging to such a collection A are *members* of the set A—in symbols, xϵA, where epsilon stands for the relation of being a member of (or element of) a class.

The membership of a set can be specified by listing the members or by citing a property possessed by all and only members of that set. Braces are used to indicate set membership. Thus, {2, 5, 9} is the set containing the numbers two, five, and nine. {x | x is even} is the class of all even numbers; the symbolic expression is read, "The set of all x such that x is even."

As we shall see from examples, the grouping of the elements to form a class may seem "natural" or "arbitrary."

<hr>

[1] For a more detailed treatment of this topic see Abraham A. Fraenkel, *Abstract Set Theory* [124], or E. Kamke, *Theory of Sets* [127].

251

Such factors have no bearing upon the status of collections as sets. The following examples all qualify: the class of all college freshmen; the class of all prime numbers; the class of all 1963 automobiles; the class of all points between one and two on a given coordinate axis; the class containing the piece of paper I just threw into the waste basket, Louis XIV, and the planet Venus. The fact that we seldom have occasion to talk about such weird collections as the last does not mean that they are not classes. Furthermore, although we may usually think of classes or sets as collections of several objects each, there are classes with just one member—these are called *unit classes*. There is, in addition, a set with no members at all—this is called the *null* or *empty set* and is symbolized by the capital Greek lambda, "Λ." The set of even prime numbers, for example, is a unit set whose only member is the number two. The class of inventors of bona fide perpetual motion machines has no members, so it is the null set.

Two sets A and B are identical—in symbols, $A = B$—if they have the same membership, that is, if every member of A is also a member of B and every member of B is also a member of A. Thus, for example,

$$\{2\} = \{\text{the number of shoes in a pair}\} =$$
$$\{x \mid x \text{ is an even prime}\}.$$

As a consequence of this definition we speak of *the* null set, for any empty set has the same members (namely, none) as any "other" empty set. Thus,

$$\{x \mid x \text{ is an inventor of a perpetual motion machine}\} = \Lambda =$$
$$\{x \mid x \text{ is a one hundred dollar bill located in my pocket}\}.$$

It is a further consequence of this definition that the order in which the members of a class are given has no bearing upon its identity; for example,

$$\{2, 5, 9\} = \{5, 9, 2\} = \{9, 2, 5\}, \text{ etc.}$$

If all of the members of a set A are also members of a set B we say that A is *included* in B or A is a *subset* of B—in symbols, $A \subseteq B$. As a consequence of this definition we say that the null set is a subset of every set, for it vacuously satisfies that condition that all of its members (of which there are none) are members of A, whatever set A may be. Moreover, every set is a subset of itself, for every member of A is a member of A. Thus, for any set A, $A \subseteq A$ and $\Lambda \subseteq A$. As a further immediate consequence of our definitions, the sets A and B are identical if each is a subset of the other; that is, if $A \subseteq B$ and $B \subseteq A$, then $A = B$. The set A is a *proper subset* of B—in symbols, $A \subset B$—if every member of A is a member of B but at least one member of B is not a member of A. Thus, no set is a *proper* subset of itself. The set of natural numbers, for example, has the following subsets, among others: the set of natural numbers, the set of even natural numbers, the set of prime numbers, the set that contains only the number twelve, and the set of all numbers that are both odd and even. The first of these subsets is not a proper subset, the next to the last is a unit set, and the last is the null set.

It is of fundamental logical importance to distinguish carefully between members of sets and subsets of sets—that is, to distinguish between the relation of class membership, denoted by "ϵ," and the relation of class inclusion, denoted by "$\subseteq$." For example, {12} is a unit set containing the number twelve as its sole member, and it is quite distinct from the number twelve itself. The number twelve is a *member* of the class of natural numbers; the set {12} is not a member but it is a *subset*. Moreover, the null set has no members, but it has one subset—itself. The distinction between members and subsets is essentially one of different logical levels. A set is on a higher logical level than its members, but it is on the same logical level with its subsets. When we use due caution in distinguishing class membership from class inclusion it is possible to construct a logical hierarchy with elements of sets on the lowest level, sets on the next, sets of sets on the next, and so on. For example, a shoe is a member of a class containing two members—a pair of shoes; this pair is, in turn, a member of a class of classes—the class of all pairs of shoes. This latter class is, of course, quite different from the class of all shoes, for the class of all shoes has shoes as members, while the class of all pairs of shoes has classes as members.[2]

It is often important to refer to the subsets of a given set A; together they constitute the set of all subsets of A, which is quite different from the class of all members of A (A itself). As a matter of fact, Georg Cantor, founder of the modern theory of sets, provided a beautiful proof that for any set A, whether null or non-null, whether finite or infinite, the *subsets* of A outnumber the *members* of A.[3] For example, {2, 5, 9} has three members, but eight subsets, namely Λ, {2}, {5}, {9}, {2, 5}, {2, 9}, {5, 9}, and {2, 5, 9}. It follows that there are infinite classes of different sizes if there are any infinite classes at all, for the class of subsets of an infinite class is a larger infinite class.

There are various operations that can be applied to sets. The *complement* A′ of a set A is the set of all entities not contained in A. The operation of complementation is usually relative to some universe of discourse. Within the universe of natural numbers, for example, the set of composite numbers is the complement of the set of prime numbers; within the universe of humans, infants and children make up the complement of the class of adults. The *sum* (or *union*) of two sets A and B—in symbols, A ∪ B—is the set of things that belong to A or B or both. The set of natural numbers is, for example, the sum of the set of odd natural numbers and the set of even natural numbers. The class of natural numbers that are even and/or prime is the sum of the class of even natural numbers and the class of prime numbers; it does not matter that the number two happens to belong to both of these classes. The *product* (or *intersection*) of two sets A and B—in symbols, A ∩ B—is the set whose members belong to

---

[2] Failure to observe some sort of type distinction between logical levels will lead to outright contradiction, as Russell has shown through a celebrated antinomy. See Bertrand Russell, *Introduction to Mathematical Philosophy* [129], chap. 13, or Raymond Wilder, *Introduction to the Foundations of Mathematics* [131], chap. 3, §2.

[3] For the proof see Fraenkel [124], chap. 2, §5, par. 3, or Kamke [127], pp. 21–22.

both sets. Thus, {2} is the set product of the set of even natural numbers and the set of prime numbers. When two classes have no members in common they are said to be *mutually exclusive;* their class product is the null set.

When we ask *how many* members a set A has, the answer is a *cardinal number*—the cardinal of the set A. The size of a set is its *cardinality.* The natural numbers, including zero, are finite cardinal numbers, but there are infinite cardinals as well. Zero is the cardinal number of the null set, and one is the cardinal number of any unit set. The cardinality of a set, like its identity, is independent of the order in which the members occur. Three is the cardinal number of {2, 5, 9}— which is the same set as {5, 9, 2} and {9, 2, 5}. It need occasion no confusion that we have referred to sets whose members are cardinal numbers, for the members of a set are quite distinct from its cardinality. For instance, one is the cardinal number of the set {12}, while twelve is the cardinal number of the set of months of the year. As we shall see shortly, the cardinal number of the set of finite cardinals is, itself, an infinite cardinal.

The fundamental concept that enables us to compare different sets with respect to cardinality is the notion of a *one-to-one correspondence.* We say that two sets have *the same number* of members—that is, they have the *same cardinal number*—if and only if it is possible to put the members of one set into one-to-one correspondence with the members of the other. On the basis of this relationship, it is possible to determine whether two classes have the same number of members without counting the members of either. For instance, we know that the number of seats in an auditorium equals the number of people in that auditorium if each seat is occupied by one and only one person, and no people are left unseated. If some people remain standing after all the seats are thus occupied there are more people than seats; if all the people are seated in separate seats and some seats remain vacant there are more seats than people.

This concept of a one-to-one correspondence provides the basis for a suitable definition of "infinity" for sets and cardinal numbers. In the case of finite sets, it is quite obvious that the set itself has a greater number of members than do any of its proper subsets. The class of scientists living in the twentieth century is a proper subset of, and has a smaller cardinal number than, the class of scientists who have ever lived at any time. If a member is removed from a finite class, the result is a smaller class. The defining characteristic of an infinite class, by contrast, is that it has the same number of members as at least one of its *proper* subclasses. An *infinite set* has some proper subset whose members can be put into one-to-one correspondence with the members of the entire set. For example, the class of natural numbers is infinite, for it can be put into one-to-one correspondence with the class of positive natural numbers, and this in turn can be put into one-to-one correspondence with the class of even natural numbers, as follows:

0	1	2	3	4	5	.	.	.
1	2	3	4	5	6	.	.	.
2	4	6	8	10	12	.	.	.

Each number on the third line is double the one directly above it, and each of these is, in turn, just one greater than the number directly above it. For each natural number we can find a corresponding positive natural number and conversely; for each positive natural number we can find a corresponding even natural number and conversely. Thus, these three sets are all infinite and all of equal cardinality. The cardinal number of the class of natural numbers is the smallest infinite cardinal; the symbol for this number is "$\aleph_0$," the Hebrew letter aleph with a zero as subscript (pronounced "aleph null"). This is the cardinal number of any class whose members can be put into a one-to-one correspondence with the natural numbers. Such classes are known as *enumerable, denumerable,* or *countably infinite* classes. Any progression developed according to a formula that provides a term for each natural number—e.g., the progression $\frac{1}{2}$, $\frac{1}{4}$, $\frac{1}{8}$, . . . generated by the rule $\frac{1}{2^{n+1}}$, where n runs through the natural numbers (including zero), which figures prominently in the "Dichotomy" and "Achilles and the Tortoise" paradoxes—has $\aleph_0$ members.

When we see that the number of natural numbers is equal to the number of even natural numbers, it should come as no surprise to learn that the number of integers, positive or negative, is also $\aleph_0$. A suitable one-to-one correspondence is easily found. (Can you find one?) A *rational number* is any number that can be expressed as a fraction with an integer as numerator and an integer as denominator. When we reflect that there are infinitely many rational numbers distributed densely between any two natural numbers, we might be tempted to guess that there are more than $\aleph_0$ rational numbers, but this would be incorrect. Cantor provided a simple proof that the number of positive rational numbers is equal to the number of positive natural numbers. To establish the appropriate one-to-one correspondence between the positive rational numbers and the positive natural numbers, let us set up a two-dimensional matrix by arranging the natural numbers in a horizontal row and again in a vertical column. Letting the numbers in the horizontal row be numerators, while those in the vertical column are denominators, our matrix provides a place for every positive rational number:

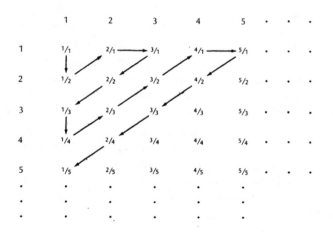

To show that these positive rational numbers can be put into a one-to-one correspondence with the positive natural numbers, we proceed to enumerate the rationals, thus assigning a natural number to each. Following the path of the arrows back and forth diagonally, we arrange the rational numbers in a sequence, skipping any number (e.g., 2/2, 4/2, etc.) that has already occurred in a different form:

$$1 \quad 2 \quad 3 \quad 4 \quad 5 \quad 6 \quad \cdots$$
$$1/1 \quad 1/2 \quad 2/1 \quad 3/1 \quad 1/3 \quad 1/4 \quad \cdots$$

This method insures that we shall reach any given positive rational number eventually, and in so doing we shall attach it to a unique natural number. In view of the above-mentioned one-to-one correspondence between the positive natural numbers and the entire class of integers, it is a simple matter to extend the above result to a complete enumeration of the entire class of rationals, positive or negative. (Can you see how to do it?)

At this point, had we not been forewarned, it might have been tempting to jump to the conclusion that all infinite sets have the same cardinal number $\aleph_0$. This is incorrect. When we consider the class of real numbers we find a higher order infinity. The rational numbers can all be written as decimals as well as in fractional form; a rational number always turns out to be a terminating decimal or a periodic decimal. Thus, $\frac{1}{2} = 0.5$, while $\frac{1}{3} = 0.333\ldots$. Actually, any terminating decimal can be written as a periodic one; for instance, $\frac{1}{2} = 0.499999\ldots$. To insure a unique representation for each number we shall adopt the non-terminating periodic form and avoid the terminating decimals. The so-called *irrational numbers*, by contrast, come out as infinite decimals which are not periodic; such numbers as pi and $\sqrt{2}$ are irrational. The set-sum or union of the set of rational numbers and the set of irrational numbers constitutes the set of *real numbers*. Cantor has given an elegant proof that the class of real numbers is not denumerable—that it has more members than the class of rational numbers. It suffices to consider the real numbers between zero and one. The demonstration proceeds by *reductio ad absurdum*. Let us suppose that some enumeration—*any* enumeration—of the real numbers could exist; it would constitute a list of real numbers corresponding to the positive natural numbers in the following manner:

1	0.2̄5978 . . .
2	0.5̄3224 . . .
3	0.43̄725 . . .
4	0.22̄897 . . .
5	0.978̄62 . . .

.
.
.

Cantor now shows us how to find a real number between zero and one that is not in the supposedly complete list. We begin by looking at the digit in the first decimal place of the first number; it is two. We choose another digit, say three, which differs from the one we found. Moreover, we always choose a digit other than zero. (Why?) Next, we look at the digit in the second decimal place of the second number; we choose another digit that is different from it and from zero. Proceeding in this way, we choose digits that differ from zero and from the digit found in the nth place of the nth number. Writing these down in order after a decimal point we get a real number between zero and one, say,

$$0.35621 . . . ,$$

which *cannot be in the list*. It differs from the first number in the first decimal place, from the second number in the second decimal place, from the third number in the third decimal place, . . ., from the nth number in the nth decimal place. Hence, the supposition that the list was complete must have been false.

To prove that two sets have the same cardinality, it is sufficient to produce any particular relationship that establishes a one-to-one correspondence. To prove that two sets differ in cardinality it is not sufficient to show that some particular relationship fails to yield a one-to-one correspondence. To prove inequality it is necessary to show that no relationship could possibly constitute a one-to-one correspondence. That is what the preceding argument shows, for it applies in precisely the same way to any relationship anyone could conceivably suggest. This establishes the fact that the cardinality of the set of real numbers is greater than the cardinality of the set of natural numbers. Sets larger than the set of natural numbers are known as *non-denumerable* or *super-denumerable* sets.

The basis for analytic geometry is the establishment of a one-to-one correspondence between the real numbers and the points on the coordinate axis. Thus, the interval or line segment between zero and one on the coordinate axis contains just as many points as there are real numbers between zero and one. We have just seen the proof that this number is larger than $\aleph_0$; it is denoted by "c," which stands for "continuum." It is easy to provide a geometric proof that the number of points in a finite interval of any size is equal to the number of points in a finite interval of any other size, and that both of these contain the same number of points as an infinite line.

Figure 1 shows how to establish a one-to-one correspondence between the points in finite intervals of different sizes. Figure 2 shows how to do it for a finite interval and an in-

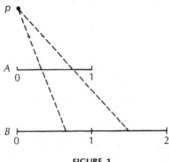

FIGURE 1

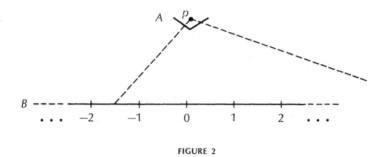

finite line. In each case, a straight line from the point p through any point in A determines a unique point in B, and a straight line from p to any point in B selects a unique point in A.[4] Moreover, it can be shown that c is also the cardinal number of points in a finite area, the cardinal number of points in a finite solid, and the cardinal number of points in the entire three-dimensional space.[5] (Can you think of a set whose cardinality is greater than c?)

Our discussion has so far focused upon the features of sets that do not depend upon the order in which the members occur. Although they may have been given in some particular order, the order could be changed without affecting such properties. The natural ordering of the rational numbers, for example, is an ordering according to magnitude. However, when we considered the cardinality of the class of positive rational numbers, we radically reordered them for the purpose of establishing a one-to-one correspondence with the natural numbers. Our reordering entirely destroyed the natural order and imposed in its stead a new and unusual ordering. We could be confident in so

[4] If a straight line is drawn from p through either end-point of A, it will be parallel with B and will fail to intersect with B at any point. In order to avoid this minor complication, we remove both end-points from A, so that we have remaining an open interval such that each of its points corresponds to a unique point of B. Removing (or adding) two points obviously has no bearing upon the cardinality of an infinite class.

[5] See Fraenkel [124], chap. 2, §6, par. 10.

doing that the rearrangement would not change the cardinality of the class. We could, indeed, be confident that reordering could not affect any property of the class *per se,* for the very identity of classes is independent of the ordering of the members.

There are, however, certain aspects of Zeno's paradoxes that depend crucially upon the ordering of the members within the sets we are considering. We must go a step beyond cardinality and introduce the concept of *order type.*[6] A class by itself has no order; order is a property of a class plus a relation.[7] The rational numbers merely as a set have no order, but the rational numbers, together with the relation of *less than* which establishes the natural order, has an order. If we ignore the relation of relative magnitude and substitute some other relation, the result may be an entirely different kind of ordering. Among the relations commonly used to order members of sets are relations of *greater than* and *less than* among numbers, *to the left of* among points on a line, and *later than* among temporally successive events.

For a precise characterization of order type, as in the case of cardinal number, we begin with a definition of equality. Again the concept of a one-to-one correspondence is fundamental. We shall say that two classes A and B have the same order type with respect to the two ordering relations R and S, where R orders the members of A and S orders the

[6] For a treatment of ordered sets see Fraenkel [124], chap. 3, Kamke [127], and Edward V. Huntington, *The Continuum and Other Types of Serial Order* [126]. If an order type is well-ordered, it is also known as an ordinal number.

[7] To be more exact, we require a relation that establishes a simple order for the class A, namely, a relation $<$ such that

1. if x and y are distinct elements of A, then either $x < y$ or $y < x$ (the relation is connexive);

2. if $x < y$ then x and y are distinct (the relation is irreflexive);

3. if $x < y$ and $y < z$, then $x < z$ (the relation is transitive).

If the class A contains at least two elements to be ordered, i.e., in all cases where order is not a degenerate concept, the foregoing conditions assure asymmetry of the relation: if $x < y$ it is not the case that $y < x$. The concept of simple order thus characterizes orderings in which it is always determinate which of any two distinct elements of a class precedes the other in the order in question. In this discussion we are concerned with simply ordered sets only.

members of *B,* provided the following *two* conditions are satisfied:

1. There exists a one-to-one correspondence between the members of *A* and the members of *B* (i.e., *A* and *B* are equal in cardinality), and

2. This one-to-one correspondence preserves corresponding relationships.

The second condition requires careful explanation. Suppose *x* and *y* are any two elements of the class *A,* while *x'* and *y'* are the elements of the class *B* associated with *x* and *y* respectively under the one-to-one correspondence of condition 1. In order for condition 2 to hold, it is necessary that *x'* have the relation *S* to *y'* whenever *x* bears the relation *R* to *y.* This is what is meant by saying that the one-to-one correspondence is relation-preserving. Some examples will help to clarify these concepts.

Consider the class of natural numbers, the class of positive natural numbers, and the class of even positive natural numbers, all of which have been shown to have the same cardinality $\aleph_0$. Taken in their natural order, each of these classes is ordered by a *less than* relation. The three classes, thus ordered, have the same order type. We see upon inspection that the one-to-one correspondences used above to establish their equal cardinality are relation-preserving. Given, for instance, two natural numbers of which one is less than the other, we find that the even natural number corresponding to the former is invariably smaller than the even natural number corresponding to the latter. The order type that these ordered classes have in common is denoted by "ω," the lower case Greek omega. It is the order type of all infinite progressions. A set exhibiting order type ω has the following outstanding characteristics: the set has a first (least) element, each element except the first has a unique immediate predecessor, and every element has a unique immediate successor (hence there is no last element).[8]

---

[8] Discrete series, including those of type ω, also satisfy Dedekind's postulate:
   If K_1 and K_2 are any two non-empty parts of K such that every element of K

Consider next the set of positive integers and the set of negative integers. These two sets can obviously be put into one-to-one correspondence with each other as follows:

$$+1, +2, +3, +4, \ldots$$
$$-1, -2, -3, -4, \ldots$$

They therefore have the same cardinal number $\aleph_0$. If both of these sets are ordered by the relation *less than,* they do *not* share the same order type. We see this immediately by noting that, while $+1$ is less than $+2$, the corresponding element -1 is *greater* than -2. If, however, we order the positive integers by the relation of *less than,* but order the negative integers by the relation of *larger than,* the one-to-one correspondence we have established is relation-preserving. Ordered by this relation, the negative integers do constitute an instance of order type ω. This fact shows once more that we cannot determine the order type of a set unless a specific ordering relation is given. With a change of ordering relation the same set may exhibit a change of order type.

The set of negative integers ordered in the normal way by the relation of *less than* has the order type of an infinite regression. In contrast to the progression, it has no first (least) element, but it does have a last (greatest). Its order type is $*\omega$. The regression $\ldots \frac{1}{8}, \frac{1}{4}, \frac{1}{2}$, which is involved in Zeno's "Dichotomy" paradox, has this order type.

An important modification of the order types ω and $*\omega$ can be made by adding an element at the appropriate end. If we take all of the positive integers in their usual order and then zero,

$$+1, +2, +3, \ldots 0,$$

we have an example of order type $\omega + 1$. This ordered set has a first and a last element. The last element comes after *all* of the positive integers, so it has no immediate predeces-

---

belongs to either K_1 or K_2 and every element of K_1 precedes every element of K_2, then there is at least one element X in K such that:

(1) Any element that precedes X belongs to K_1.
(2) Any element that follows X belongs to K_2.

Huntington [126], p. 19.

sor because there is no largest positive integer. The ordered set $\frac{1}{2}, \frac{3}{4}, \frac{7}{8}, \ldots 1$, which plays a crucial role in the discussions by Thomson and Benacerraf, also has order type $\omega + 1$. The distinction between order type ω and $\omega + 1$ is of central importance to their arguments. Notice that the addition of zero at the beginning of the sequence of positive integers would have had no effect upon the order type, for the order type of the positive integers is the same as that of the non-negative integers. Analogously, by placing zero before all of the negative integers, we create an ordered set with order type $1 + *\omega$, while the placement of zero at the end of all the negative numbers would leave the order type unchanged. In Zeno's "Dichotomy" paradox, we have to consider the set of positions $0, \ldots \frac{1}{8}, \frac{1}{4}, \frac{1}{2}$, which has order type $1 + *\omega$.

In the order types ω and $*\omega$, the elements all have next-door neighbors. In both of these order types, any element having a successor has an immediate successor, and any element having a predecessor has an immediate predecessor. When we move on to the rational numbers in their natural order (according to magnitude), we find that the nextness property is entirely absent. (We can, as we have seen, reorder them to conform to order type ω, but this is a radical departure from their usual order.) In the natural order, the set of rational numbers is *dense*. This means that between any two rational numbers there is always another, and consequently infinitely many others. No rational number has an immediate predecessor or an immediate successor. Moreover, there is no first (least) rational number and there is no last (greatest) rational number. The order type of the rational numbers in their usual order is designated by "η," the small Greek eta. The set of rational numbers in any *open* interval (e.g., the rational numbers greater than zero and smaller than one—end-points excluded) has the same order type. (Can you prove this?) It is the dense ordering of the points of space and the moments of time that gives rise to all of the difficulties Zeno found concerning infinite divisibility.

The order types so far considered are all order types of denumerable sets. As we have seen, the linear continuum, whether it is the arithmetic continuum of real numbers or the geometric continuum of points on a line, contains a super-denumerable infinity of elements. This is true of the set of numbers or points in a finite interval, as well as the entire set of real numbers or points on an infinite line. Since the cardinality of the continuum differs from the cardinality of the ordered sets we discussed above, we must have a new order type to characterize the continuum. This order type is designated by "λ," the small Greek lambda; it is the order type for any finite *open* interval as well as the entire linear continuum (as can be seen by inspection of Figure 2 above).

Like the set of rational numbers, the set of real numbers has a dense order. It is, perhaps, hard to see how a dense set can have "holes" in it. Nevertheless, as the ancient Pythagoreans discovered much to their consternation, a line consisting of points corresponding to the rational numbers alone would not be a complete continuum. Suppose that a circle, with a radius equal to the diagonal of a square whose side is one unit long, is drawn about the origin of a coordinate system.

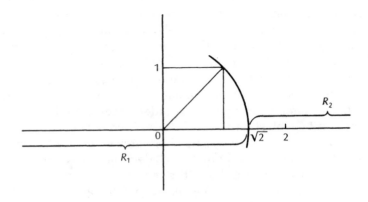

FIGURE 3

This circle would not intersect the axis at a rational point, and hence would not intersect the axis at all if that axis contained only rational points, for the distance from the center to the circumference is $\sqrt{2}$. The circle would slip through between the rational points, even though the rational points are packed densely into the line. The points of the linear continuum must be densely ordered, but they must satisfy some other conditions as well.

The circle that passes between the rational points at a distance $\sqrt{2}$ from the origin divides the whole set of rational points on the line, and by the same token the whole set of rational numbers, into two mutually exclusive subsets R_1 and R_2. Without loss we can talk about the numbers, for whatever is said applies *mutatis mutandis* to the points associated with those numbers. R_1 is the set of rational numbers less than $\sqrt{2}$; R_2 is the set of rational numbers greater than $\sqrt{2}$. Such a division in an ordered set A is a *cut*. It satisfies the following conditions:

1. Neither subset is empty.
2. The two subsets are mutually exclusive.
3. The union of the two subsets is the entire set A.
4. Each member of R_1 precedes every member of R_2 in the ordering of A.

A cut in the rational numbers might be such that R_1 had a largest element, or it might be such that R_2 had a smallest; because of the dense ordering of the rationals, no single cut could satisfy both of these conditions. Our cut, however, exemplifies a third possibility: R_1 has no greatest element *and* R_2 has no smallest element. A cut of this sort is a *gap*. A *continuum* must have a dense order and it must have no gaps. Any cut in a continuum yields either a largest member of the preceding subset or a smallest member of the succeeding subset, but not both. In order to qualify as a *linear continuum*, it must satisfy a linearity condition as well.[9]

[9] This condition requires that the set A have a denumerable subset R that occurs densely within it; that is, the cardinality of R is $\aleph_0$ and between any two

It is the linear continuum, with its super-denumerable cardinality, its dense ordering, and its absence of gaps, which lies at the foundation of our modern understanding of all of Zeno's paradoxes of plurality and motion. The paradoxes take as their point of departure the supposition that space, time, and physical processes are continua. The resolution of the paradoxes along the lines proposed by Grünbaum rests heavily upon a searching analysis of the ordinal and metrical structure of the linear continuum.

members of A there is at least one member of R. This condition is obviously satisfied by the set of real numbers in their natural order, for the set of rational numbers is denumerable and occurs densely among the real numbers. See Huntington [126], chap. 5. A continuum must also satisfy Dedekind's postulate (see preceding footnote).

BIBLIOGRAPHY

Although it would be impractical to attempt a complete bibliography of works on Zeno and his arguments, the following list of references should serve the needs of readers who wish to pursue the study of Zeno beyond the contents of this volume. Every effort has been made to mention the most important and readily available works; moreover, many cited are so well documented that the scholar should find the present bibliography, though incomplete, a fertile starting point for further research.

As an aid to the reader, the Bibliography is subdivided into four main parts. Part I is primarily historical. The works cited contain the ancient source material on Zeno, discussions of the historical significance of Zeno's arguments, and studies that attempt to reconstruct the actual content and import of the arguments as stated by Zeno. Part II mentions works that are mainly systematic. Ignoring, for the most part, niceties of historical interpretation, these works concentrate on the substantive issues that have arisen out of Zeno's arguments. Part III contains references to useful auxiliary material in modern mathematics, physics, and philosophy. They are given to provide technical background that might be needed for a full appreciation of contemporary treatments of Zeno's arguments. Part IV, Supplementary Sources, updates the Bibliography for the 2001 reprinting.

The foregoing distinctions are to some degree arbitrary, especially regarding the classification of works as primarily historical. Since much historical work on Zeno has resulted in the attribution of subtle interpretation and deep significance, several of the primarily historical works have considerable systematic interest. Furthermore, few historical treatments are completely lacking in critical analysis of the arguments.

I. Historical

Among the historical works below, Lee's *Zeno of Elea,* Cajori's "The History of Zeno's Arguments on Motion," and Vlastos' "Zeno of Elea" in *The Encyclopedia of Philosophy* stand out as comprehensive and well-documented treatments. Lee provides the primary sources, Cajori traces the arguments from antiquity to the twentieth century, and Vlastos gives a well-rounded account of the present state of scholarship on Zeno.

CLASSICAL SOURCES

1. Aristotle. *Physics.*
2. Lee, H. D. P. *Zeno of Elea.* Cambridge: University Press, 1936.
3. Plato. *Parmenides.*

HISTORIES OF GREEK PHILOSOPHY

4. Burnet, John. *Early Greek Philosophy.* 4th edn. London: Adam & Charles Black, 1948.
5. Copleston, Frederick. *A History of Philosophy.* Vol. I, *Greece and Rome.* Westminster, Maryland: The Newman Press, 1948.
6. Kirk, G. S., and J. E. Raven. *The Presocratic Philosophers.* Cambridge: University Press, 1957.
7. Robin, Léon. *Greek Thought and the Origins of the Scientific Spirit.* New York: Alfred A. Knopf, 1928.
8. Zeller, E. *A History of Greek Philosophy.* Vol. I, trans. S. F. Alleyne. London: Longmans, Green and Co., 1881.

COMMENTARIES ON PLATO AND ARISTOTLE

9. Allen, R. E. "The Interpretation of Plato's 'Parmenides': Zeno's Paradoxes and the Theory of Forms," *Journal of the History of Philosophy,* II (1964), 143–155.
10. Cherniss, Harold. *Aristotle's Criticism of Presocratic Philosophy.* Baltimore: The Johns Hopkins Press, 1935.

11. Cornford, Francis MacDonald. *Plato and Parmenides.* London: Kegan Paul, Trench, Trubner & Co., Ltd., 1939.
12. Gershenson, Daniel E., and Daniel A. Greenberg. "Aristotle Confronts the Eleatics: Two Arguments on 'The One,' " *Phronesis,* VII (1962), 137–151.
13. Greene, Murray. "Aristotle's Circular Movement as a Logos Doctrine," *Review of Metaphysics,* XIX (1965), 115–132.
14. Heath, Sir Thomas. *Mathematics in Aristotle.* Oxford: Clarendon Press, 1949.
15. Ross, W. D. *Aristotle's Physics.* Oxford: Clarendon Press, 1936.
16. Solmsen, Friedrich. *Aristotle's System of the Physical World.* Ithaca, New York: Cornell University Press, 1960.
17. Taylor, A. E. *The Parmenidés of Plato.* Oxford: Clarendon Press, 1934.
18. ———. "Parmenides, Zeno, and Socrates," *Proceedings of the Aristotelian Society,* N. S. XVI (1915–16), 234–289.

HISTORICAL STUDIES OF ZENO

19. Booth, N. B. "Were Zeno's Arguments a Reply to Attacks upon Parmenides?" *Phronesis,* I (1957), 1–9.
20. ———. "Were Zeno's Arguments Directed Against the Pythagoreans?" *Phronesis,* I (1957), 90–103.
21. ———. "Zeno's Paradoxes," *Journal of Hellenic Studies,* LXXVII (1957), 189–201.
22. Cajori, Florian. "The History of Zeno's Arguments on Motion," *American Mathematical Monthly,* XXII (1915), 1–6, 38–47, 77–82, 109–115, 143–149, 179–186, 215–220, 253–258, 292–297. Also bound together as a single reprint. Comprehensive.
23. ———. "The Purpose of Zeno's Arguments on Motion," *Isis,* III (1920–21), 7–20. An account of differing views of important historians.
24. Fränkel, Hermann. "Zeno of Elea's Attacks on Plurality," *American Journal of Philology,* LXIII (1942), 1–25, 193–

206. The paradoxes of plurality and their relation to the paradoxes of motion.

25. Gaye, R. K. "On Aristotle *Physics* Z ix 239ᵇ33–240ᵃ18," *Journal of Philology*, XXXI (1910), 95–116. The paradox of the stadium.

26. Vlastos, Gregory. "A Note on Zeno's Arrow," *Phronesis*, XI (1966), 3–18.

27. ———. "Zeno," in *Philosophic Classics: Thales to St. Thomas*, ed. Walter Kaufmann, pp. 27–45. Englewood Cliffs, N. J.: Prentice-Hall, Inc., 1961.

28. ———. "Zeno of Elea," in *The Encyclopedia of Philosophy*, ed. Paul Edwards. New York: The Macmillan Company and The Free Press, 1967. An excellent survey of the paradoxes.

29. ———. "Zeno's Race Course," *Journal of the History of Philosophy*, IV (1966), 95–108.

HISTORIES OF MATHEMATICS AND SCIENCE

30. Beth, Evert W. "The Prehistory of Research into Foundations," *British Journal for the Philosophy of Science*, III (1952–53), 58–81.

31. Boyer, Carl B. *The History of the Calculus and its Conceptual Development*. New York: Dover Publications, Inc., 1959. An excellent comprehensive history of the concepts of the derivative and the integral, and the related concepts of infinity, infinitesimals, and continuity. Shows in detail the relevance of nineteenth-century mathematics to Zeno's paradoxes. Previously published under the title *The Concepts of the Calculus*.

32. Evans, Melbourne G. "Aristotle, Newton, and the Theory of Continuous Magnitude," in *Roots of Scientific Thought*, eds. Philip P. Wiener and Aaron Noland. New York: Basic Books, 1957. Reprinted from *Journal of the History of Ideas*, XVI (1955), 548–557.

33. Heath, Sir Thomas. *A History of Greek Mathematics*. Oxford: Clarendon Press, 1921.

34. Sambursky, S. *The Physical World of the Greeks,* trans. Merton Dagut. London: Routledge and Kegan Paul, 1956.
35. Santillana, Giorgio de. *The Origins of Scientific Thought.* Chicago: University of Chicago Press, 1961.

HISTORIES OF LOGIC

36. Bocheński, I. M. *Ancient Formal Logic.* Amsterdam: North-Holland Publishing Company, 1951.
37. ———. *A History of Formal Logic,* trans. and ed. Ivo Thomas. Notre Dame, Indiana: University of Notre Dame Press, 1961.
38. Kneale, William, and Martha Kneale. *The Development of Logic.* Oxford: Clarendon Press, 1962.

II. Systematic

Some philosophers have found in Zeno's paradoxes support for fundamental logical or metaphysical doctrines; their works are cited under the heading "Logico-Metaphysical Conclusions." The remaining works mentioned in Part II are critical analyses of the paradoxes from a variety of viewpoints. Of especial importance in this category is Adolf Grünbaum's *Modern Science and Zeno's Paradoxes,* which is the only modern full-length monograph devoted to the analysis of the paradoxes, and which provides comprehensive, thorough, and detailed treatments of the associated problems.

LOGICO-METAPHYSICAL CONCLUSIONS

39. Bergson, Henri. *Creative Evolution,* trans. Arthur Mitchell. Modern Library edn. New York: Random House, 1944.
40. ———. *Matter and Memory,* trans. Nancy Margaret Paul and W. Scott Palmer. London: George Allen & Unwin Ltd., 1911.
41. ———. *Time and Free Will,* trans. F. L. Pogson. London: George Allen & Unwin Ltd., 1910.

42. Bradley, F. H. *Appearance and Reality,* chaps. 4–5. Oxford: Clarendon Press, 1930. Though making no explicit reference to Zeno, the discussion of space, time, motion, and change is thoroughly Eleatic.
43. Hegel, Georg Wilhelm Friedrich. *Lectures on the History of Philosophy,* trans. E. S. Haldane, pp. 261–278. London: Kegan Paul, Trench, Trubner & Co., Ltd., 1892.
44. James, William. *Some Problems of Philosophy,* chaps. 10–11. New York: Longmans, Green and Co., 1911.
45. Jeans, Sir James. *Physics and Philosophy.* Ann Arbor: University of Michigan Press, 1958.
46. Schaff, Adam. "Marxist Dialectics and the Principle of Contradiction," *Journal of Philosophy,* LVII (1960).
47. Weiss, Paul. *Reality.* Princeton, N. J.: Princeton University Press, 1938.
48. Whitehead, Alfred North. *Process and Reality,* Part II, chap. 2, sec. 2. New York: The Macmillan Company, 1929.
49. ————. *Science and the Modern World,* chaps. 7–8. New York: The Macmillan Company, 1946.

CRITICAL DISCUSSIONS

50. Benacerraf, Paul. "Tasks, Super-Tasks, and the Modern Eleatics," *Journal of Philosophy,* LIX (1962), 765–784. Reprinted above.
51. Benardete, José A. *Infinity; An Essay in Metaphysics.* Oxford: Clarendon Press, 1964.
52. Black, Max. "Achilles and the Tortoise," *Analysis,* XI (1950–51), 91–101. Reprinted above. Essentially the same as Essay VI in *Problems of Analysis.*
53. ————. *Problems of Analysis,* Part II. Ithaca, New York: Cornell University Press, 1954. Contains essays on "The Achilles," "The Arrow," and "The Stadium."
54. Blake, R. M. "The Paradox of Temporal Process," *Journal of Philosophy,* XXIII (1926), 645–654.
55. Broad, C. D. "Note on Achilles and the Tortoise," *Mind,* N. S. XXII (1913), 318–319.

56. Capek, Milic. *The Philosophical Impact of Contemporary Physics.* Princeton, N. J.: D. Van Nostrand Company, Inc., 1961.

57. ———. "Relativity and the Status of Space," *Review of Metaphysics,* IX (1955–56), 169–199.

58. Chappell, V. C. "Time and Zeno's Arrow," *Journal of Philosophy,* LIX (1962), 197–213.

59. ———. "Whitehead's Theory of Becoming," *Journal of Philosophy,* LVIII (1962), 516–528.

60. Chihara, Charles S. "On the Possibility of Completing an Infinite Process," *Philosophical Review,* LXXIV (1965), 74–87.

61. Chwistek, Leon. *The Limits of Science,* trans. Helen Charlotte Brodie and Arthur P. Coleman. London: Kegan Paul, Trench, Trubner & Co., Ltd., 1948.

62. DeBroglie, Louis. *Matter and Light,* trans. W. H. Johnston. New York: W. W. Norton & Company, Inc., 1939. Reprinted by Dover Publications, Inc., New York.

63. Dretske, Fred I. "Counting to Infinity," *Analysis,* XXV (1964–65), 99–101.

64. Findlay, J. N. "Time: A Treatment of Some Puzzles," in *Logic and Language* (First Series), ed. Anthony Flew, chap. 3. Oxford: Basil Blackwell, 1955. Reprinted from *Australasian Journal of Psychology and Philosophy,* XIX (1941).

65. Gale, Richard, ed. *The Philosophy of Time.* Garden City, N. Y.: Anchor Books, Doubleday & Company Inc., 1967. A comprehensive anthology on time; Section V is devoted to Zeno.

66. Greenberg, Leonard. "A Note on the Arrow in Flight," *Philosophical Review,* LIX (1950), 541–542.

67. Grünbaum, Adolf. "Are 'Infinity Machines' Paradoxical?" *Science,* CLIX (1968), 396–406.

68. ———. "Can an Infinitude of Operations be Performed in a Finite Time?" To be published by the University of Chicago Press in a collection of Monday Lectures delivered at the University of Chicago, and in the *British*

Journal for the Philosophy of Science, XX, No. 2 (Oct., 1969).

69. ———. "A Consistent Conception of the Extended Linear Continuum as an Aggregate of Unextended Elements," *Philosophy of Science,* XIX (1952), 288–306. A penetrating discussion of the paradox of plurality; precursor to Grünbaum's "Zeno's Metrical Paradox of Extension" reprinted above.

70. ———. "Messrs. Black and Taylor on Temporal Paradoxes," *Analysis,* XII (1951–52), 144–148.

71. ———. "Modern Science and Refutation of the Paradoxes of Zeno," *Scientific Monthly,* LXXXI (1955), 234–239. Reprinted above with important revisions by the author.

72. ———. *Modern Science and Zeno's Paradoxes.* Middletown, Conn.: Wesleyan University Press, 1967. British edn., which incorporates some revisions; London: George Allen & Unwin Ltd., 1968. "Modern Science and Zeno's Paradoxes of Motion," reprinted above, is taken in part from chap. 2 of the British edn. "Zeno's Metrical Paradox of Extension," also above, is taken from chap. 3.

73. ———. "Relativity and the Atomicity of Becoming," *Review of Metaphysics,* IV (1950–51), 143–186. A comprehensive treatment of the semantical issues raised by the paradoxes of motion.

74. ———. "Whitehead's Method of Extensive Abstraction," *British Journal for the Philosophy of Science,* IV (1953), 215–226.

75. Hanson, Norwood Russell. "The Tortoise Shoots Back," *Philosophical Studies,* XVI (1965), 14–16.

76. Harré, H. R. "Infinity," *Proceedings of the Aristotelian Society,* XXXVIII (1964), 57–68.

77. Hartland-Swann, John. "The Concept of Time," *Philosophical Quarterly,* V (1955), 1–20.

78. Hinton, J. M., and C. B. Martin. "Achilles and the Tortoise," *Analysis,* XIV (1953–54), 56–68.

79. Jones, Philip Chapin. "Achilles and the Tortoise," *Mind,* N.S. LV (1946), 341–45.

80. Jourdain, Philip E. B. "The Flying Arrow: An Anachronism," *Mind,* N. S. XXV (1916), 42–55. Highly amusing as well as penetrating.

81. ————. "Notes on Zeno's Arguments on Motion," *Mind,* N.S. XXVIII (1919), 123–124.

82. King, Hugh R. "Aristotle and the Paradoxes of Zeno," *Journal of Philosophy,* XLVI (1949), 657–670.

83. Lanz, Henry. "Distintegration of Integrals," *The Personalist,* X (1929), 248–255.

84. Lazerowitz, Morris. "The Paradoxes of Motion," *Proceedings of the Aristotelian Society,* N.S. LII (1951–52), 261–280.

85. Lee, Harold N. "Are Zeno's Paradoxes Based on a Mistake?" *Mind,* LXXIV (1965), 563–570.

86. Maritain, Jacques. *Bergsonian Philosophy and Thomism,* trans. Mabelle L. Andison and J. Gordon Andison. New York: Philosophical Library, 1955.

87. Maxwell, Grover, and Herbert Feigl, "Why Ordinary Language Needs Reforming," *Journal of Philosophy,* LVIII (1961), 488–498.

88. Mayo, Bernard. "Shooting It Out with Zeno," *Mind,* LXXIII (1964), 282–283.

89. McLeod, A. N. "A Problem in Philosophy," *Journal of Philosophy,* XXXIII (1936), 656–659.

90. Medlin, Brian. "The Origin of Motion," *Mind,* LXXII (1963), 155–175.

91. Metcalf, W. V. "Achilles and the Tortoise," *Mind,* N.S. LI.

92. Nelson, John O. "Zeno's Paradoxes on Motion," *Review of Metaphysics,* XVI (1963), 486–490.

93. Owen, G. E. L. "Zeno and the Mathematicians," *Proceedings of the Aristotelian Society,* N.S. LVIII (1957–58), 199–222. Reprinted above.

94. Peirce, Charles Sanders. "Achilles and the Tortoise," in *Collected Papers of Charles Sanders Peirce,* eds. Charles

Hartshorne and Paul Weiss, 6.177–184. Cambridge: Harvard University Press, 1935.

95. ———. "The Three Kinds of Sophisms," in *Collected Papers*, 5.333–340.

96. Quan, Stanislaus. "The Solution of the Achilles Paradox," *Review of Metaphysics*, XVI (1963), 473–485.

97. Reichenbach, Hans. *The Direction of Time*, chap. 1. Berkeley and Los Angeles: University of California Press, 1956.

98. Ritchie, A. D. "Why Achilles Does Not Fail to Catch the Tortoise," *Mind*, N.S. L (1941), 310–311.

99. Russell, Bertrand. *Mysticism and Logic*, chap. 5. New York: W. W. Norton & Company, Inc., 1929. Reprinted as "Mathematics and the Metaphysicians," in *The World of Mathematics*, ed. James R. Newman. New York: Simon and Schuster, 1956, pp. 1576–1590.

100. ———. *Our Knowledge of the External World*, lectures 5–7. New York: W. W. Norton & Company, Inc., 1929. "The Problem of Infinity Considered Historically," reprinted above, is taken from lecture 6.

101. ———. "The Philosophy of Bergson," *The Monist*, XXII (1912), 321–347.

102. ———. *The Principles of Mathematics*, esp. chap. 13. 2nd edn. New York: W. W. Norton & Company, Inc., 1943. An interesting arithmetical interpretation of the paradoxes of motion.

103. Ryle, Gilbert. *Dilemmas*, chap. 3. Cambridge: University Press, 1954. A distinctly "ordinary language" approach. Critically reviewed by A. Ambrose, *Journal of Philosophy*, LII (1956), 157–158.

104. Schlegel, Richard. "Quantum Mechanics and the Paradoxes of Zeno," *American Scientist*, XXXVI (1948), 396–402, 414.

105. Shwayder, David S. "Achilles Unbound," *Journal of Philosophy*, LII (1955), 449–459.

106. Siegel, Rudolf E. "The Paradoxes of Zeno; Some Similarities to Modern Thought," *Janus*, XLVIII (1959), 24–47.
107. Smith, Vincent Edward. *The General Science of Nature,* chap. 18. Milwaukee: The Bruce Publishing Company, 1958. A Thomistic textbook, treating space, time, motion, and continuity.
108. Taylor, Richard. "Mr. Black on Temporal Paradoxes," *Analysis,* XII (1951–52), 38–44.
109. ———. "Mr. Wisdom on Temporal Paradoxes," *Analysis,* XIII (1952–53), 15–17.
110. Te Hennepe, Eugene. "Language Reform and Philosophical Imperialism: Another Round with Zeno," *Analysis,* XXIII, Supplement (1962–63), 43*ff*.
111. Thomas, L. E. "Achilles and the Tortoise," *Analysis,* XII (1951–52), 92–94.
112. Thomson, James. "Infinity in Mathematics and Logic," in *The Encyclopedia of Philosophy,* ed. Paul Edwards. New York: The Macmillan Company and The Free Press, 1967.
113. ———. "Tasks and Super-Tasks," *Analysis,* XV (1954–55), 1–13. Reprinted above.
114. Ushenko, A. P. *The Philosophy of Relativity,* Appendix 2. London: George Allen & Unwin Ltd., 1937.
115. ———. "Zeno's Paradoxes," *Mind,* N.S. LV (1946), 151–165.
116. Waismann, F. "How I See Philosophy," in *Contemporary British Philosophy,* ed. H. D. Lewis. London: George Allen & Unwin Ltd., 1956.
117. Watling, J. "The Sum of an Infinite Series," *Analysis,* XIII (1952–53), 39–46.
118. White, Alan R. "Achilles at the Shooting Gallery," *Mind,* LXXII (1963), 141–142.
119. Whitrow, G. J. *The Natural Philosophy of Time.* London and Edinburgh: Thomas Nelson and Sons Ltd., 1961.
120. Williams, Donald. "The Myth of Passage," *Journal of Philosophy,* XLVIII (1951), 457–472.

121. Wisdom, J. O. "Achilles on a Physical Racecourse," *Analysis*, XII (1951–52), 67–72. Reprinted above.
122. ———. "Why Achilles Does Not Fail to Catch the Tortoise," *Mind*, N.S. L (1941), 58–73.

III. Technical Background

Works cited in this section do not, for the most part, refer explicitly to Zeno's paradoxes; rather, they deal with modern mathematical, physical, logical, and philosophical developments which are relevant to technical treatments of Zeno's arguments. Because the fields from which these materials are drawn are extensive and diverse, this section of the Bibliography is highly selected. Every effort has been made to keep these references directly pertinent, reasonably accessible, and suitably intelligible to the nonspecialist.

SETS, INFINITY, AND THE CONTINUUM

123. Cantor, Georg. *Contributions to the Founding of the Theory of Transfinite Numbers*, trans. Philip E. B. Jourdain. New York: Dover Publications, Inc., n.d. Cantor's classic work on set theory.
124. Fraenkel, Abraham A. *Abstract Set Theory*. Amsterdam: North-Holland Publishing Company, 1953.
125. Hahn, Hans. "Infinity," in *The World of Mathematics*, ed. James R. Newman, pp. 1593–1611. New York: Simon and Schuster, 1956. An excellent brief survey of basic concepts of set theory.
126. Huntington, Edward V. *The Continuum and Other Types of Serial Order*. 2nd edn. New York: Dover Publications, Inc., 1955.
127. Kamke, E. *Theory of Sets*, trans. Frederick Bagemihl. New York: Dover Publications, Inc., 1950.
128. Körner, Stephan. *The Philosophy of Mathematics*. London: Hutchinson University Library, 1960.

129. Russell, Bertrand. *Introduction to Mathematical Philosophy.* London: George Allen & Unwin Ltd., 1919.
130. Weyl, Hermann. *Philosophy of Mathematics and Natural Science.* Princeton, N. J.: Princeton University Press, 1949.
131. Wilder, Raymond L. *Introduction to the Foundations of Mathematics.* New York: John Wiley & Sons, Inc., 1952.

MATHEMATICAL ANALYSIS

132. Burkill, J. C. *The Lebesgue Integral.* Cambridge: University Press, 1953. An introduction to measure theory.
133. Courant, Richard, and Herbert Robbins. *What Is Mathematics?* New York: Oxford University Press, 1941. A superb elementary exposition of fundamental concepts of mathematics, especially functions, limits, continuity, etc.
134. Cramér, Harald. *Mathematical Methods of Statistics.* First Part. Princeton, N.J.: Princeton University Press, 1946. An excellent survey of measure theory.
135. Halmos, Paul R. *Measure Theory.* Princeton, N. J.: D. Van Nostrand Company, Inc., 1950.
136. Menger, Karl. "What is Dimension?" *American Mathematical Monthly*, L (1943), 2–7.
137. Patterson, E. M. *Topology.* Edinburgh and London: Oliver and Boyd, 1956.

PHYSICS AND PHILOSOPHY

138. d'Abro, A. *The Evolution of Scientific Thought.* 2nd edn. New York: Dover Publications, Inc., 1950.
139. Grünbaum, Adolf. *Philosophical Problems of Space and Time.* New York: Alfred A. Knopf, 1963. The most comprehensive treatise in philosophy of space and time.
140. Reichenbach, Hans. *The Direction of Time.* Berkeley and Los Angeles: University of California Press, 1956.

141. ———. *The Philosophy of Space and Time,* trans. Maria Reichenbach and John Freund. New York: Dover Publications, Inc., 1957. The twentieth-century classic in the philosophy of space and time.

142. Smart, J. J. C. *Philosophy and Scientific Realism.* New York: The Humanities Press, 1963.

143. ———. *Problems of Space and Time.* New York: The Macmillan Company, 1964. A broad anthology of writings on philosophical problems of space and time.

IV. Supplementary Sources

This section updates the Bibliography for the 2001 reprinting of this book.

144. Abraham, William E. "The Nature of Zeno's Argument against Plurality in DK 29 B I," *Phronesis,* XVII (1972), 40–52.

145. Adams, John Q. "Grünbaum's Solution to Zeno's Paradoxes," *Philosophia,* III (1973), 43–50.

146. Ahmad, Aziz. "Change and Time," *Pakistan Philosophical Journal,* XI (1973), 74–107.

147. Aktchourine, I. A. "Les Apories de Zenon, la Topologie et la Physique Contemporaine," *Revue Internationale de Philosophie,* XXV (1971), 565–574.

148. Allis, Victor, and Teun Koetsier. "On Some Paradoxes of the Infinite II," *British Journal for the Philosophy of Science,* XLVI (1995), 235–247.

149. Alper, Joseph S., and Mark Bridger. "Mathematics, Model and Zeno's Paradoxes," *Synthese,* CX (1997), 143–166.

150. Antonopoulos, Constantin. "Bohr's Reply to EPR: A Zenonian Version of Complementarity," *Idealistic Studies,* XXVII (1997), 165–192.

151. Arsenijevic, Milos. "Solution of the Staccato Version of the Achilles Paradox," in Aleksandar Pavkovic, ed., *Contemporary Yugoslav Philosophy.* Dordrecht: Kluwer, 1988, 27–55.

152. Barnes, Jonathan. *The Presocratic Philosophers: Thales to Zeno,* Vol. I. London: Routledge and Kegan Paul, 1978.

153. Barreau, Herve. "Bergson et Zenon d'Elee," *Revue Philosophique de Louvain*, LXVII (1969), 267–284.

154. ———. "Bergson et Zenon d'Elee (Suite et Fin)," *Revue Philosophique de Louvain*, LXVII (1969), 389–430.

155. Berresford, Geoffrey C. "A Note on Thomson's Lamp 'Paradox'," *Analysis*, XLI (1981), 1–3.

156. Bicknell, Peter J. "Coinage and the Presocratics II—Zeno of Elea," *Apeiron*, II (1968), 18–20.

157. Bolotin, David. "Continuity and Infinite Divisibility in Aristotle's *Physics*," *Ancient Philosophy*, XIII (1993), 323–340.

158. Borejszo, Zee. "Finding 'Finity' and Motion for Zeno," *South African Journal of Philosophy*, XIII (1994), 199–203.

159. Bostock, David. "Aristotle, Zeno, and the Potential Infinite," *Proceedings of the Aristotelian Society*, LXXIII (1973), 37–51.

160. Brook, D. "White at the Shooting Gallery," *Mind*, LXXIV (1965), 256.

161. Brown, G. Burniston. "Achilles and Dimensions," *British Journal for the Philosophy of Science*, VI (1955), 251–252.

162. Burke, Michael B. "The Infinistic Thesis," *Southern Journal of Philosophy*, XXII (1984), 295–306.

163. Butler, Clark. "Motion and Objective Contradictions," *American Philosophical Quarterly*, XVIII (1981), 131–139.

164. Chambers, Connor J. "Henri Bergson, Zenon, y la Disension Academica," *Dialogos*, VII (1971), 17–38.

165. ———. "Zeno of Elea and Bergson's Neglected Thesis," *Journal of the History of Philosophy*, XII (1974), 63–76.

166. Chari, C. T. K. "Zeno's Paradoxes Reconsidered," *Philosophical Quarterly* (India), XXVIII (1955), 153–162.

167. Cleland, Carol E. "The Difference between Real Change and Mere Cambridge Change," *Philosophical Studies*, LX (1990), 257–280.

168. Code, Murray J. "Zeno's Paradoxes I: The Standard Mathematical Response," *Nature and System*, IV (1982), 45–58.

169. ———. "Zeno's Paradoxes II: A Whiteheadean Response," *Nature and System*, IV (1982), 59–76.

170. Corbett, S. M. "Zeno's 'Achilles': A Reply to John McKie,"

Philosophy and Phenomenological Research, XLIX (1988), 325–331.
171. Curd, Patricia. "Eleatic Monism in Zeno and Melissus," *Ancient Philosophy,* XIII (1993), 1–22.
172. ———. *The Legacy of Parmenides: Eleatic Monism and Later Presocratic Thought.* Princeton: Princeton University Press, 1998.
173. Dejnozka, Jan. "Zeno's Paradoxes and the Cosmological Argument," *International Journal for Philosophy of Religion,* XXV (1989), 65–81.
174. Douglass, Paul. "Deleuze and the Endurance of Bergson," *Thought,* LXVII (1992), 47–61.
175. Edgar, William J. "Locations," *Canadian Journal of Philosophy,* IX (1979), 323–333.
176. Eells, Ellery. "Quentin Smith on Infinity and the Past," *Philosophy of Science,* LV (1988), 453–455.
177. Evans, David. "Socrates and Zeno: Plato 'Parmenides', 129," *International Journal of Philosophical Studies,* II (1994), 243–255.
178. Faris, J. A. "Zeno's Dichotomy and Achilles Paradoxes," *Irish Philosophical Journal,* III (1986), 3–26.
179. Feyerabend, Paul. "Some Observations on Aristotle's Theory of Mathematics and of the Continuum," *Midwest Studies in Philosophy,* VIII (1983), 67–88.
180. Forrester, James William. "The Argument of the 'Porphry Text'," *Journal of the History of Philosophy,* XI (1973), 537–539.
181. Furley, David J., and R. E. Allen, eds. *Studies in Presocratic Philosophy,* Vol. 2: *The Eleatics and Pluralists.* London: Routledge and Kegan Paul, 1975.
182. Furley, David J. "Anaxagoras in Response to Parmenides," *Canadian Journal of Philosophy,* supp. II (1976), 61–85.
183. Gardner, Martin. "Mathematical Games," *Scientific American,* CCXXV, no. 6 (Dec. 1971), 97–99.
184. Gerber, William. "Another Window into Zeno's Antinomies," *Indian Philosophical Quarterly,* XX (1993), 115–119.
185. Gorr, Michael. "Vlastos and the New Race Course Paradox," *Australasian Journal of Philosophy,* LIV (1976), 244–249.

186. Grattan-Guinness, I. "Achilles is Still Running," *Transactions of the Charles S. Peirce Society,* X (1974), 8–16.
187. Groarke, Leo. "Zeno's Dichotomy: Undermining the Modern Response," *Auslegung,* IX (1982), 67–75.
188. Gruender, C. David. "The Achilles Paradox and Transfinite Numbers," *British Journal for the Philosophy of Science,* XVII (1966), 219–231.
189. Grünbaum, Adolf. "Some Recent Writings in the Philosophy of Mathematics," *Review of Metaphysics,* V (1951), 281–292.
190. ———. "Reply to J. Q. Adams' 'Grünbaum's Solution to Zeno's Paradoxes'," *Philosophia,* III (1973), 51–57.
191. Hager, Paul. "Russell and Zeno's Arrow Paradox," *Russell,* VII (1987), 3–10.
192. Hahn, Robert. "Continuity, Discontinuity, and Some Paradoxes of Motion: Zeno's Arguments in the Light of Quantum Mechanics," *Southwest Philosophical Studies,* VII (1982), 115–123.
193. Harrison, Andrew. "Zeno's Paper Chase," *Mind,* LXXVI (1967), 568–575.
194. Harrison, Craig. "The Three Arrows of Zeno," *Synthese,* CVII (1996), 271–292.
195. Heath, Thomas Little. *Mathematics in Aristotle.* Oxford: Clarendon Press, 1949.
196. Ingram, Clive. "Aristotle's Dilemma," *Philosophical Studies* (Ireland), IX (1959), 27–35.
197. Johnson, P. O. "Wholes, Parts, and Infinite Collections," *Philosophy,* LXVII (1992), 367–379.
198. Kaiser, D. Nolan. "Language and the 'Achilles Paradox'," *Philosophia Mathematica,* V (1968), 11–23.
199. ———. "Russell's Paradox and the Residual Achilles," *Apeiron,* VI (1972), 39-48.
200. Kluge, Eike Henner W. "Infinite Divisibility, Ontology, and Spatial Relations," *Dialogue,* IX (1970), 356–365.
201. Knorr, Wilbur R. "Zeno's Paradoxes Still in Motion," *Ancient Philosophy,* III (1983), 55–66.
202. Lalumia, Joseph. "From Science to Metaphysics and Philosophy," *Diogenes,* LXXXVIII (1974), 1–35.

203. Lear, Jonathan. "A Note on Zeno's Arrow," *Phronesis,* XXVI (1981), 91–104.

204. Lee, Harold N. "Comment on 'The Infinitistic Thesis'," *Southern Journal of Philosophy,* XXIII (1985), 399–400.

205. ———. "Zeno Cannot Be Caught on His Own Racetrack," *Mind,* LXXX (1971), 269.

206. Lenzen, Victor F. "Peirce, Russell, and Achilles," *Transactions of the Charles S. Peirce Society,* X (1974), 3–7.

207. Makin, Stephen. "Zeno on Plurality," *Phronesis,* XXVII (1982), 223–238.

208. Mar, Gary, and Paul St. Denis. "What the Liar Taught Achilles," *Journal of Philosophical Logic,* XXVIII (1999), 29–46.

209. Massey, Gerald J. "Toward a Clarification of Grünbaum's Conception of an Intrinsic Metric," *Philosophy of Science,* XXXVI (1969), 331–345.

210. Maziarz, Edward Anthony, and Thomas Greenwood. *Greek Mathematical Philosophy.* New York: Ungar, 1968.

211. McKie, John R. "The Persuasiveness of Zeno's Paradoxes," *Philosophy and Phenomenological Research,* XLVII (1987), 631–639.

212. ———. "Zeno's Paradox of Extension," *Southern Journal of Philosophy,* XXIX (1991), 69–86.

213. McLaughlin, William I. "Thomson's Lamp Is Dysfunctional," *Synthese,* CXVI (1998), 281–301.

214. McLaughlin, William I., and Sylvia L. Miller. "An Epistemological Use of Nonstandard Analysis to Answer Zeno's Objections against Motion," *Synthese,* XCII (1992), 371–384.

215. Molina-Jiminez, Carlos. "Antonio Machado y la Segunda Aporia de Zenon de Elea," *Revista de Filosofia de la Universidad de Costa Rica,* IX (1971), 243–247.

216. Mookerjee, S. "Problem of Change—Old and New," *Journal of the Philosophical Association,* IX (1962), 93–98.

217. Moor, Donald. "Has Lee Finally Caught Zeno?" *Mind,* LXXVII (1968), 430.

218. Moore, A. W. "A Problem for Intuitionism: The Apparent Possibility of Performing Infinitely Many Tasks in a Finite

Time," *Proceedings of the Aristotelian Society,* LXXXX (1990), 17–34.

219. Moreno, Antonio. "The Calculus and Infinitesimals: A Philosophical Reflection," *Nature and System,* I (1979), 189–201.

220. Mourelatos, Alexander P. D., ed. *The Pre-Socratics: A Collection of Critical Essays* (Revised Edition). Princeton: Princeton University Press, 1994.

221. Mueller, Ian. "Zeno's Paradoxes and Continuity," *Mind,* LXXVIII (1969), 129–131.

222. O'Brien, James F. "Zeno's Paradoxes of Motion," *Modern Schoolman,* XL (1963), 105–138.

223. Owen, G. E. L. "Aristotle on Time," in *Motion and Time, Space and Matter,* Peter K. Machamer and Robert G. Turnbull, eds. Columbus: Ohio State University Press, 1976, 3–27.

224. Owen, G. E. L., and Martha Nussbaum. *Logic, Science and Dialectic: Collected Papers in Greek Philosophy.* Ithaca: Cornell University Press, 1986.

225. Papa-Grimaldi, Alba. "Why Mathematical Solutions of Zeno's Paradoxes Miss the Point: Zeno's One and Many Relation and Parmenides' Prohibition," *Review of Metaphysics,* L (1996), 299–314.

226. Pena, Lorenzo. "Partial Truth, Fringes, and Motion: Three Applications of a Contradictorial Logic," *Studies in Soviet Thought,* XXXIX (1990), 283–312.

227. Peterson, Sandra. "Zeno's Second Argument against Plurality," *Journal of the History of Philosophy,* XVI (1978), 261–270.

228. Petrov, I. U. "Some Problems in the Logic of Motion," *Soviet Studies in Philosophy,* III (1964), 35–42.

229. Pickering, F. R. "Aristotle on Zeno and the Now," *Phronesis,* XXIII (1978), 253–257.

230. Pozsgay, Lawrence J. "Zeno's Achilles Paradox," *Modern Schoolman,* XLIII (1966), 375–396.

231. Priest, Graham. "On a Version of One of Zeno's Paradoxes," *Analysis,* LIX (1999), 1–2.

232. Qfiasco, Flash. "Another Look at Some of Zeno's Paradoxes," *Canadian Journal of Philosophy,* X (1980), 119–130.

233. Quan, S. "The Solution of Zeno's First Paradox," *Mind,* LXXVII (1968), 206–221.

234. Raju, P. T. "Some Reflections on Activism and Zeno's Paradoxes," *Philosophical Quarterly* (India), XXVIII (1955), 49–72.

235. Ray, Christopher. "Paradoxical Tasks," *Analysis,* L (1990), 71–74.

236. Rickless, Samuel C. "How Parmenides Saved the Theory of Forms," *Philosophical Review,* CVII (1998), 501–554.

237. Robinson, Abraham. "The Metaphysics of the Calculus," in *The Philosophy of Mathematics,* J. Hintikka, ed. London: Oxford University Press, 1969, 153–163.

238. ———. *Non-Standard Analysis.* Amsterdam: North-Holland, 1966. 2nd ed., 1974.

239. Rogers, Ben. "On Discrete Spaces," *American Philosophical Quarterly,* V (1968), 117–123.

240. Rossetti, Livio. "The Rhetoric of Zeno's Paradoxes," *Philosophy and Rhetoric,* XXI (1988), 145–152.

241. ———. "Sull'intreccio di logica e retorica in alcuni paradossi di Zenone di Elea," *Archiv für Geschichte der Philosophie,* LXXIV (1992), 1–25.

242. Sainsbury, R. M. *Paradoxes.* Cambridge: Cambridge University Press, 1988. 2nd ed., New York: Cambridge University Press, 1995.

243. Salmon, Wesley C. "An 'At-At' Theory of Causal Influence," *Philosophy of Science,* XLIV (1977), 215–224.

244. ———. *Causality and Explanation.* New York and Oxford: Oxford University Press, 1998.

245. ———. "A New Look at Zeno's Paradoxes," *Space, Time, and Motion: A Philosophical Introduction,* Encino: Dickenson, 1975, chap. 2. 2nd ed., Minneapolis: University of Minnesota Press, 1980.

246. ———. "Zeno of Elea," in *A Companion to Metaphysics,* Jaegwon Kim and Ernest Sosa, eds. Oxford: Basil Blackwell, 1995, 518–519.

247. Schoenberg, Judith. "The Respecting of Indeterminacy," *Mind,* LXXIX (1970), 347–368.

248. Seaton, Robert. "Zeno's Paradoxes, Iteration, and Infinity," *Nature and System,* VI (1984), 229–236.

249. Shamshi, F. A. "A Note on Aristotle, 'Physics' 239^{b}5–7: What Exactly Was Zeno's Argument of the Arrow?" *Ancient Philosophy,* XIV (1994), 51–72.

250. ———. "Victor Brochard on Zeno's Arguments against Motion," *Indian Philosophical Quarterly,* XV (1988), 1–18.

251. ———. "Zeno's Paradoxes: A Solution Hazarded," *Pakistan Philosophical Congress,* XV (1968), 143–156.

252. Sherry, David M. "Zeno's Metrical Paradox Revisited," *Philosophy of Science,* LV (1988), 58–73.

253. Shibles, Warren A. *Models of Ancient Greek Philosophy.* London: Vision Press, 1971.

254. Sinnige, Theo-Gerard. *Matter and Infinity in the Presocratic Schools and Plato.* Assen: Van-Gorcum, 1971.

255. Skyrms, Brian. "Zeno's Paradox of Measure," in *Physics, Philosophy and Psychoanalysis,* R. S. Cohen and L. Laudan, eds. Dordrecht: Reidel, 1983, 223–254.

256. Smith, Joseph Wayne. "Zeno's Paradoxes," *Explorations in Knowledge,* II (1985), 1–12.

257. Smith, Quentin. "Infinity and the Past," *Philosophy of Science,* LIV (1987), 63–75.

258. Smolenov, Hristo. "Zeno's Paradoxes and Temporal Becoming in Dialectical Atomism," *Studia Logica,* XLIII (1984), 169–180.

259. Solmsen, Friedrich. "The Tradition about Zeno of Elea Reexamined," *Phronesis,* XVI (1971), 116–141.

260. Stogre, Michael. "Mathematics and the Paradoxes of Zeno," *Modern Schoolman,* XLV (1968), 313–319.

261. Sviderskii, V. I. "On Contradiction in Mechanical Motion," *Soviet Studies in Philosophy,* I (1963), 31–35.

262. Szekely, Laszlo. "Motion and the Dialectical View of the World: On Two Soviet Interpretations of Zeno's Paradoxes," *Studies in Soviet Thought,* XXXIX (1990), 241–255.

263. Teloh, Henry. "Parmenides and Plato's 'Parmenides' 131A–132C," *Journal of the History of Philosophy,* XIV (1976), 125–130.

264. Toth, Imre. "The Dialectical Structure of Zeno's Arguments," in *Hegel and Newtonianism*, Michael John Petry, ed. Dordrecht: Kluwer, 1993, 179–200.

265. Turnbull, Robert G. "Zeno's Stricture and Predication in Plato, Aristotle, and Plotinus," in *How Things Are*, James Bogen, ed. Dordrecht: Reidel, 1985, 21–58.

266. Van Valen, Leigh. "Zeno and Continuity," *Mind*, LXXVII (1968), 429.

267. Van-Bendegem, Jean-Paul. "Zeno's Paradoxes and the Tile Argument," *Philosophy of Science*, LIV (1987), 295–302.

268. Vlastos, Gregory. "Plato's Testimony Concerning Zeno of Elea," *Journal of Hellenic Studies*, XCV (1975), 136–162.

269. Warhadpande, N. R. "A Little about Zeno's Paradoxes," *Journal of the Philosophical Association*, VII (1960), 15–20.

270. Wedeking, G. A. "On a Finitist Solution to Some Zenonian Paradoxes," *Mind*, LXXVII (1968), 420–426.

271. White, Michael J. "The Spatial Arrow Paradox," *Pacific Philosophical Quarterly*, LXVIII (1987), 71–77.

272. ———. "Zeno's Arrow, Divisible Infinitesimals, and Chrysippus," *Phronesis*, XXVII (1982), 239–254.

273. Whitrow, G. J. "On the Foundations and Application of Finite Classical Arithmetic," *Philosophy*, XXIII (1948), 256–261.

274. Wilbur, James R., and Harold J. Allen, eds. *The Worlds of the Early Greek Philosophers*. Buffalo: Prometheus, 1979.

275. Zangari, Mark. "Zeno, Zero and Indeterminate Forms: Instants in the Logic of Motion," *Australasian Journal of Philosophy*, LXXII (1994), 187–204.

276. Zinkernagel, Peter. "A Note on S. Quan 'The Solution of Zeno's First Paradox'," *Mind*, LXXX (1971), 144.

277. ———. "Was Zeno Right?" *Inquiry*, VIII (1965), 292–300.

278. Zwart, Paulus Johannes. *About Time: A Philosophical Inquiry into the Origin and Nature of Time*. Amsterdam: North-Holland, 1976.

INDEX

Since one of the chief values of this anthology is the bringing together of views of different authors on common problems, the index has been constructed with the aim of facilitating the tracing of important themes throughout the book. It is relatively detailed, and is liberally sprinkled with cross-references. Especially significant entries are given in boldface numerals: in the case of an author, the boldface entry indicates a passage, other than a brief quotation, from his own writings; in the case of a technical term, the boldface indicates a formal definition; in the case of any of the paradoxes, the boldface indicates the actual statement or paraphrase of it; and in other cases, the boldface simply indicates a particularly significant or extended discussion of the topic in question. The index does not contain entries referring to the Bibliography, but only to the citations of such works within the text.

Soul, purity of, 105
Source, psychological, of discrete conception of time, 173
Space: analytic geometry of, 176; cardinality of, 261; concept of, 5; consisting of points, 54–55; continuity of, 175, 268; discrete, 175, 244; mathematical description, 84, 178; in quantum theory, 174–175; 244–247; theories of, 54. *See also* Continuum
Space-atoms, 12. *See also* Atomicity; Atomism; Atoms
Space variable, range of, 21, 35, 171
Spatio-temporal entities, 80
Special relativity. *See* Relativity
Specious present, 37
Spectrum, discrete vs. continuous, 245
Speculation, on spatio-temporal atomicity, 174–175, 245–247
Speed. *See* Velocity
Spin, discreteness of, 246
Square circle, difficulty of drawing small one, 71
Staccato runner. *See* Runners
Stade. *See* Stadium
Stadium, paradox of, **11–12,** 30, 46, **51–54,** 141, 148–151, 244, 246–250
Stages, in division, 135, 145
Standard theories, 185, 187, 194–196, 209
Star-omega, **ω. See* *Omega
State, change of, 131. *See also* Transition
States, successive, 62–63
State variable, of lamp, 236
Stationarity, of arrow. *See* Arrow
Statistics, 173–174, 195
Steele, D. A., 177
Steps, infinite series of, 69, 71
Stone, thinking, 128
Stop, at point. *See* Be at point

Stream of consciousness, 173
Strength, insufficiency for super-task, 225
Subdivision. *See* Division
Sub-interval: impossibility of terminal, 207; possibility of super-denumerable set, 193. *See also* Interval
Subsequent state, following infinite sequence, 49, 57–58, 146, 207
Subset, **252;** dense denumerable, 267–268; number of, 254; proper, 190–191, **253;** same cardinality as set, 256
Succession, in, 156
Successor, immediate, 37, 248, 263, 265. *See also* Discrete order; Nextness
Sum: denumerable, via limit, 168; of divergent series, 111; finitary, 168; infinite, 14–15, 31, 143; of infinite series, *see* Series, sum; of infinite set of equal positive terms, 14–15, 143, 178; lengths of degenerate intervals, 192; partial, *see* Partial sums; physical counterpart of, 29, 34; set-theoretic, 180, **254;** super-denumerable infinity of terms, 169, 192–193. *See also* Addition
Summation: geometrical, 169, 196; of parts, 155; of zeros, 14, 143, 165, 177–178. *See also* Addition
Super-denumerability: logical importance of, 168–169, 195, 198; proof of, 258–259
Super-denumerable infinity, 35, 37, 167–169, 192–199, **258–259,** 266. *See also* Continuum
Super-denumerable set. *See* Sets
Super-duper-task, **113–114,** 116, 121
Super-machine, 225, 232–233
Super-task, 90–100, 106, 111–116, 120–124, 128, 220, 225, 229–230;